On 15th June 2007
the United Nations General Assembly
unanimously resolved to observe

October 2

the birth anniversary of Mahatma Gandhi as the

International Day of Non-violence

The idea of promoting the resolution originated from the
Declaration adopted at the international conference on
"Peace, Non-violence and Empowerment—Gandhian Philosophy
in the 21st Century" convened in New Delhi in January 2007
to commemorate the centenary of Satyagraha

Celebrating Hundred Years of 'Satyagraha' (1906-2006)

GANDHIAN

Peace, Non-violence and Empowerment

WAY

INDIAN NATIONAL CONGRESS

EDITED BY
ANAND SHARMA

PUBLISHED BY
ACADEMIC FOUNDATION

Published in 2007

by: ACADEMIC FOUNDATION

4772-73 / 23 Bharat Ram Road, (23 Ansari Road),
Darya Ganj, New Delhi - 110 002 (India).
Tel : +91-11-23245001/02/03/04.
Fax : +91-11-23245005.
E-mail : academic@vsnl.com
www.academicfoundation.com

Photographs appearing in the volume, courtesy:

Gandhi Smriti, New Delhi
Indian National Congress
Nehru Memorial Museum and Library, New Delhi
Nelson Mandela Foundation, Johannesburg
Press Information Bureau (PIB), Government of India, New Delhi

The publishers gratefully acknowledge creative inputs from
Dr. Savita Singh, Dr. Amit Banerjee and Dr. Anand Prakash.

Cataloging in Publication Data--DK
  Courtesy: D.K. Agencies (P) Ltd. <docinfo@dkagencies.com>

Gandhian way: peace, non-violence and empowerment
  / edited by Anand Sharma.
    p.   cm.
  Contributed articles.
  "Celebrating hundred years of 'Satyagraha'
  (1906-2006)"--Half t.p.
  ISBN 13: 9788171886487
  ISBN 10: 8171886485

  1. Gandhi, Mahatma, 1869-1948.--Philosophy.
  2. Passive resistance. 3. Conflict management.
  4. Peace-building. 5. World politics.   I. Sharma,
  Anand. II. Indian National Congress.

DDC 322.409 54   22

Designed and typeset by Italics India, New Delhi.
Printed and bound in India.

10 9 8 7 6 5 4 3 2 1

Contents

Section II
A Non-violent Approach to
Conflict Resolution and Peace Building

Section III
Gandhian Philosophy for Poverty Eradication,
Education and People's Empowerment

I know the path.

It is straight and narrow.

It is like the edge of a sword.

I rejoice to walk on it.

I weep when I slip.

God's word is:

'He who strives never perishes.'

— M.K. Gandhi

Phones : 23019080

ALL INDIA CONGRESS COMMITTEE
24, AKBAR ROAD, NEW DELHI - 110 011

Sonia Gandhi
President

FOREWORD

IT gives me and my colleagues at the Indian National Congress a sense of fulfilment in sharing with citizens of the world Mahatma Gandhi's humane philosophy and empowering principles through this publication.

His revolutionary concept of Satyagraha, based on the simple weapons of truth and non-violence, unleashed an indomitable moral force which not only aroused Indians to free themselves from colonial oppression and social injustice, but inspired millions of people all over the world in their quest for freedom, justice and a life of dignity. It continues to do so to this day.

Mahatma Gandhi's courage of conviction, his all-encompassing compassion and spirit of service to humankind, his renunciation of power and its worldly trappings, and his unwavering self-discipline in practicing what he preached, imbued all his words and actions with a compelling moral authority. In a world riven with ethnic and religious conflict, terrorism, and growing emphasis on economic prosperity at the cost of human, social and environmental factors, his philosophy provides tangible answers to many of the dilemmas and problems of modern society.

The decision of the Indian National Congress to commemorate the Centenary of Satyagraha was an opportunity to reaffirm our collective commitment to the enduring principles of Mahatma Gandhi. His philosophy provides the foundation without which we believe our social, economic and political progress would be devoid of moral direction and anchor.

The International Conference convened on this occasion brought together eminent world personalities, philosophers and Gandhian scholars. The Satyagraha Conference had aimed to inspire individuals and institutions in different parts of the world to build a coalition of conscience to address contemporary issues and concerns. It was immensely rewarding to find that deliberations resonated with the collective resolve of present and future leaders of the world to invoke the Gandhian way to resolve current conflicts between peoples and cultures, and to liberate humankind from the misery of poverty and hunger.

Great leaders leave behind a rich inheritance for posterity, making their indelible mark on the annals of world history. In this respect, Mahatma Gandhi was surely the towering figure of our times, whose philosophy of Satyagraha was a supreme example of the invincibility of the human spirit. His message is universal, timeless and eternal. His philosophy embraced all mankind, and was never confined by the narrow divides of national boundaries or barriers of religion or culture.

This volume is an attempt to bring together the essence of Satyagraha, and the enriching contributions of all those who had come together at New Delhi in January 2007 to join in our commemoration of the Centenary of Satyagraha. With the challenges confronting the world today, we believe it is imperative for the leaders of today, and especially for youth, to nurture and sustain Gandhian values for the generations to follow, so that Mahatma Gandhi's legacy continues to be our guiding light through the 21st century.

May 30, 2007
New Delhi

Introduction

ANAND SHARMA

ONE hundred years ago on the 11th of September, 1906, Mohandas Karamchand Gandhi, a young Barrister from India, gave a stirring call for peaceful resistance against discrimination, oppression and injustice at a public meeting in Johannesburg, South Africa. Over the years, "Satyagraha—the firmness of force of truth" became a powerful tool in the movement of the people which gave voice to millions of men and women, who were subjugated and viewed as weak and helpless. His philosophy and commitment to human freedom and dignity inspired the people of India and liberated them from the shackles of colonialism. It also had a profound influence on leaders and liberation struggles worldwide

To commemorate the centenary of the Satyagraha, the Indian National Congress convened an international conference "Peace, Non-Violence and Empowerment—Gandhian Philosophy in the 21st Century" in New Delhi on 29-30 January, 2007. It was an occasion to recall the momentous struggle led by Gandhi, to acknowledge the historic contribution of Satyagraha and to renew people's commitment to the noble principles of peace and non-violence espoused by him.

The "Satyagraha Conference" generated worldwide interest and enthusiastic response. This was reflected in the participation of leadership delegations from 91 countries and 122 organisations. The representative gathering of leaders including Nobel laureates, philosophers and leaders of civil society organisations, it underscored the enduring legacy of Gandhi and the continuing relevance of his message. The Conference deliberations and final Declaration presented by a hero of the South African liberation struggle and former prisoner of conscience Ahmed Kathrada, articulated the collective yearning of the participants for a new way forward to address the problems of hunger and dehumanising poverty, which continue to plague humanity, to confront the threat of violence and terrorism and for building a just and equitable world where people live with dignity and in peace and harmony with each other in diverse and pluralistic societies.

Presenting the enriching thought exchange at the Conference together with the original illustrations of Satyagraha, this book brings out the positive energy and hope associated with the Gandhian way.

Section I   Gandhian Philosophy in the 21st Century

ELA GANDHI

MANMOHAN SINGH

SONIA GANDHI

NELSON MANDELA

KENNETH KAUNDA

DESMOND TUTU

PRANAB MUKHERJEE

A.K. ANTONY

LECH WALESA

MUHAMMAD YUNUS

ANAND SHARMA

NASSER AL-KIDWA

Section I

Gandhian Philosophy in the 21st Century

This section comprises addresses delivered at the Inaugural Plenary and the Concluding Plenary of the international conference "Peace, Non-violence and Empowerment: Gandhian Philosophy in the 21st Century" held at Vigyan Bhawan, New Delhi on January 29-30, 2007.

Conference Chairperson: Sonia Gandhi
Conference Vice Chairperson: A.K. Antony
Conference Secretary General: Anand Sharma
Conference Rapporteur General: Mani Shankar Aiyar
Conference Secretary: Mukul Wasnik

1

The Sacred Warrior

NELSON MANDELA

I am delighted to be addressing this conference from Johannesburg, the City where Mahatma Gandhi launched the Satyagraha just over a 100 years ago. This conference on Gandhian Philosophy in the 21st century comes at a critical juncture. We in South Africa owe much to the presence of Gandhi in our midst for 21 years. His influence was felt in our freedom struggles throughout the African continent for a good part of the 20th century. And he greatly inspired the struggle in South Africa led by the African National Congress.

His philosophy contributed in no small measure to bringing about a peaceful transformation in South Africa and in healing the destructive human divisions that had been spawned by the abhorrent practice of apartheid. It is very appropriate, therefore, that India and South Africa are jointly celebrating the centenary of Satyagraha, which is the legacy shared by both our countries. I also had the opportunity of meeting Prime Minister Manmohan Singh, when he visited South Africa last October for the joint commemoration.

I am aware that a series of events have been planned both in South Africa and India to mark 100 years of Satyagraha. We recently had a conference on Robben Island, a place of oppression and exile, to reflect on the legacy of Gandhi. This conference in New Delhi marks an important milestone in those celebrations and I hope it will articulate the aspirations of all those who lay faith in the years that Mahatma Gandhi preached and lived for. I am especially happy that the conference has chosen to focus on Satyagraha as a tool for empowerment of the masses. Gandhi's insistence on self-sufficiency is the basic economic principle that if followed today could contribute significantly to alleviating Third World poverty and stimulating development. It is a strange coincidence that Mahatma Gandhi

Video address by Nelson Mandela to the Satyagraha Centenary Conference held on 29-30 January 2007 at Vigyan Bhawan, New Delhi.

launched the Satyagraha on September 11, 1906 at the Empire Theater, Johannesburg. Today, at the turn of this century 9/11 has an entirely different and horrific connotation.

When Time Magazine asked me to write about one of the 100 most influential persons of the 20th century, I had no hesitation in choosing Gandhi. I called him the "sacred warrior" because of the manner in which he combined ethics and morality with a steely resolve that refused to compromise with the oppressor.

In a world driven by violence and strife, Gandhi's message of peace and non-violence holds the key to human survival in the 21st century. He rightly believed in the efficacy of pitching the soul force called the Satyagraha against the brute force of the oppressor, and in effect converting the oppressor to the right and moral point.

I hope that this conference will be able to come up with creative solutions, that suit our world today and create a new paradigm for the application of the Indian trinity of *Satyagraha*, *Sarvodaya* and *Ahimsa*, to create a just, peaceful and tolerant world for the present and succeeding generations.

The Fort Prison Complex where Mahatma Gandhi
was imprisoned on multiple occasions.

Some historic landmarks in South Africa...

11 Albermarle Street, Troyeville
where Mahatma Gandhi moved in 1904.

Gaiety Theatre, where Mahatma Gandhi addressed mass meetings of
Transvaal Indians, exhorting them to burn their registration certificates.

Empire Theatre, Johannesburg, where Satyagraha was launched on
11 September, 1906 at a mass meeting chaired by Mahatma Gandhi.

Mahatma Gandhi and Khan Abdul Ghaffar Khan at a
meeting with Muslim Leaguers, Jahanabad, March 28, 1947.

Nelson Mandela

Martin Luther King Jr.

2

Rediscovering the Mahatma's Way

SONIA GANDHI

THE Satyagraha movement changed the course of history. It first won respect, though limited, for Indians living in racist South Africa. It then brought freedom to India from the mightiest colonial power of the day. It went on to serve as a guiding spirit to some remarkable personalities in their own struggles. Badshah Khan, Nelson Mandela and Martin Luther King come readily to mind.

September 11 in our own times has become a watershed date. Ironically, it was also on the 11th day of September in 1906 in Johannesburg that a young lawyer, dissatisfied with the idea of mere passive resistance, unveiled the concept of "Satyagraha". The lawyer Mohandas Karamchand Gandhi described Satyagraha as a "force which is born of truth and love of non-violence." For him, it was the end of a quest for a moral equivalent of war. In his own words:

> Non-violence is the greatest force at the disposal of mankind. It is mightier than the mightiest weapon of destruction devised by the ingenuity of man.

In his design of Satyagraha, the empowerment of the weakest was fundamental and means were as crucial as ends. With Satyagraha, Mahatma Gandhi ushered in the age of the 'common man' in history (and I should add, 'common woman' as well to an unprecedented degree). He did not claim to have originated any new principle or doctrine. He was always at pains to point out that, in his own way, he was trying only to apply the eternal truths to daily life and its problems. Satyagraha and all that it entailed was a completely novel mode of mass mobilisation and non-violent action. Over the years, it was used with wondrous effect. It showed how the individual can bring about social and political change.

Of course, we all know that with Mahatma Gandhi, more than with any other individual, the life was itself the message. A lightness of spirit was combined with seriousness of purpose. Respect for tradition was combined with bold iconoclasm. A life of contemplation was lived with galvanic energy. A personality unyielding in principle was also flexible in approach. Austerity was his hallmark, transparency his creed. Everything he thought, everything he did was open to public scrutiny. No freedom of information act was needed to shed light on his motives and actions.

Never has there been a man who was so merciless in self-criticism and self-reproach. Never has there been a man more unremitting in self-analysis and self-healing. He once remarked that self-purification was fundamental to Satyagraha. Thus, while we reflect on what he taught us, we should not forget how he lived. It is this coming together of thought, word and deed that is unique.

But we are not here just to celebrate Mahatma Gandhi once more, or to simply add to the Gandhian bibliography, so to speak. We are here today not just to recall what Mahatma Gandhi said and did yesterday but to explore what he might say and do today. We are congregated here to learn from each other, to share our experience, to reignite the spark of hope amidst the indifference and cynicism that surround us.

Although much of what he did has to be seen in the specific context of his times, the core of his philosophy reverberates even more strongly today.

To help us along, the Conference will have four specific but inter-related themes. First, a non-violent approach to conflict resolution and peace building. Second, the Gandhian philosophy for poverty eradication, education and people's empowerment. Third, dialogue among peoples and cultures. Finally, towards a nuclear weapons-free and non-violent world order. Let me briefly cover each of these four areas.

I

The end of the Cold War has not seen a worldwide resurgence of peace as we might have hoped. Democracy has certainly spread. But sometimes democratic forms can mask undemocratic practices. There has certainly been a growth of nationalism. But, too often, this nationalism, in the guise of building pride, is stoking prejudice with horrifying consequences. We continue to witness outbreaks of large-scale violence across the world targeting innocent men, women and children. Millions have been killed and displaced from their homes.

We are today faced with the scourge of terrorism fuelled by religious, political, ethnic or sectarian conflict. In too many parts of the globe, societies are in discord, nations are at war, human security at risk. In a number of cases, violence is the cry of the oppressed and the exploited. It is a sad reality that in many instances violence has to be resorted to in order to be heard.

While the underlying causes of conflict have to be understood, it does humanity no good to rationalise, let alone romanticise, violence in any way. It provides no lasting solutions. It leads to untold suffering and atrocities. Mahatma Gandhi was decidedly against the idea that violence is the only answer to violence. As he famously remarked: "An eye for an eye only ends up making the whole world blind."

It is only natural to ask the question: is the Gandhian way feasible at all today? Can it prevail against terrorism and extremism? It would, I suggest, be a grave error to writeoff the Gandhian approach as irrelevant to our age. There are individuals and groups who are trying to adapt and adopt Satyagraha to deal with changing circumstances and situations. The challenge for us now is to find creative inspiration from the Gandhian way to evolve a Satyagraha appropriate to our times.

II

Globalisation has had both positive and negative effects. It has certainly expanded opportunities for many in the developing world but it has also left many poor countries behind. Moreover, even in the countries that have reaped the fruits of economic expansion, there are regions and communities that have become poorer, at least in the relative sense. Our own country, for instance, has made spectacular gains over the past decades and is being rapidly transformed. But destitution, poverty, malnutrition and illiteracy are still widespread. Inequality is very visible.

We live in an age of incredible scientific achievement and awesome technological advance. But are not the fruits of this achievement and advance still inequitably distributed? Is it not the case that a few enjoy the gains, while many bear the pains? We must accelerate economic growth. But should we not be mindful of possible adverse consequences of that progress and take steps to deal with them? Can we not satisfy material wants and aspirations without threatening ecological security and planetary survival?

Does economic progress have to be necessarily accompanied by the spread of social bigotry, as we see in many places? Must gender and disadvantage continue to be synonymous? To be equitable, economic growth has to be sustainable. To be sustainable, economic growth has, in turn, to be all-inclusive. All-inclusive is no longer the "greatest good of the greatest number". It is actually "sarvodaya", or "the rise of all". Mahatma Gandhi saw this as essential to Satyagraha itself. He insisted that such a rise must be respectful of land in harmony with nature and the earth's long-term future.

III

A noted anthropologist has recently said that while the very idea of a clash of civilisations is wrong, a civilisation of clashes is today's reality. That is what makes dialogue among cultures and peoples urgent. But dialogue to be meaningful has to proceed in a spirit of give and take. Dialogue to be meaningful has to be infused with a spirit of accommodation and compromise.

Mahatma Gandhi once declared that intolerance is the worst form of violence. Without genuine tolerance, without that tolerance that springs from within, no dialogue can have an impact.

Of course dialogue is between peoples and among cultures. But Mahatma Gandhi did more than this. His external engagement proceeded from a ruthless internal interrogation of himself. That is what made his approach unique. He was not always successful, as he himself admitted more than once. But he never abandoned the pursuit.

For us to follow in his footsteps, we need to rid our minds of stereotypes that condition us to act with hostility towards others. Where are the roots of hatred sown? Where is the poison of prejudice first injected? Without doubt, in young and impressionable minds.

That is why personally I believe that education and the values it inculcates and instils are so very important. Sometimes, I just feel that if we were to rewrite history text-books together, nations that confront each other could reduce distrust, setting the stage for reconciliation.

IV

In the immediate aftermath of Hiroshima, Mahatma Gandhi had said that "the moral to be legitimately drawn from the supreme tragedy of the bomb is that it will not be destroyed by counter-bombs, even as violence cannot be destroyed by counter-violence. Mankind has to get out of violence only through non-violence."

Since then, nuclear weapons have become even more of a terrifying reality. They have become the very currency of power. The world's nuclear weapon states have more than adequate atomic arsenal to destroy humanity many times over. And it is not just nuclear weapons. We also confront the spectre of chemical and biological weapons.

In October 1988, my late husband Rajiv Gandhi had presented a blueprint for a comprehensive, universal nuclear disarmament at the United Nations. Just a few days ago, four influential Americans who held very different views whilst in office, including Henry Kissinger and George Shultz, have drawn attention to his impassioned plea and called for urgent action.

Yes, India has nuclear weapons. This became a strategic compulsion for us, born out of the failure to persuade the world to abolish nuclear weapons. But the commitment to comprehensive, universal nuclear disarmament remains our profound conviction which we intend to carry forward.

The relevance of Mahatma Gandhi is not the real issue. Our preparedness for him is. The question is not whether Mahatma Gandhi is relevant for us. Instead, it is whether we are ready to embrace him once again. It is not a question of going back to Mahatma Gandhi as much as it is of going forward with him.

This is not as simple as it sounds. While he fascinates and enchants, we have to admit that it is difficult to emulate him. It is easy to make him an icon. But it is infinitely more exacting to make him our beacon. He did not provide us with final answers. He wanted us to find our own and make our own experiments with truth.

The task before us is how we, individually and collectively, launch an organised, disciplined mass movement for peace, non-violence and empowerment, which is the very essence of Satyagraha.

In his own lifetime, it was the youth who were particularly drawn to that rare combination of passion and compassion, of candour and courage. Likewise, it is today's young men and women who have to take the Gandhian torch forward. We look to them for initiative and leadership.

Let the message go forth that men and women from across the world assembled here, and resolved to rediscover the Mahatma's way for peace and harmony. Let the message also go forth that we met here to rekindle the flame of Gandhian action with its array of revolutionary ideas and techniques. Let the world know that there are men and women, in governments and outside, who are determined to propagate Gandhian values.

Plurality preserves us. Diversity defines us. For that plurality to survive, for that diversity to prosper, we need a new global compact, a new global covenant. I submit to you that the foundations of this new edifice can be found in what Mahatma Gandhi preached and practised, in what Mahatma Gandhi lived for and died for.

My life is my message.
— M.K. Gandhi

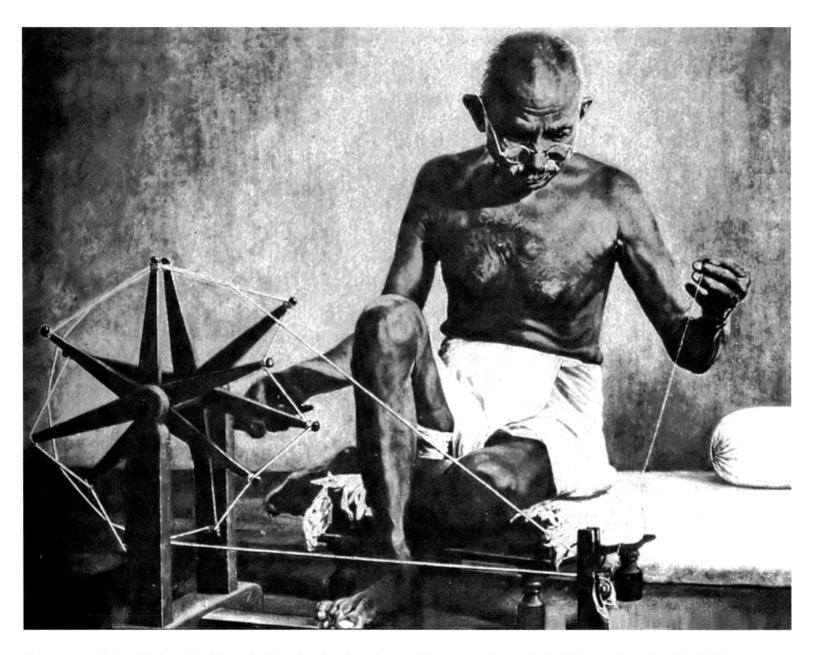

The message of the spinning-wheel is much wider than its circumference. Its message is one of simplicity, service of mankind, living so as not to hurt others, creating an indissoluble bond between the rich and the poor, capital and labour, the prince and the peasant. That larger message is naturally for all. — M.K. Gandhi

3

Celebrating Satyagraha

Assertion of Human Dignity and Spirit

MANMOHAN SINGH

THE ideas that Mahatma Gandhi is remembered for are based on universal ideals. Many "Isms" battle for our minds, but few succeed in touching our hearts. Many political ideologies have come and gone over the past century, some with doubtful legacies and others with terrible consequences. The only political philosophy that I believe will remain relevant for as long as humankind seeks peace—peace in our societies, peace between nations and peace with nature—will be the ideas and values we associate with Mahatma Gandhi.

These ideas and values are today remembered not just when we gather to celebrate the life and teachings of Gandhiji. They are remembered across the world when people gather to honour the legacy of his many disciples—like Martin Luther King, Nelson Mandela, Bishop Desmond Tutu, Vaclav Havel, Lech Walesa, and scores of others who have opted for the path of non-violence in the struggle for purposeful social change.

I salute the Gandhian vision of Nelson Mandela and Archbishop Desmond Tutu who inspired South Africans to practise what Mahatma Gandhi preached. The great liberation of South Africa and the end of apartheid have shown that it is possible to resolve even the bitterest of differences with a spirit of reconciliation. I am, therefore, delighted that we have in our midst Archbishop Desmond Tutu.

Why do we celebrate Satyagraha? We do so because of the timeless relevance of this unique form of assertion of the human dignity and the human spirit. Gandhiji himself explained the term Satyagraha in these words:

> Truth (*Satya*) implies love, and firmness (*agraha*) engenders and
> therefore serves as a synonym for force....the force which is born
> of truth and love or non-violence.

As long as we live in a world of conflict, as long as human societies are divided by differences, as long as people resort to might to assert their right, there will always be a Gandhian to remind us of the power of truth, of love, of compassion, of peace. That is why I believe Mahatma Gandhi was the most modern thinker of the 20th century.

The essence of Gandhiji's political philosophy was the empowerment of every individual, irrespective of caste, class, creed or community. Representative democracy is the institutional form in which modern societies have sought to empower individuals. Democracy is not just about periodic elections. Democracy is not just about keeping alive democratic institutions. Democracy is about respecting the innate rights of all human beings. Democracy is about tolerance. Democracy is about asserting the right to dissent. Democracy is about protecting the dignity and self-respect of every human being.

There is no corner of the world where the message of the Mahatma is still not relevant. It is a message that we also associate with the teachings of all the great religions of the world. No religion teaches intolerance. No religion preaches violence. No religion advocates injustice. Every religion echoes the deep and abiding faith of humankind in the power of peace and compassion. That message must go forth to every corner of the world.

When I say Mahatma Gandhi was the most modern thinker of the 20th century, I say so because of the overwhelming relevance today of the key ideas that Gandhiji put forth. *Satyagraha* and *Ahimsa*—peaceful resistance and non-violence were two such ideas. As I said, we have seen the wonders they continue to perform in transforming diverse societies across all continents. They have been able to give shape to dissent in a manner that has enabled peaceful transition through bloodless revolutions.

We must respect the value of dissent. But those who dissent must also respect the value of building a viable consensus. We must foster tolerance for the other point of view. Every one has a right to be heard, and must be heard. We must learn to listen to the other point of view. Violent conflict never allows this. Violence deafens us. Non-violence helps us to hear. A civilised society must offer space for discussion and dialogue. All human progress must be based on the firm foundation of societal consensus. But in a modern democracy, we must respect the role of institutions that seek to create and translate that consensus into policy action.

Satyagraha should never be viewed as a means of obstructing dialogue or obstructing change. I believe Gandhiji always viewed Satyagraha as a means to a dialogue, as an instrument of change and progress. Satyagraha was, therefore, not an end in itself. It was a means to an end. That end being the liberation of all people, their peaceful coexistence and, above all, their well-being and progress.

There are other ideas of Gandhiji that are also of great relevance today. They are relevant to the way we wish to organise our societies and our polity. They are relevant to the way we wish to conduct national and international affairs. They are relevant to the path of development we wish to pursue.

One such idea is captured by Gandhiji's statement that "the Earth provides enough to satisfy every man's need, but not every man's greed." In this simple statement on sustainable development Mahatma Gandhi showed us the value of high thinking and simple living. The concern for our environment that now envelops civil society across the globe is best articulated by this simple statement. I do sincerely believe that the world cannot sustain the lifestyles of the affluent. We need a new development paradigm that caters to everyone's need and can keep in check human greed.

A second idea of equally great relevance to our world today, an idea that can foster peace between peoples, cultures, nations and civilisations, is captured by Gandhiji's statement, and I quote: "I do not want to stay in a house with all its windows and doors shut. I want a house with all its windows and doors open where the cultural breezes of all lands and nations blow through my house. But I refuse to be blown off my feet by any." This pluralism, this liberalism, this commitment to an open society and an open polity, I believe also an open economy, is what shaped our national movement under Gandhiji's leadership. These wise words must guide us all in this era of globalisation.

If there is one message India should be remembered for, and identified with, it is the message of the Mahatma. The message of tolerance, of pluralism, of the need to "live and let live". Every civilised society must respect human freedoms, must care for the poorest of the poor and must enable the coexistence of all religions, all languages, all colours and creeds.

Our pluralism is our biggest and most enduring tribute to the Father of our Nation. As long as the 'idea of India' lives in our hearts and minds, the legacy of the Mahatma will live on. This 'idea of India' is the idea of 'unity in diversity'. The idea of pluralism, the idea that there need be no 'conflict of civilisations', the idea that it is possible for us to facilitate and work for a 'confluence of civilisations'. These ideas, I believe, have a universal, a truly global relevance. In a world enveloped by the darkness of conflict and hatred, these ideas come as rays of sunshine, lighting up our lives, giving us hope, renewing our faith in our common humanity.

I sincerely hope we can convey this message to the world.

4

Poverty, Injustice and World Peace

MUHAMMAD YUNUS

MAHATMA Gandhi's Satyagraha Movement, the historical movement of civil disobedience, passive resistance and a struggle for upholding the truth has shaped not just the history of the subcontinent but indeed of the world. Mahatma Gandhi's life and example have influenced deeply the values of modern civilisation and remain an inspiration for us all even one hundred years after the movement began. In these troubled times that we live in, his memory and message are as important as they were before.

Poverty and Peace

The significance of this year's Nobel Peace prize is that in a powerful way it links poverty and peace. It recognises poverty as a threat to peace. This year's Nobel Peace prize has focused the world's attention on what is, in my view, the most important issue of the day—poverty, what the Mahatma emphasised long back. It is impossible for us to think of a peaceful world when 60 per cent of the world population lives on 6 per cent of the world income only and half of the world population lives on under two dollars a day.

At the United Nations, the world had united in the year 2000 to adopt the Millennium Development Goals which aimed to reduce extreme poverty by half before 2015. This was a bold and ambitious goal, the pursuit of which was derailed at the start of the millennium by the war on terrorism. I believe we have to fight terrorism. But to do that, it should not be by military action. We should be addressing terrorism by its root causes which, in many cases, are poverty and injustice.

Financial Apartheid

I have long argued that poor people remain poor not because of any fault of their own, but because we have designed institutions and policies in the wrong way. No matter how hard the poor masses try or how hard they work, they remain trapped in poverty because of these institutions and because of these policies. A major example of this is the financial institutions that we have created all over the world. Two-thirds of the world's population does not have access to financial services from the conventional financial institutions.

That we systematically exclude poor people from financial services is tantamount to financial apartheid. What Grameen Bank has sought to do over the 30 years since its inception is to provide financial services to the very poor on terms that are suited to them. Grameen Bank's microcredit, in its very essence, challenges this unjust global financial system.

Grameen Bank

What began as a tiny project in a small village called Jubra in Bangladesh, is now a nationwide programme through the Grameen Bank which gives collateral free loans to nearly seven million poor people—97 per cent of them are women—in all the villages of Bangladesh. Grameen Bank gives income-generating loans, housing loans, student loans and micro enterprise loans to the poor families and offers a host of attractive savings including pension funds and insurance products for its members. Since it introduced them in 1984, housing loans have been used to construct over 700,000 houses.

In a cumulative way the Bank has given loans totalling over six billion US dollars worth of Bangladeshi currency. The repayment rate is 99 per cent. Grameen Bank routinely makes profit. Financially, it is self-reliant and has not taken donor money since 1995. Deposits and own resources of Grameen Bank today amount to 143 per cent of all the outstanding loans. According to Grameen Bank's internal survey, 58 per cent of our borrowers have crossed the poverty line. Most importantly, it has proved that the poor, indeed the poorest people are creditworthy and bankable in the deepest meaning of the term.

Social and Economic Empowerment

In Bangladesh, we have made progress in improving the lives of the poor and especially in empowering the poor women. Through provision of microcredit, combined with social mobilisation, microcredit programmes have become a vehicle which has changed the lives and the outlook of the poor in Bangladesh forever. We have created a revolution, one that is silent and non-violent.

Microcredit network has provided a framework for bringing dramatic changes in the lives of the people beyond merely economic ones. Grameen Bank focused on women not only because they repaid the loans better but we have found without exception that loans going to the families through women invariably bring about deeper and more lasting changes in the families.

Research has shown that women's participation in microcredit programme has resulted in their steady empowerment over time. Women have much greater role in decision-making in their families today as an outcome of participating in the programmes. They have greater independence of movement, greater participation in social activities and so on. And as a result, they are more confident in themselves and in the future of their families.

A powerful impact of women's participation in microcredit programme is the impact it has on the children. Mothers always give topmost priority to their children. That is why we first look at our children to see what has been the impact of our work. We always encourage children of our members to go to school and over the years, all the children of our members have enrolled in schools. Not only did they enroll in schools, but they became the top students in their classes and their schools. We began providing scholarships and student loans to the children of Grameen Bank's borrowers who, we are delighted to discover, are attaining the highest levels of achievement in professional and other education. These children are the first literate generation in their families and are poised to make a historical break in the generational poverty and illiteracy.

Expansion of Microcredit

Microcredit has been shown to contribute in a significant way to poverty reduction. Globally, nearly 100 million of the worlds' poorest have now been reached with microcredit. Although the expansion of microcredit to the poor is encouraging, there are still a number of constraints that prevent microcredit spreading even more quickly.

Bangladesh is still the only country where microcredit outreach to the poor families is over 75 per cent. In most of the countries it has not even reached 10 per cent of the poor families. To make a significant dent in global poverty, each country must reach out to 50 per cent of the poor families within the country. Therefore, there is a lot of catching up to do. Two major issues are always discussed in connection with the institutionalisation of microcredit in Bangladesh and elsewhere. They are: 1) financing of microcredit; and 2) legal and regulatory framework for integrating microcredit with the national financial system. Both issues are inextricably linked with each other. If the issue of appropriate legal and regulatory framework for microcredit institutions is resolved, then the funding issue becomes much easier to address.

Microcredit programmes through Grameen Bank type programmes as well as the widespread Self-Help Group system are helping to bring poor people into the mainstream economy in India. Without these opportunities for the poor to join the ranks of the middle class, we cannot hope for a stable future in our countries.

India has already taken many important initiatives in the field of finance for the poor. The government, NGOs and private sector are joining hands to expand the outreach. The whole world is looking to India to take the lead in organising the requisite funding mechanisms for support of microcredit as well as the supportive legal and regulatory framework that will kick start the sector in this country.

Regional Cooperation

In Bangladesh we have made great strides in human development. We have reduced infant mortality and maternal mortality. We have created good opportunities for participation of women in the economy. Our non-resident Bangladeshis are contributing to the national exchequer in a more significant way than ever before. We have made great strides in telecommunications in Bangladesh. Through Grameenphone we have provided nearly 300,000 mobile phones to poor women in every village of Bangladesh, connecting them to the rest of the world. We are now working on bringing information and communication technology to the masses.

In this regard we look at India with great admiration in what it has achieved by harnessing the talents of Indians in India as well as Indian diaspora. We look forward to creating a framework with India and SAARC countries for poverty alleviation for the region. In this respect, I am happy to report that Grameen Bank will be opening, in just a few days, an office in Mumbai as a way of bringing Grameen Bank in Bangladesh closer to development organisations in India.

I look forward to a Bangladesh which works very closely with India for a common future of prosperity for the peoples of our two countries. I have been advocating the creation in Bangladesh of a mega port in Chittagong together with an international airline hub which all countries in the region can benefit from.

I share with His Excellency Prime Minister Dr. Manmohan Singh the excitement about building a highway network to connect all the SAARC countries where Bangladesh becomes an intersection that connects Nepal, Bhutan, Eastern India,

Pakistan as well as Myanmar, Thailand and China in the eastern side. With borders opening up, highways criss-crossing the region and businesses growing, we can create mutual trust and cooperation among all the countries of the region to work towards a regional water management plan in conjunction with the plan for regional production and distribution of electricity. Fortunately, this region has an enormous capacity to produce hydroelectricity. With growing political understanding, Bangladesh can meet her ever-growing electricity needs from a mutually beneficial arrangement with Nepal, Bhutan and India.

Social Business

I have been talking about creating social businesses which will be a kind of business introduced in the market place with the objective of making a radical difference to the world. I am arguing that all businesses do not have to be profit-maximising entities. By asserting that businesses, by their very nature, are only one kind, that is the profit-maximising kind, and by practising it as an axiom we have created a world where social problems remain unaddressed or sometimes partially addressed by philanthropy or left to be addressed by the concerned Government alone.

A social business, designed and operated as a business enterprise to pass on all the benefits to the customers, replaces the profit-maximisation principle by a benefit-maximisation principle. In a social business, benefits of the business are passed on to the target group rather than translated into profit for the investors. Investors in the social business could get back their investment money, but will not take any dividend from the company. Instead, profit would be ploughed back into the company to expand its outreach and improve the quality of its product or the service. A social business will be a non-loss, non-dividend company.

Young people all around the world, particularly in rich countries, or in rich families will find the concept of social business very appealing since it will give them a challenge to make a difference by using their creative talents. Almost all social and economic problems of the world can be addressed through social businesses. Social business is important because it addresses very vital concerns of humankind. It can change the lives of the bottom 60 per cent of the world population and help them to move out of poverty.

Even profit-maximising companies can be designed as social businesses by giving full or majority ownership to the poor. This constitutes a second type of social business. Grameen Bank falls under this category of social business. It is owned by the poor. The poor could get the shares of these companies as gifts by donors, or they could buy the shares with their own money. The borrowers buy Grameen Bank shares with their own money, and these shares cannot be transferred to non-borrowers. A committed professional team does the day-to-day running of the bank. Bilateral and multilateral donors could easily create this type of social business. When a donor gives a loan or a grant to build a bridge in the recipient country, it could create instead a 'bridge company' owned by the local poor. A committed management company could be given the responsibility of running the company. Profit of the company will go to the local poor as dividend, and towards building more bridges. Many infrastructure projects, like roads, highways, airports, seaports and utility companies could all be built in this manner.

Grameen Bank has created two social businesses of the first type. One is a yogurt factory, to produce fortified yogurt to bring nutrition to malnourished children. It is a joint venture with Danone. It will continue to expand until all malnourished children of Bangladesh are reached with fortified yogurt. Another is a chain of eye-care hospitals. Each hospital will undertake, on an average, 10,000 cataract surgeries per year at differentiated prices to the rich and the poor.

I have even been advocating the creation of a separate social stock market where only the shares of social businesses will be traded.

I support globalisation and believe it can bring more benefits to the poor than any of its alternatives. But it must be the right kind of globalisation. The rule of "strongest takes it all" must be replaced by rules that ensure that the poorest have a significant share in the action, without being elbowed out by the strong. Globalisation must not become financial imperialism. Powerful multinational social businesses can be created to retain the benefit of globalisation for the poor people in Third World poor countries.

I believe that social businesses, particularly multinational social businesses, will radically transform the nature of capitalism, which in its present incarnation does not create enough opportunities for the poor, and which in fact threatens the global environment through ever increasing materialism and consumerism.

Creating a Poverty Free World

Within a framework that encompasses Gandhiji's philosophy of tolerance and non-violence, compassion for all humanity and peaceful coexistence, we can work together to create a world that our grandchildren and our great grandchildren can be proud of. We can create a world where we can achieve peace, not through war but through dialogue and cooperation. We can create a world where we prefer to use resources on improving the lives of the poor rather than spend on weapons. We can create a world which is prosperous where we all live together in peace. We can create a world where each individual has the opportunity to unleash the unlimited potential that he or she is born with to achieve what he or she dreams of.

We can create a world where poverty exists only in the museums. Let us dream of such a world and work to make it happen.

Pietermaritzburg railway station, where Gandhi was evicted from the first class railway compartment despite having a valid ticket.

5

The Spirit of Togetherness

DESMOND TUTU

AS I stand before you, I feel immensely privileged to be part of this august and auspicious gathering, clearly imbibing every moment of this very moving and significant event. We, as invitees, must convey our profound gratitude to the Indian National Congress for this opportunity. I must congratulate Prime Minister Manmohan Singh and his government for steering India to what is distinctly one of the success stories of our globe; a country that is enjoying remarkable economic growth. I also want to acknowledge how deeply moved many of us were to observe the graciousness, magnanimity and the spirit of sacrifice exemplified by Madam Chair, Mrs. Sonia Gandhi in keeping with the true tradition of her inspiring leadership and of protecting the national interest of her country. Let me also recall the visit of Minister Anand Sharma who was able to come to our country at a very traumatic period of Boipatong massacre in 1992 that nearly sabotaged the whole negotiation process. He came as a Gandhian and gave comfort to us.

We South Africans boast that we have a rather substantial share in the great soul—the Mahatma, whose philosophy, life and actions have inspired us greatly. As you know, within 10 days of his arriving in our beautiful South Africa, at the beginning of the 20th century, he suffered the humiliation of being ejected from a first class compartment of the train in which he was travelling, despite possessing a valid ticket. This happened in a place called Pietermaritzburg. He later himself described that particular event as the most creative experience of his life for it opened his eyes to the plight of Indians in South Africa and led him to evolve his Satyagraha—adherence to truth through non-violent action.

He was instrumental in the founding of the Natal Indian Congress and his non-violent method achieved much improvement in the lot of South African Indians. So, we legitimately lay a claim to a fairly significant part of Mahatma Gandhi. He was pivotal in the struggle against South African racism and honed his political skills in South Africa. He returned to his homeland and was absolutely pivotal to the defeat of the colonialism of the British *raj* and the emergence of India as a free and democratic land, the world's largest democracy. He also campaigned effectively against casteism, identifying with the so-called untouchables whom he called the "Harijan", God's children, the Dalits. He thought that revenge, retribution, reprisal are all self-defeating. An eye for an eye makes all the people blind.

When will we ever learn that the most effective way of dealing with differences, with conflict, with disagreement is not through force, not by annihilating the others? But it is through forgiveness, through negotiation, through compromise, through trying to see the point of view of the other, recognising and respecting the essential, irreducible human spirit which is common to us all.

But when will we learn this vital truth? It is said, we learn from history that we do not learn from history. In the bad old days they used to tell in South Africa what they called van der Merve stories. The story goes that a friend of this van der Merve took him to a movie and the movie was a western. This friend laid a bet with van der Merve and said—you know, you are going to see this film, where the villain is going to be riding a horse and then at one point during the movie, he is going to be hit by a branch and will fall down. They laid their bets. Sure enough, the bad guy got his comeuppance. He was hit by the branch and fell to the ground. Then the friend became somewhat remorseful and said to van der Merve, I am sorry, I was actually cheating you; I did see this film before. To which, van der Merve replied, well, I am sorry too, I had also seen the movie but I did not think that this guy was so stupid that he would again come and allow himself to be hit by the branch.

Do we not seem to be those who do not learn? We keep being hit by the same branch time after time. See what Hitler did. He blamed the economic wars of Germany, at a time, on the Jews and so clobbered them as he did the gypsies, homosexuals and blacks. They were all different. He wanted to deal with diversity by eliminating it. It led to the horror of the holocaust. Eventually, that nightmare ended after the defeat of the Nazis and thereafter Germany has been living with diversity and on the whole has prospered.

There was the evil of apartheid. The supporters of apartheid used violence and brutality to enforce this vicious system. Although committed to non-violence, those opposed to the apartheid system eventually resorted to violence too. Almost everybody predicted that—OK, that poor country! It is going to be overwhelmed by a racial system. It should have. But it did not. Did violence do the trick? No. The resolution of our almost intractable problem happened when the antagonists sat down and parleyed and negotiated and disagreed and compromised. It was then that the new South Africa emerged and it has become, in a way, a kind of paradigm of forgiveness and reconciliation. Nelson Mandela, who has been referred to earlier, emerged as a universal icon of magnanimity and forgiveness.

In 1994, there was the ghastliness of the genocide in Rwanda when the Hutus taking to violence climbed into Tutsis with gay abandon. Nearly a million people were killed. Now they are doing what they should have done right at the beginning. They are seeking a way through the morass. They are looking for accommodation of one another. They are looking for peace. They are looking for reconciliation. We could multiply the examples—the aftermaths of the so-called ethnic cleansing in Bosnia, the sinning intractable madness in the Middle East, the sectarian strife in Northern Island, the civil war in Sri Lanka, the Democratic Republic of the Congo, Columbia, Chechnya, Sudan, Somalia, Burma, etc. The catalogue is so long that you become intensely conscious of the catastrophe that ought not to have happened.

In Iraq and in virtually all of these places, the antagonists have resorted to violence and yet, in the end, they will realise that they will find peace, stability, prosperity only through the non-violent ways of negotiation, talking to one another, compromising, trying to enter into the shoes of the other. Martin Luther King Junior, a disciple of the Mahatma summed it up all succinctly. The choice, he said, is between non-violence and non-existence. This is a moral universe. There is no way that injustice, oppression and evil can ever have the last word. Ultimately, truth, goodness, love, laughter, compassion, caring and sharing, these are what will prevail. Those who used power for their self-aggrandisement, for perpetrating injustice, for oppressing others have fallen. They always ultimately bite the dust and do so ignominiously. Where are they today—those who used to be the cocks of the walk, seemingly invincible, the Hitlers, the Amins, the Mussolinis, the Stalins, the perpetrators of apartheid, the Pinochets, etc.? We ask again—where are they? They have become the flotsam and the jetsam of history.

We revere, we hold in the highest possible regard and esteem not the macho, not the aggressive; no. We hold in the highest possible esteem deep reverence for a person like Mahatma Gandhi, a Mother Teresa, a Dalai Lama, an Aung San Suu Kyi, a Nelson Mandela. We hold them in high regard because they are good and we are made for goodness, for compassion, for caring. We are those who are made for fellowship, for family. There is no way that we will ever win what we call the war against terror as long as the conditions in the world that make some desperate to treat our sisters and brothers, members of our own families as if they were rubbish. We are made for togetherness, for harmony. At home we have something that is difficult to translate—*Ubuntu* which speaks about generosity, about hospitality, about gentleness, about caring. *Ubuntu* is the essence of being human and we say a person is a person through other persons. For you see, we are all bound together in the bundle of life.

There is an old film—most of you are too young to know of—*The Defiant Ones*. It shows two escaped convicts, one is black and the other is white. They are manacled together and they fall down a slippery slope. And then, one tries to clamber out and he makes his attempts to get up and he nearly gets up; but he cannot make it because he is bound to his fellow convict. The only way they can ever make it is together—up and out together.

Mahatma Gandhi would say, yes, we can be free only together; we can be safe only together; we can be prosperous only together; we can be human only together; otherwise not.

In 1893 Mahatma Gandhi arrived in South Africa to practise law. Instead, he practised humanity. Putting his life to risk, he took active part in organising Indian Ambulance Corps for the British during the Boer War (1899), a role for which he received recognition in the form of prestigious medals. Soon thereafter, he plunged himself into leading peaceful revolts against British atrocities and discriminatory policies towards the Indian community working in South Africa. Thus, began the life of a true 'satyagrahi'.

On 16 August 1908, outside the Hamidia Mosque in Johannesburg, thousands gathered in response to Gandhi's call and publicly burnt their registration certificates protesting against the 'Black Act'.

C.S.O. 187

Transvaal Asiatic Registration Certificate.

Name in full... Mohandas Karamchand Gandhi...

Race... Br. Indian... Age... 37... Height... 5-7¾

Description... Scar left cheekbone...

Registrar of Asiatics.

Right Thumb Impression.

Date of Issue 10ᵗʰ February 1908

Holder's Signature... M.K.Gandhi

Name of Wife... Kasturbai... Residence... India

SONS and MALE WARDS under the age of 16 years.

NAMES.   AGE.   RESIDENCE

6

Building a New World Order

ELA GANDHI

HUMANKIND today stands at crossroads. The stark reality facing us is to make us choose between conserving the world through constructive programmes or destroying it through exploitation of both people and resources. We really need a comprehensive solution and I believe that Gandhiji offered us such a solution. It is a solution based on faith in humankind. His appeal is a universal appeal that aims to bring on surface the goodness that lies in all of us. It is an appeal that we ignore at our own peril.

So, as we deliberate today on the complexities of non-violence, of eradication of poverty, of empowerment and of peace, let us consider some of the most practical and immediate steps which each one of us can take in order to achieve our aims. Let us come up with a practical solution, a practical blueprint, a pathway to attain these goals. I believe that a new world order is possible, a new ethos and a new worldview is possible if we collectively endeavour to attain it.

Satyagraha is based on faith in all human beings, in our ability to bring to surface the good in all of us and in our firm commitment to fearlessly pursue truth, a truth which we can all see if we allow ourselves to be objective, to be sincere and to be determined. The greatness of Gandhiji lies not in his philosophy but in his ability to translate his beliefs into action and to mobilise the masses to likewise act on their beliefs.

We have gathered here as people who have power within our countries, within our societies and in the world. The challenge lies in our ability to make a commitment, build a new world order based on the principles of equity, non-violence and love for our world and the universe.

Farewell to South Africa (1914).

7

Re-launching the Satyagraha Movement

KENNETH KAUNDA

MAHATMA Gandhi was our torch bearer without whose guidance the history of our struggle for freedom and national independence would have taken a different course. It is therefore, fitting that all men and women of goodwill the world over should not only acknowledge his role in shaping the course of history, but also renew our commitment to the values he espoused and his noble mission of building a world that enjoys peace and harmony deeply rooted in justice for all. His historic contribution to human development has added significance in our region because it is this great visionary who kicked off the fight for justice that triggered the struggle against apartheid in South Africa, the last bastion of racism, oppression and foreign domination. He fuelled the spirit for the nascent independence movement.

Mahatma Gandhi was a legend of extraordinary quality, endowed with a depth of vision, humility and wisdom without parallel, with exemplary passion for justice, an indefatigable fighting spirit for what was right, courage to face any risk and readiness to make the supreme sacrifice in the service of mankind. Nothing that touched humanity was foreign to him. Jawaharlal Nehru said of this towering figure: "The manner of his death was the culmination and perfect climax to an astonishing career."

Gandhi's epoch-making career gave birth to the Satyagraha Movement dedicated to promoting non-violence and passive resistance against powerful forces of the colonial, oppressive and racist regimes that created conditions for violent change among the world's peoples.

The World Faces Dangerous Time Ahead

Today, in a world facing turmoil, a world in which senseless and unjust wars are raging with catastrophic consequences, the relevance of the Gandhian message, embodied in Satyagraha, is even greater and more challenging than in his time.

The world has become a more dangerous place than earlier and needs leaders embracing the Gandhian spirit and values.

Yet this should be an exciting century in human development. The 20th century's phenomenal advances in science and technology are without parallel in history. The 21st century promises even more progress propelled by new accomplishments that improve the quality of life.

Advances in information technology and communication, in medicine, among others, have all revolutionised the way the world is developing, the way we think, live and work. What a wonderful world it would be if these tremendous achievements were attended by and nurtured under conditions of perfect peace! Regrettably, while vast opportunities for a better world abound, we have made no headway in changing human behaviour. The incurable cancer of greed, heartlessness and insatiable appetite for power and desire to impose one's will on others, to dominate and control the world, to dictate the terms of peace, stability, security, cooperation and development among nations still persists among world leaders. Massive financial resources, in trillions of US dollars which should support efforts in human development, are diverted to futile destructive wars. The beneficiaries are arms manufacturers and arms dealers in developed countries. The poor in the developing countries are the worst victims. Look at the destruction in the killing fields of Iraq, Afghanistan, Lebanon, Palestine, Darfur, Somalia, Sierra Leone, Ivory Coast, Liberia, the Congo D.R., Sri Lanka and many other parts of the world. The list is endless.

UN Resolutions and countless others adopted in many other fora calling for peaceful end to conflicts have done little to stop the senseless massacres of the innocent in countless numbers. Modern technology, designed to improve the quality of human life, has changed the art of war. Conventional warfare with limited killing capacity has been replaced by weapons with immeasurable destructive capacity. The ingenuity of modern technology has been abused and is easily accessible even to militants conducting war without borders. Suicide bombers have become a new force in insurgency operations. Millions continue to suffer and die in the name of national interests, ideology, religion or some perceived personal glory. Dialogue is spurned to satisfy the egos of those powerful but dangerous war mongers backed by massive military machines and financial resources.

Science and technology, the very instruments for advancing the welfare of mankind have become the weapon for man's destruction.

Degrading Poverty Breeds Fertile Ground for Instability, Revolution and Terrorism

Unfortunately, these unprecedented advances in science and technology have not improved the devastating social and economic conditions of the world's poor. The recent World Social Forum held in Nairobi, Kenya, reaffirmed the global concern about the vast majority of the world's people who are still in the vice-like grip of abject poverty. This concern has been echoed again at the recent meeting of world leaders in Davos where the failed promises to reduce global poverty have been reviewed. Millions of people have yet to benefit from the tremendous progress recorded by modern science and technology. Poverty levels and associated abject social conditions in most parts of the world remain dangerously high and provide cause for frustration, anger, militancy and violence that fuel conflicts. International terrorism finds fertile ground for the spread of the ideology of hatred and senseless killing of innocent people. Extremism by nations and organisations in pursuit of ideological and personal interests is identified with virtue and is glorified.

We, therefore, need to address critical issues of conflict resolution and poverty eradication as foundations for sustainable peace, security, stability, cooperation and development. In doing so, we need the Gandhian message embodied in Satyagraha. Gandhi used non-violence to mould and move enormous masses of people against injustice. He won. His victory was an inspiration to many in the world. Martin Luther King Jr. adopted non-violence in the United States and won. We adopted it in Zambia and we won. So his victory became our victory. Southern Africa was an exception. Liberation movements only took up arms because the minority racist regimes used armed repression to frustrate African aspirations. The nationalist armed response was predictable, giving proof to the dictum: "Those who prevent peaceful change make violent change inevitable."

The re-launching of the Satyagraha Movement, therefore, provides an opportunity to tell the war mongers that: Enough is enough. Stop the wars; start talking. Spare innocent lives. Stop the war games and play 'peace games'. Stop the blame game and save innocent lives instead of saving face. An unjust war, however well prosecuted, brings no honour to the victor. Americans, with massive superior power, learned valuable lessons in Vietnam. The US primacy in world affairs may be unquestionable, but will not give Americans power to control and dominate the world. Iraq, a country smaller than many US states, has just proved it.

It is now time to deal with the root causes of conflicts and not merely to manage the consequences or treat the symptoms as the world drifts towards Armageddon. Let us therefore sound the clarion call to all men, women and youth of goodwill to unite and work for an end to the era of invasions, fratricidal conflicts, terrorism, military coups and oppression. Let us call for a stop to the senseless deaths of young men and women in uniform and the helpless millions of victims of collateral damage in the theatres of conflict.

I appeal to President George Bush, to Prime Minister Blair and their allies to stop these wars. Military strategies and campaigns have obviously failed at great cost in life, property and opportunities for development. No one with any sense of humanity and responsible leadership can stand the sickening devastation shown on our television screens.

These costly wars are not in US and British interests. The US and UK are less safe today than before the wars in Iraq and Afghanistan. Israel is even less secure. The rights of Americans and British people have been eroded by the demands of national security.

I also appeal to the al-Qaeda leadership, Islamist militants and other combatants engaged in conflicts to end the pursuit of their objectives through the terrorist path. Islam espouses love and peace. The military or insurgency options will not produce the desired results. It is time to pursue the path of peace, not war; the path of dialogue, not military confrontation.

I call upon those financing the senseless catastrophic wars to turn their massive resources and efforts to the war against poverty, hunger, ignorance, HIV/AIDS, malaria, tuberculosis and other debilitating diseases as well as the exploitation of the vulnerable by the powerful and acquisitive minority.

As we re-launch the Satyagraha Movement worldwide, we must re-dedicate ourselves to the preservation of freedom, peace, justice and development. Let us join hands with progressive Governments, Parliaments, national and international civil society movements, institutions and concerned citizens the world over. Let us stand up with a united voice and say 'no' to war; 'no' to terrorism; 'no' to war-mongers, war lords and arms dealers trading in weapons of death; 'no' to Government leaders seeking to glorify themselves by sending young men and women to die for senseless causes.

We must specifically address the Middle East crisis as a threat to international peace and security. The cloak of verbiage that characterised diplomatic shuttles in the midst of senseless destruction of Lebanon and Palestinian cities added nothing to stop the carnage. The fact is that the Israeli-Palestinian issue is the cradle of the conflict in the Middle East and West Asia in which Islamic militancy and terrorism preoccupying the world today find their genesis. Indeed, the Israeli-Palestinian conflict is at the core of tension in the Middle East. It is therefore important to recognise the fact that until the Israeli-Palestinian issue is resolved, it will continue to shape and even radicalise the historical events in the region which reverberate in many parts of the world.

We understand the need for Israel to have secure borders. We condemn terrorism in every shape and form. But the root cause lies with those who prevent peaceful change and refuse to recognise the Palestinian state. We must appeal to Israel and the Israeli lobby, particularly in the United States, to deal with the future of Palestine, honestly and resolutely. The US policy of play-acting and double-dealing diplomacy will not bring sustainable peace to Israel and the region. Terrorism will not disappear. Threats to US interests and security will continue to grow. The price will be paid by ordinary people.

The fratricidal conflict between Hamas and Hezbollah is unacceptable and must stop. It complicates the road to durable peace and security, thus giving Israeli authorities reason for prevarication. It frustrates those genuinely engaged in the peace making process. The worst victims of years of Israeli-Palestinian conflict are millions of innocent people even beyond the borders of the region.

Nuclear proliferation cannot be ignored and must be addressed fairly and without favour. It defeats the purpose of the Satyagraha Movement.

Finally, let me underline this: The current destructive and costly wars are unnecessary and must end. Military options have failed to achieve their objectives. Short of annihilating of whole nations, nuclear arsenals will not lead to domination of the world by any one nation. War games must point to one viable option, namely: dialogue and negotiation to end the conflicts. Most men in uniform will attest to this reality. There will be no victors; only the vanquished who are dead and those who will continue to die in the theatres of battle. To save humanity from destruction in the 21st century, the world must be armed, not with weapons of mass destruction, but with the values and wisdom espoused by Gandhi and embodied by the Satyagraha Movement as the hope of the future. As citizens of this global village, let us do our bit towards peace and security and commit ourselves to non-violence and dialogue and in unity declare: Let there be love, peace and joy shared among us.

8

Overcoming the New Divisions

LECH WALESA

MANKIND throughout history has been creating divisions—some divisions that were extremely nasty and other divisions that were very threatening. The divisions that Mahatma Gandhi struggled to overcome were not only nasty and threatening but also deep-rooted. Through 'Satyagraha' he found an effective method to overcome those divisions. Following Mahatma Gandhi's approach, Nelson Mandela overcame a very nasty division called apartheid. He can certainly be regarded as a great hero, the follower of Mahatma Gandhi. But is it not that Mr. de Clark is also a great follower of Mahatma Gandhi? He agreed to share his power with Blacks and released Nelson Mandela from prison, aware that he will lose his personal and political power.

I too consider myself a follower and a student of Mahatma Gandhi. However, the divisions that I tried to overcome were different. The division that I struggled against was the division of one-half of the world in favour of communism and the remaining against it. But when I say communism, I have the Soviet communism in mind. There are some other variants of communism in some parts of the world that can be tolerated.

Until 1970, I had not believed that the methods of Mahatma Gandhi could be effective. I could not believe that the Soviet communist empire could be defeated with peaceful measures. It was an empire that affected more than 200 million people. Incidentally, apartheid killed almost as many.

However, when I was faced with my struggle, I stood no chance. It seemed that no victory was possible, because, on the Polish territory alone we were controlled by 200,000 Soviet soldiers based there permanently and over 1 million armed Soviet soldiers in all the surrounding countries plus the nuclear missiles all around Poland. Actually it was this military potential that convinced me to adopt peaceful non-violent measures. Had I tried to struggle against communism through nonpeaceful measures, I could have blown up the whole world. It is true that in 1940s and 1950s we tried to oppose the communist system with arms. We lost in those attempts. We then tried to oppose the communist system with violent strikes and protests. We lost in those attempts, too.

Finally, following the example of Mahatma Gandhi we found that by adopting peaceful, non-violent measures we could reorganise the society, and empowered by the resulting solidarity and togetherness we could effectively lead that struggle. We did not lose in this attempt.

Our generation has seen the end of the era of division of the world into antagonistic blocks. We have seen the world embracing the era of intellect, information, Internet and globalisation. We have been successful in overcoming and eliminating many of the 'old divisions' that hampered world progress.

But 'new divisions' have immediately emerged. And these divisions are neither apparent nor definable. Through the legacy of Mahatma Gandhi's movement, we need to identify and verbalise these new divisions in the world. Once we are able to identify and define these 'new divisions', let this movement try to find measures to overcome these divisions.

There is a great rescue available to this world which I can see in globalisation, but certainly not through the globalisation that we see in the world today. What we have is more of a caricature than the globalisation in the true sense. The countries that have been oppressing and exploiting us are now trying to do so through globalisation. So, perhaps, the task for the followers of Mahatma Gandhi's movement would be to identify and formulate the correct shape of globalisation. To identify what should be our own individual role, the role of India and the role of the United States in this globalised world.

Our generation has succeeded in accomplishing a lot following Mahatma Gandhi's legacy. We should be able to face and find solutions to these new challenges also. I do hope that with our combined efforts we will find solutions to the new challenges facing the 21st century.

To conclude, I would like to stress: Please do not appropriate Mahatma Gandhi and limit him to South Africa and India only. His impact is felt throughout the world.

I would not like to live in this world if it is not to be one world.
— M.K. Gandhi

Addressing the Inter-Asian Relations Conference
in New Delhi on April 1, 1947.

No municipality can cope with insanitation and congestion by the simple process of taxation and paid services.
This vital reform is possible only by wholesale and voluntary co-operation of the people, both rich and poor.

— M.K. Gandhi

9

Immortality of Gandhian Philosophy

PRANAB MUKHERJEE

IT was exactly one hundred years ago when the mighty mind of Gandhiji forged an instrument of Satyagraha based on truth, non-violence and power of self-suffering. These instruments helped India to shed the yoke of colonialism and showed the path to many other countries also suffering under the oppressive rule of colonial powers to march towards Independence.

What is its relevance today? On 11th of September, 1906 at a mass meeting in the Empire theatre in Johannesburg in South Africa, Gandhiji launched Satyagraha to resist the Ordinance, which the apartheid regime in South Africa sought to impose upon the Indian immigrants. What was his weapon? It was peaceful resistance— non-violence. Barely 95 years after that incident, on the same 11th September in 2001, the whole world found a new form of weapon using human beings together with aircraft as the missiles and symbols of quantum violence. Therefore, I entirely agree with Lech Walesa when he says that Gandhi is not mere history but Gandhi is very much relevant even today. What did he conceptualise by Satyagraha? Gandhiji called it "the soul force." In his own words, "Satayagraha is a vindication of truth, not by infliction of suffering on the opponent but on one's own self that requires self-control; the weapon of Satyagraha is within reach." For Gandhiji the cause was as important as the way.

Driven by this conviction, Gandhiji stepped forward to take on the collective might of the State. He was the first *Satyagrahi* in the world to go to jail for upholding human rights. Gandhiji described the evolution of Satyagraha in the following words: "I myself am daily growing in the knowledge of Satyagraha. I have no readymade textbooks to consult in time of need." The struggle in South Africa lasted for eight years and ultimately the mighty colonial power had to yield.

After his return to India in 1914, Gandhiji practised Satyagraha on a number of occasions ranging from the very local issue of Birangam customs to the Indian

Immigration Act, Champaran Satyagraha, struggle for the mill hands of Ahmedabad, Kheda struggle against Rowlatt Act, Khilafat movement, etc. Over the years, Satyagraha evolved as a powerful expression of the wills and aspirations of the people of India.

When Gandhiji returned to India in 1914, the Indian National Congress was almost 30 years old. On the advice of Shri Gokhale, Gandhiji set out on his travels to understand and identify with the masses in India. It was during this period that Gandhiji metamorphosed into a true Indian. He adopted the austere lifestyle of the common man and learnt to empathise with common man's struggles, sufferings, simple joys and sorrows. With his keen intuition and sensitive heart, he understood the psyche of the nation. His great quality of first practising in his own life what he preached to others made him the real great Mahatma. The real strength of the Mahatma lay in the total and implicit confidence the masses reposed in him. It was his crusade against communalism in Noakhali which inspired Lord Mountbatten to comment: "Fifty thousand soldiers cannot maintain peace on the western frontier and prevent communal riots from reckless violence while on the eastern sector there is no ripple of violence because of the presence of one man boundary force in Gandhiji." He appealed to both the intellect and the heart of the masses. He epitomised the aspirations of 400 million Indians when against the British imperial forces, he declared on 8th August, 1942, two words "Quit India." With these two words the whole country was galvanised and Independence was achieved within five years.

Gandhiji evolved with time and his ideas changed. But there were three constants. These were: truth, non-violence and self-sacrifice. His ideas and his way of life permeated the collective conscience of India and found expression in all the democratic institutions that we have built up over the years. When we drew up our Constitution, concepts such as fundamental rights, directive principles to the States, abolition of untouchability, rights for underprivileged and the marginalised were all inspired by Gandhian thoughts and values.

Our foreign policy, which is based on Panchsheel, propounded by Pandit Jawaharlal Nehru was itself drawn from the Gandhian philosophy of peace and non-violence as well as the five principles of peaceful coexistence or respect for each other's territorial integrity, non-aggression, non-interference in each other's internal affairs, equality and peaceful coexistence. These are not only the basic tenets of India's foreign policy, but have now become the accepted norms of relations between nations and stand recognised throughout the world. Even in our security policy, non-aggression is the basic tenet.

India's commitment to work for universal disarmament has its roots in the doctrine of peaceful coexistence. Even though India is a nuclear weapon State today, it has affirmed its intention to maintain a credible minimum nuclear deterrent. As a responsible nuclear power it has exercised self-imposed moratorium on further tests and its commitment to no first use and no use against the non-nuclear weapon States. Another institution which has evolved in India today on the basis of the Gandhian philosophy is Panchayati Raj where the Village Councils or Village Parliament will assume more responsibility than the national Parliament or Lok Sabha. The principle of 'From Gram Sabha to Lok Sabha', which was the motto of Gandhiji, was sought to be effectively put into action by another illustrious follower of Gandhiji, the late Prime Minister Rajiv Gandhi.

Today, while listening to some of the observations made in this conference I am struck with the relevance of Gandhian philosophy in today's context. When Prof. Yunus explained his concept of social business, I found it close to the concept of Gandhiji's trusteeship in industry. Mr. Lech Walesa very correctly pointed out that this great man could never be confined either to South Africa or to India, but was a world force. The man was relevant in the 20th century; he is relevant to the 21st century.

I will conclude my observations by narrating a small incident which took place just on the eve of the Second World War. Rabindranath Tagore, the great poet, was in Europe at that time. It was before September 1939. Hitler had taken total control of Germany. The fascist forces had unleashed their operations. Einstein had been driven out of Germany. Books of Nobel Laureate Thomas Mann were burnt on the streets of Berlin. Naturally, a sensitive mind of a poet was hurt. He wrote about this to his friends all over the world. Many replies came. One reply was striking and I will just quote it. A friend of Tagore responded by stating: "I share your anguish; but at the same time I would like to remind you, the courses of civilisation have never been determined by the brutal forces. Courses of civilisation have been determined by the forces of humanity. Therefore, neither the brown shirt of Hitler nor the black shirt of Mussolini are going to determine the course of civilisation in the contemporary period. The course of civilisation is going to be determined by a person who has no shirt, he is Mahatma Gandhi. He lives in India."

Mahatma Gandhi was relevant yesterday, he is relevant today.

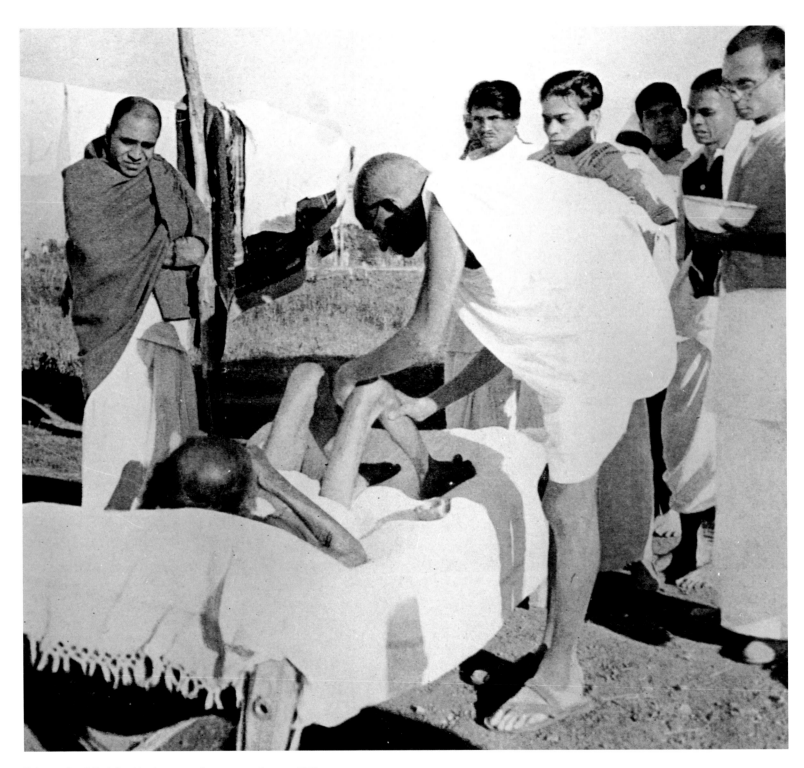

Mahatma Gandhi's daily attendance on a leprosy case, Segaon, 1939.

10

Promoting Gandhian Philosophy

NASSER AL-KIDWA

AS a Palestinian, as a son of the people who have lived through deprivation, pains and horrors for the last 100 years, I am here today to try once more to learn from the great philosophy of Gandhi. I am also here to express a special bond the Palestinians feel towards the Indian people and India—India of Mahatma Gandhi, of Jawaharlal Nehru and of course India of Indira Gandhi and Rajiv Gandhi—the distinct friends of our people, and along with Nelson Mandela, dear friends of our historic leader the late President Yasser Arafat.

The region of the Middle East has been suffering wars and foreign occupation. It has suffered from terrorism, extremism and religious intolerance. As such, it does pose very serious threats to international peace and security. So, let us hope that we can draw the necessary lessons from Gandhi's philosophy and let us try to promote those lessons; let us deepen dialogue and negotiations.

Let us raise our preparedness for Gandhi's philosophy and let us push for the application of that philosophy. While doing so, I am sure we can achieve justice for the Palestinian people and I am sure that we will be able to achieve peace and security for all peoples of the region and all states of the region including Palestine and Israel. By doing that, we will have contributed greatly in achieving peace and security the world over. Let us dream of the world that Muhammad Yunus has described to us. Let us draw upon Gandhi's philosophy and let us make our dream happen.

I have no weapon but love to
wield authority over anyone.

— M.K. Gandhi

11

True World Citizenship

ABDELAZIZ BOUTEFLIKA

THE active spirituality of Gandhi, an iconic world figure, symbolises non-violence, tolerance and the fight against discrimination. These were causes, which, he was wont to say, deserved that one should die for but not kill anyone for their sake. He was a man whose faith, purity and detachment from material benefits bring to mind the great Sufi masters of Islam, an Islam that Gandhi indeed recognised as being a religion of peace and wherein the Hadiths of Prophet Muhammad "are", said Gandhi, "a treasure of wisdom, not only for Moslems but for all mankind."

Anyway, how could I not follow up on an invitation of the Congress Party whose illustrious representative, Pundit Nehru, gave his precious support to Algeria's fight for freedom as early as 1955, during the Afro-Asian Conference in Bandoeng? His love for freedom and his vision made him say that: "Idealism is but tomorrow's realism." It was in this "tomorrow's" freedom that independent Algeria had the distinct honour of welcoming, in Algiers, the late Indira Gandhi at the Ministerial Conference of the Group 77 in 1967. We greeted her as the follower of her late Father in his path towards Non-Alignment, a path on which our two countries have continuously been fellow travellers. A great lady she was indeed, as she launched a visionary appeal for increased environmental awareness during the Stockholm Conference on Human Environment in 1972. This appeal still echoes in our minds. Referring to human improvidence concerning the environment, she warned that: "It is obvious that the crisis awaiting us will deeply alter the destiny of our planet."

This appeal is more topical than ever now as we are threatened by the eerie silence of a permanent summer brought forth by the greenhouse effect as well as by this nuclear winter that her son the late Rajiv Gandhi wanted to ward off by campaigning ceaselessly for "a nuclear-free and non-violent world."

Message read at the conference by H.E. Idriss Jazairy, Special Envoy of H.E Abdelaziz Bouteflika, President of Algeria.

Beyond the adjustments called for by rapidly changing circumstances, we see continuity in the values which have guided the steps of these prestigious leaders. As members of the same spiritual family, whether they were related or not, they are thus the worthy heirs of a great tradition of civilisation, that of eternal India.

By organising the present conference, Shrimati Sonia Gandhi, the Chair of the Conference, has afforded upcoming generations of the Congress Party that she is leading, while remaining true to this precious heritage, an inspiration drawn from the most limpid sources.

Thus, as the young cadres of your Party are called upon to take over, they will become able to better assess the challenges which assail our contemporary world and to make contributions to the international community, which are no less crucial than those of their forebears.

At the forefront of these challenges stand those that relate to peace, to human rights and to development, which are the three themes on which I would like to make some remarks.

Let me first refer to our common aspirations for peace, a peace that does not boil down to the connotation of the sole concept of security. Mahatma Gandhi said: "Peace will not come from the clash of arms but from justice." We realise this today more than ever in the Middle-East conflict where a sophisticated and implacable war machine is unable to overcome the thirst for justice and freedom for the Palestinians, a thirst that the United Nations can help to quench in the short-term through engaging more resolutely in the Quartel framework. A thirst that can also be addressed in other geographic regions through the work of the General Assembly and of the Security Council as well as through that of the new Peace building commission, provided sufficient resources are made available to it. I have no doubt that India will be provided in this new institution with a choice opportunity to pursue its Gandhian calling of support to non-violence.

As Indira Gandhi used to say: "Peace is not only the absence of war." In the medium-term it calls for the equitable and non-selective implementation of international instruments on disarmament.

While our circumstances differ, Algeria aspires, as India does, for the advent of an era governed by conventions that prohibit resorting to nuclear weapons and calling for the destruction of existing stockpiles with a view to achieving the total elimination of this weapon as of all other weapons of mass destruction. For current international instruments, whose basic logic was already detrimental to non-nuclear States, are being selectively implemented in a manner which further tips the disequilibrium to the detriment of the latter. Thus, the pursuit of the destruction of stockpiles, which is legally mandatory for nuclear States, is being postponed indefinitely. Meantime, constraints imposed on non-nuclear States become more compelling, their right to produce fissile material for civilian purposes being even challenged.

At the same time, we are witnessing a trend to deprive multilateral disarmament institutions of their substance, with only the non-proliferation component of their mandate being salvaged and transferred to more restricted clubs with a view to its forced imposition. A unilateral approach of this nature might well trigger retaliation and thus give rise to grave dangers. A saying attributed to Mahatma Gandhi would be particularly apposite: "An eye for an eye would make the whole world blind."

Thus, despite the end of the East-West ideological confrontation, we have not succeeded in rebuilding confidence, as one had expected, in order to re-launch the dynamics of peace through disarmament.

We intend to, indeed we must, make nuclear technology for peaceful purposes a theme for cooperation and no more for confrontation. Therefrom perhaps confidence will be reborn.

We are in a position to be precursors on this path through reinforcing South-South cooperation in the field of the peaceful uses of nuclear energy and technologies. I therefore welcome the decisions that we took jointly towards this end during the last G-15 Summit in Havana.

Let me now refer to the second challenge which relates to the promotion and protection of human rights.

I see this as a promising field of endeavour which can be a meeting point, regardless of North-South divisions or of oppositions of rival powers, a meeting point for all those that partake in the same universal values of freedom and dignity of individuals and of groups in their diversity.

None better than Mahatma Gandhi was able to assert through non-violence the civil and political rights of an oppressed nation, its economic, social and cultural rights as well. He thus blazed the trail that was later followed by Martin Luther King and Nelson Mandela.

Depending on whether one hails from rich or from developing countries, emphasis will tend to be put either on civil and political rights or on economic, social and cultural rights as well as on the right to development. It will be incumbent on the United Nations multilateral human rights mechanisms to demonstrate their readiness to see to the equitable promotion and protection of all these rights.

Peace and prosperity are more conducive to the blossoming of human rights. Yet under such circumstances, violations do occur even if they are occasionally glossed over. *A fortiori* in times of conflict, whether countries involved are rich or poor, serious violations do occur that are more readily raised at the international level in some cases than in others. Bitter experiences of combating terrorism to which a number of our countries have been subjected are reminders of how difficult, indeed how heart-rending may be the action that is called for to reconcile security and liberty. In the face of what is often a cruel dilemma, India and Algeria have not ceased to advocate at the United Nations the conclusion of a comprehensive convention against international terrorism.

As to the Human Rights Council, we need to insulate it from any manipulation so that it may become the conscience of the United Nations. To this end, we need to exercise vigilance so that the noble values of our common humanity, of which the Council should be the ultimate promoter and protector, be not instrumentalised for political purposes whereby might would have precedence over right.

The third challenge, which the rising forces of your party, as all of us, are confronted with, is that of development.

The strategy that we followed together at the United Nations in the seventies in pursuit of a more equitable new international economic order was undermined by the loss of the pivotal role of the Non-Aligned Movement in the East-West ideological competition, a competition that is no more. Yet, we must also endorse a part of the responsibility for the loss of momentum, recognising that we did not pursue with sufficient determination at the internal level the socioeconomic reforms that were called for. Gandhi's example comes to mind. He repeatedly resorted to the symbol of the spinning wheel to put emphasis on self-reliance, such self-reliance as should enable today all nations to be actors and not simply targets of globalisation. "The spinning wheel" he used to say "is my sword." We must now recognise that we will not achieve improved global governance through laments or mere advocacy of justice or even through the accumulation of our votes at the United Nations. We will achieve it solely through unleashing the creative energy of our peoples, through providing impetus to our production and to our trade. For those developments will increase our weight in the global economy and thereby our international audience.

The revolution of the new information and communication technologies affords us an opportunity to do so. Thanks to the Indian Institutes of Technology inaugurated by Jawaharlal Nehru, thanks also to the allocation of 2 per cent of its GNP to research and to a policy to make the most of its emigrated scientists, your country stands as a pioneer in this field. Africa which is determined to follow suit has just made the commitment in Algiers this month to devote already a minimum of 1 per cent of its GNP to scientific research, in spite of its limited means.

Thus, we are witnessing today, not without some measure of conflict, the first stirrings of a process of shift of global economic power from the North to the South, towards Africa and especially towards Asia where emerging economies are advancing at impressive growth rates. Our emerging economies will not let themselves be co-opted by the global oligarchies. They will be keen to remain true to the traditions of our countries, to give a voice to the voiceless, to articulate loud and clear the aspirations of the most vulnerable. Indeed our countries will continue to advocate global governance that will be, at one and the same time, more democratic and better attuned to current realities. And we will continue to demand for the most deprived countries, the special and differential treatment they are entitled to in international trade.

We have decided that globalisation will be for our countries what we will it to be, and we are headed towards winning this bid. It is now the turn of the North to address its mind to the issue. Its policy makers are busy seeking palliatives to problems that they now face in the wake of globalisation, be it social stratification, protectionist withdrawal or compunctions about the inflow of labour and even of capital, originating in the Third World.

With an enhanced economic status on the international scene, we will be able to contribute to reinventing globalisation so that it is beneficial to all, democratic and also compatible with diverse identities and cultures. In other words, we will be able to see to it that globalisation begets a concept of true world citizenship.

The Algerian-Indian declaration on strategic partnership, which was signed during my visit to India in 2001, provides the ideal framework for us to fine-tune our strategies in the face of these challenges at the multilateral level. The strategic partnership which binds us should also offer a framework for the elaboration of a bilateral cooperative scheme that could be a model between two emerging countries.

Section II A Non-violent Approach to Conflict Resolution and Peace Building

GENE SHARP

ABUNE PAULOS

AHMED KATHRADA

FRANCESCO RUTELLI

JANEZ DRNOVŠEK

JUSUF KALLA

GEORGE PAPANDREOU

M.A. GAYOOM

RADHA KUMAR

Section II

A Non-violent Approach to Conflict Resolution and Peace Building

This section corresponds to the Subject Session I of the international conference "Peace, Non-violence and Empowerment: Gandhian Philosophy in the 21st Century" held in New Delhi on January 29-30, 2007.

Chairperson: Lia Diskin (Brazil)
Session Secretary: Pawan Kumar Bansal (India)
Session Rapporteur: Rajni Patil (India)
Paper Presenter: Gene Sharp (USA)

Participants:
Francesco Rutelli (Italy), Ahmed Kathrada (South Africa), Radha Kumar (India), George Papandreou (Greece), Maumoon Abdul Gayoom (Maldives), Janez Drnovšek (Slovenia), Jusuf Kalla (Indonesia), Abune Paulos (Ethiopia), Liu Hongcai (China), Pawel Zalewski (Poland), Lyonpo Khandu Wangchuk (Bhutan), Ramesh Chennithala (India), Farooq Sattar (Pakistan), Navnit Dholakia (United Kingdom), Sadok Fayala (Tunisia), Mohamed Ali Rustam (Malaysia), Pradip Giri (Nepal), Karen Balcázar Cronenbold (Bolivia)

12

Gandhi's Answer

Neither Peace Nor War but Non-violent Struggle

GENE SHARP

IN a world that often seems filled with violence and oppression, it is relevant to recall that a hundred years ago the Indian minority in South Africa at the Empire Theatre protest meeting in Johannesburg on September 11, 1906 resolved to disobey the draft Asiatic Law Amendment Ordinance by means of non-violent defiance. Their actual struggle began after the bill became law in July 1907.

It is also appropriate that this anniversary observance conference is sponsored by the Indian National Congress. It was the Congress that led the predominantly non-violent Indian struggle for independence from the strongest empire that the world had ever seen, and won.

It is important both that the Congress itself remembers, and that it calls attention to that struggle that happened a hundred years ago. Its lessons are very relevant to the peoples of the 21st century.

It sounds easy to call attention to these struggles, and it can be done and should be done. However, paying attention to their importance for the 21st century, beyond mere recognition of their historical occurrence, is unlikely to be easy, and may even be painful. The easy path is to comfort ourselves by standing amazed at those movements and those that followed, not only in South Africa but also very importantly in India itself.

As we reflect on those movements, it is not difficult to feel humble before the memory of the remarkable man who played such an important role in those movements. However, in honouring Mohandas K. Gandhi, there is a danger that we revere him without taking seriously his insights and example. They are of extreme importance.

Neither War Nor Peace

Modern thought widely assumes that the peaceful alternatives to violence and war consist of negotiations, dialogue, diplomacy, compromise, conciliation, and such other tools of conflict resolution.

Those are all good and useful tools in many situations and they need to be explored and developed further. However, that list does not include the full range of alternatives to violence. It does not give recognition to Gandhi's views and experience in the development of Satyagraha and the important wider historical practice of non-violent struggle in social, economic, political, and international conflicts.

Gandhi's important contributions about how to deal with conflicts do not fit smoothly into established modern thought and practice. The assumption usually is that in serious conflicts one ultimately must choose between surrender to a force using violence, and refusal to participate on pacifist grounds.

Gandhi was no advocate of surrender to oppression, but neither was he a supporter of violence and war, nor was he a simple conscientious objector. He was a crucial contributor to the continued development of what Krishnalal Shridharani called "war without violence."[1]

Gandhi's views differ significantly from the answers to conflict espoused by those who rely on war and other violence in extreme conflicts. His views also differ significantly from the answers offered by most practitioners of Western conflict resolution, peace research, and pacifism.

The contributions of conflict resolution and peace research are important for some conflicts, especially those with issues of secondary significance. However, those contributions are inadequate when dealing with acute conflicts.

Gandhi's Answer

Gandhi's answer was to identify those conflicts where the issues are fundamental. Those are the conflicts that occur at a time when moral principles, human rights, and justice are at stake and when compromise is not possible or desirable. Then the primary task of the exponent of non-violent means is to assist the oppressed people to become empowered by learning how to apply Satyagraha, or non-violent struggle, to change their situation, as Gandhi insisted. Most Western conflict resolution advocates, pacifists and peace researchers have not yet fully grasped

Dandi March: Salt Satyagraha, 12 March 1930.

As part of the ongoing Salt Satyagraha Movement a mass raid of Dharasana salt depot was organised.
Gujarat, May 21, 1930.

Breaking the salt law: Gandhi picks up a
lump of natural salt, Dandi, April 6, 1930.

this great contribution to the resolution of acute conflicts.

Gandhi on Power

We need to remember that Gandhi was no naïve romantic playing at politics, imagining the world to be one of sweet harmony, gentleness, and love. The times in which he lived and worked had many of the characteristics of our own times. Those characteristics include the existence of acute conflicts, dictatorships, great violence, mass killings, and communal and racial hatreds.

We often forget that Gandhi was tough and realistic. He fully recognised the role of power in political conflicts. Indeed, it seems that he understood power far better than those leaders of today who dogmatically believe that violence and military might are the only real source of political and international power.

In the January 23, 1930 issue of his journal *Young India*, Gandhi wrote: "The British people must realise that the Empire is to come to an end. This they will not realise unless we in India have generated power within to enforce our will."[2]

"The English Nation responds only to force..." Gandhi wrote at the beginning of the 1930-1931 civil disobedience campaign.[3]

On March 2, 1930, Gandhi wrote a letter-ultimatum to the Viceroy, Lord Irwin, rejecting the idea that the issues between India and Britain could be resolved by a conference. He wrote:

> It is not a matter of carrying conviction by argument. The matter resolves itself into one of matching forces. Conviction or no conviction, Great Britain would defend her Indian commerce and interest by all the forces at her command. India must consequently evolve force enough to free herself from that embrace of death.[4]

Such an incisive was possible because Gandhi understood political power very well. He wrote:

> ...[N]o Government, much less the Indian Government, can subsist if the people cease to serve it.[5]

> Even the most despotic government cannot stand except for the consent of the governed which consent is often forcibly procured by the despot. Immediately the subject ceases to fear the despotic force, his power is gone.[6]

A Humble Learner

This was the insight into the basic nature of political power and all governments on which Gandhi developed the political aspect of Satyagraha—his application of non-violent struggle. He had already grasped this insight by 1905. Non-cooperation and disobedience as means of struggle to achieve liberation were rooted in his insights into political realism, not primarily in the political application of *ahimsa*.

Gandhi was humble enough not to think that he had no need to learn from the experiences of others. Gandhi was also wise enough not to think he could originate everything that was important concerning how to respond to serious conflicts, and that he could do everything himself. He also understood that the participation of the masses of people suffering under oppression was needed to lift the burden of oppression from society. By participating in non-violent struggles against the injustices, the oppressed could become empowered.

Continuing Relevance

Gandhi's insights and the experiences of those movements have great relevance today and for the centuries ahead of us. Humanity has not yet solved the problems of violence and war, oppression and dictatorships. Despite some gains, we still face them. Past peace movements and programmes to achieve greater freedom and social justice have not been adequate to remove these conditions. This may be because many peace and reform advocates have offered merely hopes and dreams instead of effective means to produce a better society.

Today's realities differ only in degree from those that confronted Gandhi, and everyone else, in South Africa, India and elsewhere. Gandhi's response to these realities was not simply to be peaceful. He did not advise infinite patience by the oppressed. In acute conflict situations he did not merely seek more skilful ways to negotiate, nor did he search for a "win-win" solution with the perpetrators of violence and oppression. Gandhi did not deny the reality of the power of oppressors, but he did not ignore either the plight of the suffering powerless or their potential for self-liberation. He recognised that there were relevant insights and experiences elsewhere that could help in formulating wise and responsible ways to move forward in the existing situation.

Viewing Gandhi in Historical Context

We can gain greater understanding of Gandhi's significance and the potential of his insights and experiences if we viewed him and the struggles in which he was so important in historical context.

It is obvious from Gandhi's own account of the Empire Theatre meeting on September 11, 1906 that the attendees were already familiar with earlier non-violent protests and resistance by the Indian minority in South Africa. In his journal *Indian Opinion* on October 6, 1906 Gandhi reminded his readers of their earlier resistance. They had refused to move to the assigned location, and had also rejected the demand that they carry passes: "The Indian people refused to accept the passes...and the Regulation had to be withdrawn,"[7] he wrote. Gandhi was also familiar with previous instances of African and mixed-race resistance: "The pass law applies to them as well, but they do not take out passes," he said two days before the Empire Theatre meeting, speaking at the Hamidiya Islamic Society.[8] He also cited the African refusal to pay taxes to the European oppressors.

Chinese, Russian, and Other Models

Equally importantly, Gandhi was aware of the use of non-violent resistance methods in other parts of the world. He saw such cases to be relevant to the current plight of Indians in South Africa. Gandhi had previously referred to the Chinese use of the economic boycott more than a year earlier on August 19, 1905 in an article concerning Lord Curzon's proposal for the partition of Bengal. Gandhi wrote that if the proposal was not changed, "Indian merchants should stop all trade with Great Britain. We must admit that our people have learnt these tactics from China."[9]

The year-long Russian 1905 Revolution was predominantly, but not completely, non-violent. Gandhi referred to that vast struggle, especially by implication the Great October General Strike that had forced the Tsar to grant a limited parliament. He compared this strike to earlier Russian violence: "This time they have found another remedy which, though very simple, is more powerful than rebellion and murder. The Russian workers and all the other servants declared a general strike and stopped all work." He later continued in the same article: "We, too, can resort to the Russian remedy against tyranny." Gandhi compared the Russian strike movement to the anti-partition movement in Bengal: "The governance of India is possible only because there exist people who serve. We also can show the same strength that the Russian people have done."[10]

Gandhi referred to the "strong movement" in Bengal against partition that was using the boycott of British goods and the consumption of only Indian produced goods (swadeshi): "The movement in Bengal for the use of swadeshi goods is much like the Russian movement." Gandhi also had paid much attention to the Irish resistance movements, including boycotts and rent strikes.[11]

Gandhi also referred to cases of individuals practising religious disobedience and tax refusal in England and the earlier objection of American colonists to English taxation.[12] All this indicates that Gandhi was eager to learn from both past and current non-violent struggles. In counselling how to proceed and in helping to lead non-violent struggles in South Africa and India, he recognised that he and his contemporaries could draw on the experiences of non-violent struggles by others who had come before.

Gandhi and the Indian minority in South Africa clearly knew of all these cases of non-violent struggle well before the important Empire Theatre meeting. Gandhi's own article in Indian Opinion referred to the non-violent resistance and revolutionary movements in China on August 19, 1905, in Russia on November 11, 1905, in Bengal on September 16, 1905, in the American colonies on September 30, 1905, and in South Africa by Africans on November 25, 1905. These references range between nine-and-a-half and thirteen months before the Empire Theatre meeting of September 11, 1906. Knowledge of the other cases of non-violent struggle also was clearly antecedent to calculations by the Indians on how to respond to the draft Asiatic Law Amendment Ordinance.

Further, Gandhi recognised that various individual methods of non-violent action—economic boycotts, strikes, and disobedience—had a great deal in common with each other. They were parts of a broad approach to the conduct of serious conflicts.

Reasoning from Political to Political

It should be noted that Gandhi's own reports of these conflicts demonstrate that at this time he was not calculating how to apply ahimsa to political conflicts. He was reasoning from several previous pragmatic non-violent struggles to current and future applications of non-violent struggle in South Africa. Said another way, Gandhi was reasoning from political applications of non-violent struggle in other countries to its prospective political application in South Africa.

Gandhi also clearly viewed Satyagraha, or non-violent struggle—to the development of which he contributed so much—as a technique of great importance, not only in the immediate situation but beyond his lifetime. He anticipated its further development and practice in other parts of the world.

Some Historical Examples

A comprehensive history of the practice of non-violent struggle throughout the world does not exist. However, it is important to try to place Gandhi and his "experiments" in the historical context.

There may never have been a beginning to non-violent struggle. Its basic operation is extremely simple. It seems to be primarily based on human stubbornness, refusal to do what one is supposed to do and doing what is forbidden.

We do know, however, that from the late 18th century through the 20th century, the technique of non-violent action was widely used in highly diverse conflicts: colonial rebellions, international political and economic conflicts, religious conflicts, and anti-slavery resistance.

During the years up to the present, this type of struggle has been used to gain national independence, to generate economic gains, to resist genocide, to undermine dictatorships, to gain civil rights, to end segregation, and to resist foreign occupations and coups d'etat. American colonists conducted three strategically planned non-violent struggle campaigns against British regulations, taxation, and rule from 1765 to 1775.

In the late 19th century and the early 20th century in various countries workers widely used strikes and economic boycotts to gain trade union recognition and economic gains. Similar methods were also used in various other conflicts.[13]

For example, Chinese boycotts of Japanese products occurred in 1908, 1915, and 1919. In 1920, massive non-cooperation by Germans defeated the Kapp Putsch, a pro-monarchist coup d'etat against the new Weimar Republic. Germans in the Ruhr in 1923, resisted through non-cooperation the French and Belgian occupation of the region with major effect.

From the 1920s to the 1940s, Indian nationalists used non-violent action in their struggles against British rule, often under the leadership or inspiration of

Mohandas K. Gandhi. Contemporaneously, but independently, with the struggles in India that Gandhi led or inspired, a remarkable predominantly Muslim non-violent struggle movement developed in the North-West Frontier Province of British India. It was led by Khan Abdul Ghaffar Khan and shook British control of that region.

At the same time that Satyagraha was being practised in South Africa and later in India, methods of non-violent struggle were being used on a large scale in other countries. In several countries methods of non-violent action were used in Europe to achieve universal manhood suffrage. Later, especially in Britain and the United States, strong women's movements struggled by such means and other peaceful methods to get women the right to vote also.

Gandhi clearly saw that non-violent struggle would spread to other parts of the world. In 1936, he told a visiting African-American scholar that it might be through their community in the United States that the message of non-violent action in conflicts might spread to the world.[14]

From 1940 to 1945, in various European countries, especially in Norway, Denmark, and the Netherlands, the populations used non-violent struggle to resist Nazi occupation and fascist rule. The Norwegian resistance during the Nazi occupation is one of the most significant cases, especially the teachers' resistance. Clergymen, sportsmen, trade unionists, and others also participated in it.

Other important cases include major aspects of the Danish Resistance 1940-1945, including the successful general strike in Copenhagen in 1944, major aspects of the Dutch Resistance 1940-1945 including large-scale strikes in 1941, 1943 and 1944. Non-violent action was used to save Jews from the Holocaust in Berlin, Bulgaria, Denmark, and elsewhere. The military dictators of El Salvador and Guatemala were ousted through brief non-violent struggles in the spring of 1944.

After India's independence, her example of how to escape the British Empire inspired Nigerians under the leadership of Nnamdi Azikiwe and Africans in the Gold Coast (later, Ghana) led by Kwame Nkrumah. Nkrumah urged people to struggle for their freedom by "positive action" (by a combination of non-violent resistance, education, and electoral politics).

Since Gandhi's passing away, non-violent struggle has continued to spread and increase in power and potential. The American civil rights struggles against racial segregation and discrimination, especially in the 1950s and 1960s, with the participation of Dr. Martin Luther King, Jr. and many others changed laws and long-established segregation policies, especially in the United States South.

In April 1961, non-cooperation by French conscript soldiers in the French colony of Algeria, combined with popular demonstrations in France and defiance by the Debre-de Gaulle government, defeated the military coup d'etat in Algiers before a related coup in Paris could be launched.

Facing Extreme Dictatorships

Contemporary with the spread of Gandhi-inspired non-violent action in other parts of the world, there emerged in Communist countries independent demonstrations of the technique under exceedingly difficult circumstances.

The East German Rising of June 1953 included women in the city of Jena sitting down in front of Soviet tanks; strikes occurred in Soviet political prisoners' camps also in 1953, especially at Vorkuta; and major aspects of the Hungarian Revolution of 1956-1957 were non-violent.

In 1968 and 1969, following the Warsaw Pact invasion, Czechs and Slovaks held off full Soviet control for eight months with improvised non-violent struggle and refusal of collaboration. From 1953 to 1991, dissidents in Communist-ruled countries in Eastern Europe, especially in East Germany, Poland, Hungary, Latvia, Estonia, and Lithuania used non-violent struggles for increased freedom.

Non-violent struggle brought about the end of Communist dictatorships in Poland and Czechoslovakia in 1989 and in East Germany, Estonia, Latvia, and Lithuania in 1991. The Solidarity struggles in Poland began in 1980 with strikes to support the demand for a legal free trade union, and concluded in 1989 with the collapse of the Polish Communist regime. The attempted "hard-line" coup d'etat in Moscow in 1991 was defeated by non-cooperation and defiance.

In South Africa, non-violent protests and mass resistance were highly important in thwarting the apartheid policies and European domination, especially between 1950 and 1990.

In July and August 1988, Burmese democrats protested against the military dictatorship with marches and defiance, and brought down three governments. Finally, the struggle succumbed to leadership problems, a new military coup d'etat, and mass slaughter.

In 1989, Chinese students and others in over three hundred cities (including in Tiananmen Square, Beijing) conducted symbolic protests against government corruption and oppression, but the protests finally ended following massive killings by the military. The Marcos dictatorship in the Philippines was destroyed by a non-violent uprising in 1986. In early 2001, President Estrada, who had been accused of corruption, was ousted by Filipinos in a "People Power Two" campaign.

During parts of 1991 and 1992, the Thai population in various parts of the country waged a vigorous struggle by mass marches, occupations of many thousands of people, and individual hunger strikes blocked the establishment of a new military government despite deaths and injuries caused by repression.

Starting in November 1996, Serbs conducted daily parades and protests in Belgrade and other cities against the autocratic governance of President Milosovic, and secured correction of electoral fraud in mid-January 1997. Serb democrats, however, at the time lacked a strategy to continue the struggle, and failed to launch a campaign to bring down the Milosovic dictatorship. Serb democrats rose up against Milosovic in early October 2000 in a carefully planned non-violent struggle led by Otpor, a movement of mostly young people, outside of the political parties, and the dictatorship collapsed.

In Kosovo, the Albanian population between 1990 and 1999 conducted a non-cooperation campaign against repressive Serbian rule. When the *de facto* Kosovo government lacked a non-violent strategy for gaining *de jure* independence, a guerrilla Kosovo Liberation Army initiated violence. This was followed by extreme Serbian repression and massive slaughters by so-called "ethnic cleansing," which led to NATO bombing and intervention.

Remarkable additional struggles to oust authoritarian regimes succeeded following Serbia in 2000, in Georgia in 2003, and in Ukraine in 2004. There have been a large number of additional important cases. This review has only been a brief sampling.

Such struggles of the past need to be studied and analysed carefully, but they ought not to be simply imitated. Many of these serve as firm evidence that a record of major achievements of non-violent struggle exists, although some doctrinal believers in the omnipotence of violence try to deny it.

Uses of New Knowledge

Of course, not all attempts to use non-violent action in conflicts have succeeded in gaining the objectives sought. Neither have all attempts to struggle with some form of violence worked effectively. Additionally, non-violent actionists in earlier conflicts have usually been improvising their struggles. They have lacked significant understanding of the means of conflict they were using. They had no handbooks on this technique, no guides to action, and no instructions on how to plan strategies to make their efforts more effective.

The dynamics of how this type of struggle operates have been little understood, and the range of available non-violent methods and tips on how to use them successfully remained generally unknown. There were no lists of the factors that contribute to success or failure. Additionally, there was only limited knowledge of the experiences of others who had struggled by related means.

Not only has there been a lack of availability of important information and guidance on non-violent struggle, but there also has been an abundance of misconceptions and misrepresentations. Nevertheless, a remarkable percentage of these non-violent struggles contributed significantly to gaining the intended goals.

Increasing Effectiveness

Most past cases of non-violent struggle—before Gandhi's involvement, independently during his lifetime, and since his passing—did not have the benefit of Gandhi's natural strategic acumen. Also, most of those past cases were improvised rather than carefully planned and prepared. The fact that despite these limitations highly important successes have nevertheless occurred is remarkable.

Although these successes have often been impressive, greater effectiveness at lower cost is desirable. Success in non-violent struggles does not occur by chance, nor is it determined by purity of beliefs. Instead, the results are in part tied to the existence of favourable external conditions, to the presence of a wise strategy, to changes in the conflict situation produced by the resisters, and to the pre-conflict relative strengths of the contending groups. In the future, the non-violent resisters can have an impact on all these conditions and can change the established power relationships.

However, the fact remains that the past lack of planning and of preparations meant that the participants were unprepared for the future situations they would face and the roles they might play in the conflict. Very often, neither the actionists nor the leaders (if any) understood even the major characteristics of the technique of action they were employing, and what was required if they were to have a chance of success.

While spontaneity has some positive qualities, more often it has had disadvantages. Frequently, the non-violent resisters have not anticipated the brutalities inflicted by their opponents so that they not only suffered gravely but also sometimes the resistance collapsed. At times, the lack of planning has left crucial decisions to chance, with disastrous results. Even when the oppressive system was brought down, the absence of planning on how to handle the transition to a better system has contributed to the emergence of a new dictatorship or other oppression.

Past resisters have usually launched non-violent action without careful strategic planning that could have made the resistance more effective. Poor planning, lack of carefully developed strategy, and unwise actions and use of resources, have reduced the chances of success in many past non-violent struggles.

Nevertheless, increasingly, this technique is being recognised to be a type of action requiring understanding, courage, tenacity, discipline, organisational capacity, and great strategic skill. All these qualities were emphasised by Gandhi and he contributed greatly to the recognition of their importance and to the capacity of people to achieve them.

The Role of Wise Strategic Planning

There is another option in place of improvisation and spontaneity: deliberate steps to increase the effectiveness of non-violent action. This option requires increased understanding of its major characteristics, capacity, requirements, and strategic principles. This makes possible wise strategic planning that is identifying the characteristics of the present situation, what needs to be done, why, when, and how to do it, and how to counter the opponents' actions and repression.

Beneficial changes in the conditions of the conflict, and in the relative power of the contending groups, can be produced by actions of the non-violent struggle group. These can be achieved principally through the skilful choice and application of wise strategy. Wise strategy can greatly increase the effectiveness of non-violent struggle and its capacity to undermine oppression.

A strategic non-violent struggle can be targeted to apply the strengths of the population against the weaknesses of the oppressors in order to change power relationships. The oppressed population can be strengthened, the domination can be undermined, and even highly repressive regimes can be weakened, and even disintegrated. As the population's strength grows, it becomes possible for them to move from initial small victories to large successes. Already this technique has moved far from its role in politics when Gandhi began his experiments with it in South Africa and years later in India.

Now, some social scientists and strategists operating with the most meagre resources are attempting to study this technique and to learn its nature, its dynamics, the requirements for success with it against various types of opponents, and to examine its future potentialities to resolve individual grave problems realistically.

Most past cases appear to have been independent developments, sometimes stimulated by comparable movements in neighbouring countries or by news of the power of this technique. However, directly and indirectly, there have been influences from Gandhi's thought and actions on a number of these cases. In turn, some of these more recent struggles have contributed, simply by their existence to the development of additional applications of non-violent struggle.

Assisting Empowerment

Gandhi was well aware that participation in non-violent struggles can contribute to empowering the powerless victims of oppression and injustices.

True, Gandhi believed that "pure" non-violent individuals could wield such immense power that could make organised mass non-violent struggles unnecessary. However, he was also convinced that the community as a whole ought to learn how to use non-violent action. This would make the community conscious of its collective strength and enable it to solve problems through its own efforts. Therefore, even if a pure *satyagrahi* existed, such a person's responsibility was to educate the masses in the use of Satyagraha.[15] They needed to be shown how they could act despite difficulties and in face of the power of their opponents.

It is also true that Gandhi saw serious problems with the practice in Indian non-violent struggles and the disaster of massive migrations and killings following the partition at the time of Independence. However, this did not mean that Gandhi concluded that he should have taken a different course and instead should have sought believers in non-violence as a moral principle instead of counselling political non-violent struggle. To the contrary, Gandhi remained convinced that: "I did well to present to the Congress non-violence as an expedient." He wrote in 1942, "I could not have done otherwise, if I was to introduce it into politics."[16]

Gandhi long insisted—especially in his later years—that the "non-violence of the brave" did not contain the weaknesses he saw in the Indian practice. The impression is widespread that this type of non-violence can be equated with belief in non-violence as an ethical or religious principle. An examination of Gandhi's own descriptions of the "non-violence of the brave" does not confirm this simple interpretation however.[17]

The truth is more complex and more significant for the future. Gandhi was an innovator in politics. He had a considerable understanding of political realities. He relied on this and his intuition, as well as his constant experiments. His useful insights and experiences can give us important understandings to help us now and in the future. Gandhi did more to advance the development of non-violent struggle than any other single person in the 20th century. He and the movements in which he was involved also contributed immeasurably to the world-wide recognition of the existence and potential of non-violent struggle against oppression.

During Gandhi's lifetime, and certainly more so in recent decades, significant research has been underway that greatly helps this process. Historical accounts, analyses of the dynamics of this type of conflict, and strategic development are all important. These make possible the deliberate refinement of non-violent struggle to make it more effective than the improvised cases of the past, and even the independent planned cases during and since Gandhi's lifetime.

The Potential of Continuing Studies

The several major elements of these studies need to include the following:

1. Recognition, discovery and dissemination of the realisation that Satyagraha, non-violent struggle, is an important contribution of world significance when people face acute conflicts.

    Negotiations, dialogue, compromise on lesser issues, the tools revealed by studies of international relations, social conflicts, peace research, and conflict resolution studies are important. However, in cases of crucial issues, some means of pursuing those issues in open conflict are needed. Apart from violence, non-violent struggle is the clear option.

Condemnations of violence and repetition of moral precepts have done little or nothing to remove violence. People will not give up reliance on violence unless they see that there exist powerful non-violent alternative means of struggle that can be effective. Gandhi understood this very well.

2. Research and analysis can give us increased understanding of the workings and dynamics of non-violent struggle. These studies can reveal both that violence is not needed and that it can contribute to defeat of the people struggling for greater justice and freedom. Instead, there exists a vast history of non-violent struggle, under various names, that, if wisely applied, can be substituted for violence for meeting a variety of needs and be used in extreme crisis situations.

3. Gandhi was a master pioneering strategist. His work and insights point toward the importance of strategic analysis and planning to make an anticipated non-violent struggle as effective as possible. They also point to some of the strategic principles and insights that if applied can be incorporated into the preparations of strategies for future non-violent conflicts.

4. Policy studies are now also needed for dealing with several important types of conflict situations. The planned and prepared substitution of non-violent action for violent means has been recommended for the following purposes:

    • Dismantling dictatorships.

    • Blocking new coups d'etat and preventing new dictatorships.

    • Defending against foreign aggression and occupations.

    • Lifting social and economic injustices.

    • Developing, preserving and extending democratic practices and human rights.

    • Incorporating in additional ways non-violent means into democratic societies; and

    • Preserving the existence and ways of life of indigenous peoples.

Major progress has already been made in developing such policies and the broad means of action required for them, such as civilian defence (civilian-based defence), blocking coups d'etat, and disintegrating dictatorships. Pioneering struggles have also occurred on additional issues.

The Responsibility Continues

In the future, as in the past, non-violent struggle may be used for objectives that many of us would not support. Even that is a major advance. Would we prefer that those same objectives were supported by violence?

As non-violent struggle spreads, it is replacing reliance on violence and war and also is empowering people who have often felt helpless before the violence of their oppressors. Much has already been done in the past hundred years since the Empire Theatre meeting to advance the application of non-violent struggle to which Gandhi contributed so powerfully. A great deal more remains to be done.

Now that we are at this point in history, what are we to do?

A heavy responsibility continues to rest on all of us who respect Gandhi and take his insights and example seriously.

End Notes

1. Krishnalal Shridharani. *War Without Violence: A Study of Gandhi's Method and Its Accomplishments*. New York: Harcourt, Brace and Co., 1939; London: Victor Gollancz, New York: Garland, 1972; Revised edition, Bombay: Bharatiya Vidya Bhavan, 1962.

2. Gene Sharp, *Gandhi Wields the Weapon of Moral Power*. Ahmedabad: Navajivan Publishing House, 1960, p.52; *Young India*, January 23, 1930, p.28.

3. Gene Sharp, *Gandhi Wields the Weapon of Moral Power*, p.67; Bhogaraju Pattabhi Sitaramayya, *The History of the Indian National Congress*, Vol. I (1885-1935), p.638. Madras: Working Committee of the Congress, 1935.

4. Gene Sharp, *Gandhi Wields the Weapon of Moral Power*, p.64; *Congress Bulletin*, No.5, March 7, 1930.

5. Gene Sharp, *Gandhi as a Political Strategist with Essays on Ethics and Politics*. (Boston: Porter Sargent Publishers, 1979 and New Delhi, India: Gandhi Media Centre, 1999). p.44; *Young India*, May 5, 1920, quoted in M.K. Gandhi, *Satyagraha*, p.116. Ahmedabad: Navajivan Publishing House, 1951.

6. Gene Sharp, *Gandhi as a Political Strategist*, p.44; *Young India*, June 30, 1920; quoted in Nirmal Kumar Bose. *Selections from Gandhi*, p.116. Ahmedabad: Navajivan, 1948.

7. Gene Sharp, *Gandhi as a Political Strategist*, p.34; *Indian Opinion*, October 6, 1906; M.K. Gandhi, *The Collected Works of Mahatma Gandhi*, Vol. V. p.462. Delhi: Publications Division, Ministry of Information and Broadcasting, Government of India. (Hereafter The Collected Works).

8. Gene Sharp, *Gandhi as a Political Strategist*, p.34; *Indian Opinion*, September 2. 1906; M.K. Gandhi, *The Collected Works*, Vol. V. p.418.

9. Gene Sharp, *Gandhi as a Political Strategist*, p.28 (see also p.30); *Indian Opinion*, August 19, 1905; M.K. Gandhi, *The Collected Works*, Vol. 5, p.44.

10. Gene Sharp, *Gandhi as a Political Strategist*, p.29; *Indian Opinion*, November 11, 1905; M.K. Gandhi, *The Collected Works*, Vol. V, pp.131-132.

11. Gene Sharp, *Gandhi as a Political Strategist*, pp.31-32; M.K. Gandhi, *The Collected Works*, Vol. V, p.132.

12. Gene Sharp, *Gandhi as a Political Strategist*, p.32.

13. For bibliographies of many of these struggles see Ronald McCarthy and Gene Sharp, with Brad Bennett, *Non-violent Action: A Research Guide*. (New York: Garland Publishing, 1994) and April Carter, Howard Clark and Michael Randle, *People Power and Protest since 1945: A Bibliography of Non-violent Action*. (London: Housmans Bookshop, 2006).

14. Homer A. Jack, editor, *The Gandhi Reader*, p.316. Bloomington, Indiana: University of Indiana Press, 1956.

15. Gene Sharp, *Gandhi as a Political Strategist*, pp.92-93; *Young India*, Vol. I. p.262; *Harijan*, August 18, 1940 and September 8, 1940; Gopi Nath Dhawan, *The Political Philosophy of Mahatma Gandhi*. pp.165-166. Third revised edition, Ahmedabad: Navajivan, 1962.

16. Gene Sharp, *Gandhi as a Political Strategist*, p.103; *Harijan*, September 29, 1940; Dhawan, *The Political Philosophy of Mahatma Gandhi*, p. 165.

17. Gene Sharp, *Gandhi as a Political Strategist*, p.105-106.

Other Select Relevant Writings by the Author

Gandhi Wields the Weapon of Moral Power. Foreword by Albert Einstein. Introduction by Dr. Bharatan Kumarappa. Ahmedabad: Navajivan Publishing House, 1960.

Gandhi as a Political Strategist, with Essays on Ethics and Politics. Introduction by Coretta Scott King. Boston: Porter Sargent Publishers, Extending Horizons Books, 1979.

Civilian-Based Defense: A Post-Military Weapons System. Princeton, New Jersey and London: Princeton University Press, 1990.

The Politics of Non-violent Action. Introduction by Thomas C. Schelling. Now only available in three volumes: "Part One: Power and Struggle"; "Part Two: The Methods of Non-violent Action"; "Part Three: The Dynamics of Non-violent Action". Boston: Porter Sargent Publishers, Extending Horizons Books, 1973 and later editions.

Co-editor, *Resistance, Politics, and the American Struggle for Independence, 1765-1775*. Boulder, Colorado: Lynne Rienner Publishers, 1986: Out of Print.

Social Power and Political Freedom. Introduction by Senator Mark O. Hatfield. Boston: Porter Sargent Publishers, Extending Horizons Books, 1980.

Waging Non-violent Struggle: 2nd Century Practice and 21st Century Potential. Boston: Porter Sargent Publishers, Extending Horizons Books, 2005.

Co-author with Bruce Jenkins, *The Anti-Coup*. Boston: Albert Einstein Institution, 2003.

"Civilian-Based Defense" in Roger S. Powers and William B. Vogele (eds.), *Protest, Power, and Change: An Encyclopedia of Non-violent Action*, pp.101-104. New York and London: Garland Publishing, 1997.

From Dictatorship to Democracy. Bangkok: Committee for the Restoration of Democracy in Burma, 1993 and Boston, Massachusetts: Albert Einstein Institution, 2002 and 2003.

"Non-violent Action" in Joel Krieger (ed.), *The Oxford Companion to the Politics of the World*, pp.603-605. Second Edition. Oxford and New York: Oxford University Press, 2001.

"Non-violent Action" in Lester Kurtz (ed.), *The Encyclopedia of Violence, Peace, and Conflict,* Vol. 2, pp.567-574. San Diego: Academic Press, 1999.

"Non-violent Struggle and the Media" in *The Encyclopedia of International Media and Communication*, Vol. 3. San Diego: Academic Press, 2003.

There Are Realistic Alternatives. Boston: Albert Einstein Institution, 2003.

Other publications by the author and others and many translations are available on the website, www.aeinstein.org

13

Restoring the Theme of Non-violence

FRANCESCO RUTELLI

THE globalised world is seeking efficient institutions, pluralism, tolerance and respect for individual peace through greater social justice and by expanding opportunities. Dialogue and cooperation with India will be instrumental in achieving these ends in this 21st century.

I should also like to talk about the fascination which the life and experience of Mahatma Gandhi and his non-violent struggle for Indian independence exerted on some people of my own generation. It was not only fascination but also a profound educational formative experience. Some of us held Gandhi's courage, consistency, dedication and personal detachment as a familiar, and by no means an abstract benchmark to try to follow. This was the man who defeated British colonialism with the Satyagraha and other forms of civil disobedience, non-cooperation and non-violent action; and who after having studied British law, set his sights on home rule, *Swaraj*, which, as he wrote in 1909 was much more than simply "wanting English rule without the Englishman; the tiger's nature but not the tiger." Being such an innovator while remaining so totally Indian, Gandhi's thinking and work will never cease to be of universal appeal. As Ramji Singh has said, Gandhi had a global mind and, therefore, drew widely, as he himself never hesitated to admit, on both the West and the East.

I just said that Gandhi inspired some members of my own generation. I would have been more accurate however, to say, a minority of my generation. The majority of the young Europeans who engaged in politics at that time were strongly drawn to an ideology which, like Jean Paul Sartre, believed that non-violence was passivity that only serves to take the side of the oppressors. There was also, unfortunately, a tiny minority that advocated violence leading to the experience of political terrorism. From this scourge, European countries only managed to emerge by standing up with tough and determined counter-measures.

When I first got involved in politics, I found it logical to study Gandhi's life and writings including Gene Sharp's books and articles. At the age of 25, in the wake of the assassination of the Italian statesman, Aldo Moro, I joined a minority party which was waging struggle under the banner of non-violence; even using Gandhi's effigy and rallying support to combat hunger and poverty in the pursuit of civil and human rights. I also published a number of elementary writings to familiarise the public with Gandhi and his ideas and experiences, such as, the Satyagraha. A linkage developed between passion for freedom and democracy and Gandhi's thoughts and works.

Italy's leading political thinker of that time Norberto Bobbio wrote, "the time has come to restore the theme of non-violence to its place of honour and to begin considering it as the fundamental theme of our age." But Gandhiji's topical relevance, also in the West, is not only linked to defeats of the advocates of a revolution growing out of the barrel of a gun but also to the embracing of non-violence by many people who had previously frowned on it. The core of his message on the need to harmonise means and ends, the seed and the tree, the need for transparent and participatory democracy which more effectively protects rights and clearly indicates duties, is also extremely relevant today. The need for a secular faith is also highly relevant today. The need to reconcile religious beliefs, pluralism and tolerance—India's daily challenge to integrate, respect and prevent discrimination against the various sources of spiritual inspiration—is increasingly becoming a touchstone against extremists and fundamentalists, and the resurgence of conflicts based on religion in many parts of the world.

However, Europe cannot claim to be extraneous to these. Not only because of its past centuries of conflicts and bigotries culminating in the carnage of the 20th century European wars but also because Europe has quite recently experienced religious violence in the Balkans, for instance, as well as the threat of fundamentalist terror in our cities. How then can Europe whose moral unity has been built on the rejection of war and which advocates genuine soft power; which includes the commitment to the abolition of capital punishment worldwide, refrain from explicitly referring to the experience of Gandhi. How could the followers of Gandhi fail to admire European Union's successful completion of political unity which now comprises half a billion citizens as its democratic institutions have moved peacefully forward. Anyone who remembers Stalin's dismissive words about the Roman Pope—how many divisions has he got—cannot fail to point out that the dictatorship of the Soviet Union was toppled by non-violent revolutions. Solidarity's revolution in Poland which drew its inspiration from John Paul-II; Prague's Velvet revolution; and the Berlin wall that was brought down by the hands of young people and not by military might, are equally relevant instances.

Many young people in the West today are familiar with Gandhi, more so than previous generations, thanks to several superb films, the television and the internet, which have brought progress about which Gandhi could never have imagined. The possibility to multiply people's aspirations to achieve village democracy—*panchayat*—into a global village with billions of visitors today bringing information, and often the truth directly to them personally is overwhelming.

I recall a remarkable advertisement for a major Italian telecommunication company made in 2004 by Director Spike Lee recreating an imaginary world in which it was possible to watch a live television broadcast by Gandhi in every part of the world. It is true that challenges, problems, backwardness, injustices, violence and opportunities have radically changed since the time of Gandhi's non-violent struggle. But we must never forget that he was a man who knew how to communicate through his own body, to put across the values, convictions and aims. Only examples set by great men and women can change the world, as Mother Teresa, in Kolkata, has done.

As Gandhi said, true morality consists not in following the beaten track but in finding out the true paths for ourselves and in fearlessly following it today. I vow henceforth to commemorate September 11 not only in remembrance of the devastating painful Twin Towers of New York. We shall always remember those victims but we shall honour them and all the victims of the world more fittingly by recalling that September 11 is first and foremost anniversary of that day 100 years ago on which a slightly-built Indian rallied thousands of Indians and Asians together in Johannesburg, South Africa, to assert their rights to dignity and justice; the day he convened his first Satyagraha and thus changed the history of the world.

Addressing a mass meeting, Bengal, 1946.

I claim to know my millions. All the 24 hours
of the day I am with them. — M.K. Gandhi

14

Power of Peaceful Transformation

AHMED KATHRADA

IN my young days it was commonly said that the sun never set on the British Empire. Some time later, someone was asked: "Why is it that the sun never sets on the British Empire?" and the reply was, "The good Lord does not trust what the British would do in the dark."

The history of South Africa ever since the colonial days has been replete with violence by the colonialists. Right from the time that Jan van Riebeeck landed in South Africa, the indigenous people tried by all means possible to resist. The colonialists were defeated by the power of Gandhi. Subsequent to that, there were years and years of non-violent efforts to bring about redress but they failed.

The apartheid regime in South Africa worked according to what you may imagine as a ladder; on top of the ladder were the Whites who enjoyed all the privileges and rights that were denied to all the oppressed people, and then under the ladder were the Indians and the coloured people, and at the bottom of the ladder were the black majority, the African people. But inherent in the violence of the oppressors were the seeds of continuous conflict. It was in this situation that Gandhiji arrived in South Africa and it would be interesting to know that Gandhiji formed the first liberation organisation in 1894—The Natal Indian Congress. The African National Congress was formed in 1912.

I would not speak about the Satyagraha struggle of Mahatma Gandhi since that has all been said over and over again. But we are very proud to come from South Africa which nurtured the thoughts of Mohandas Karamchand Gandhi and gave to India the making of what became Mahatma Gandhi, who led the Independence movement of India. Right through the years of Mahatma Gandhi's negotiations with the regime in South Africa, he achieved some redress. But the hypocritical government backed out on all the promises made and resorted to continuous repression soon after Mahatma Gandhi left. After Gandhiji's departure, Indian politicians of South Africa, contrary to the practice of Mahatma Gandhi, took the road of deputations, petitions and resolutions, all to no avail.

In 1945 and 1946, two Indian doctors Yusuf Dadoo and Monty Naicker returned to South Africa, and they swept into power in the Indian Congress in South Africa. In 1946, once again the spirit of Mahatma Gandhi was revived in a passive resistance struggle conducted by the Indian Congress. Over 2000 Indian volunteers went to prison. At the same time, the Indian Congress in South Africa appealed to India to help in their struggle. Although it was still the interim government, India responded to the requests made by the Indian Congress in South Africa to break trade and diplomatic relations with South Africa. When people talk of the boycott of South Africa, they talk of the 1970s and the 1980s when some countries broke off trade relations, though not completely with South Africa. India broke off trade, diplomatic and cultural relations with South Africa in 1946. India also raised the question of discrimination at the United Nations in the same year. So, as I said, 2000 volunteers went to prison in 1946. But it was an experience that went on to influence the later struggle.

After the 1946 passive resistance of the Indian community, the African National Congress and the South African Indian Congress jointly launched in 1952 a non-violent defiance campaign against certain laws. Among the first volunteers in that struggle were Nelson Mandela who was the volunteer-in-chief, and Ismail Ahmed Cachalia who was the deputy volunteer-in-chief. About ten thousand volunteers went to prison in that campaign, but repression never ended. In the face of all non-violent efforts, repression just increased. In 1960, the two liberation organisations, the African National Congress and the Pan African Congress, were declared illegal so that the avenues for non-violent protests just about came to an end. Some of our leadership was sent into exile. Oliver Tambo, Dr. Yusuf Dadoo and quite a few others were sent into exile while other leaders like Nelson Mandela, Walter Sisulu, Govan Mbeki and others remained behind to carry on the struggle in the country which eventually led to the imprisonment of Mr. Mandela on Robben Island for 27 years.

Long after he was in prison and consistent with the policy of the African National Congress, Mr. Mandela decided under very difficult circumstances to make the first move to speak with the enemy. That first move was endorsed by the ANC leadership in exile and thereafter the matter was taken forward. Mr. Mandela's demands for the release of political prisoners, withdrawal of the ban on the organisations, return of the exiled, and negotiations were accepted by the government of the day. In 1989 and 1990, the prisons were emptied of political prisoners and negotiations started in earnest by the other side. Mr. Mandela emerged from prison without bitterness or idea of revenge but with the message of reconciliation and forgiving the enemy in the interest of a united nation of South Africa. Since then, of course, much has happened.

After the first Government of National Unity, a new constitution was adopted and we now look back at 13 years of South African democracy. I would not go into what has been achieved except to say that this democracy has ushered in dignified existence for the oppressed people who were humiliated and deprived of all social standing for 350 years. They now walk tall in dignity. Thirteen years of democracy also meant liberating the white people because all those who ruled the country, were insecure people. They were ashamed to leave South Africa and say they were Whites or they were South Africans. Now they too live under the same flag, proud to be South Africans.

We have also achieved gender equality. If you see, almost half of our Cabinet consists of women. Some of our ambassadors, e.g., our Ambassador in the USA, in Britain and in many of the countries of the world, are women. Our Parliament has got about 30 to 40 per cent women members.

Under apartheid, there was no religious freedom. We have now passed legislation for complete freedom of religion and freedom of speech. What I am saying is that we have achieved much through a peaceful transformation, like very few other countries have. People from different countries in the world come to South Africa to find out how this miracle took place. It is not for us, it is not for our Government to prescribe to other countries how they should achieve their goal, but to say that 20 years ago none would have believed that South Africa was going to undergo a peaceful transformation. But South Africa did succeed in the face of great odds, to achieve a peaceful transformation.

I would just end with the hope, the wish, the prayer that all countries of conflict in the present-day world—be it the Northern Ireland, countries of the Middle-East or Latin America, will achieve negotiated, peaceful transformation in their countries.

At Juhu beach, Bombay, 1944.

I deny being a visionary. I do not accept the claim of saintliness. I am of the earth, earthly... I am prone to as many weaknesses as you are. But I have seen the world. I have lived in the world with my eyes open. I have gone through the most fiery ordeals that have fallen to the lot of man. I have gone through this discipline.

— M.K. Gandhi

15

Relevance of Gandhi in the Political World Today

RADHA KUMAR

I am struck by the enormous range of relevance that Gandhi's life as well as his writings have for us in the political world today. Dr. Sharp has pointed out that Gandhi's engagement with and support for non-violent protests against oppressive regimes was worldwide and global. His interests and engagements were with countries all over the world. But Gandhi also engaged in politics on a number of occasions in a more traditional or formal level. I am remembering, for example, the League of Nations Conference after the end of World War-I in which the world had decided on what to do with the territories of the former Austro-Hungarian as well as the former Ottoman Empire. Gandhi had sent a delegation to that Conference in which the Congress's point of view was put forward suggesting that the same rights of self-determination or independence that were being offered to the territories of the former Austro-Hungarian empire should be offered to the territories of the Ottoman Empire. Instead, of course, as we know, those territories were re-divided and handed over to different empires—the British and the French—most notably at that point.

Thinking about that particular moment in history, I am tempted to raise an important question. If Gandhi's advice had been heeded, even if not taken on board fully, would we be actually looking at the kind of conflicts that we have in the Middle-East today? My own sense is that perhaps there has been a period in which either form of trusteeship envisioned by Gandhi might certainly have meant that 50 years down the road there would have been a series of regional relationships of the Middle-East and of West Asia which would have, to some extent, protected them from the kinds of vulnerabilities that those countries face today. I have in mind the possibility of the emergence of the independent nations much earlier in that part of the world. Gandhi's specific view of trusteeship would have meant something different to them. I also think that Gandhi underlined the importance of political timing. He said that under some conditions non-violence was impossible; that it was important to know how you can, over a period of time build your strength so that when the political moment is ripe, you are able to achieve success through non-violent means. I think the most telling example of that is actually East Europe. The non-violent resistance movements in Hungary, Poland, Czechoslovakia from the late 1950s to the late 1960s, were all met by brute force. But in the late 1980s and the early 1990s, the moment had clearly come in these movements which could actually bring in independence and self-determination.

Writing about Gandhi in the year 2000, Nelson Mandela called him a sacred warrior and he pointed out—a point that I think Mr. Rutelli made as well—that Gandhi's real political brilliance lay in going against the prevalent wisdom of any particular moment in time. And this is what Mandela says: "At a time when Freud was liberating sex, Gandhi was reining it in; when Marx was pitting worker against capitalist, Gandhi was reconciling them; when the dominant European thought had dropped God and soul out of the social reckoning, he was centralising society in God and soul; at a time when the colonised had ceased to think and control, he dared to think and control; and when the ideologies of the colonised had virtually disappeared, he revived them and empowered them with a potency that liberated and redeemed."

Several speakers have referred to the events of September 11, 2001. I actually lived in New York at that time and I lived only two blocks from the World Trade Centre. So, my building was also rather badly affected. What I do recall, in fact, in the immediate aftermath of those days. For those of you who know New York might remember that in Union Square in New York, there is a very beautiful statue of Gandhi that was built by the trade unions of America. Everyday there must have been 500 or 600 bouquets around that statue. People went to Union Square and to Gandhi statue to somehow seek a way of dealing with the violence of 9/11 that would not be retaliatory or vengeful in any way. I think that was a very important point. Something else we should recall is that in the aftermath of 9/11—and this is not to do with the US Administration, it is to do with perhaps different collections of American people—six states in America introduced Gandhian teachings into their textbooks, which is something. Of course I hope that our country is going to follow suit with.

The points that Gandhi made are so relevant to us even today. In 1947, talking about India, Gandhi said: "If India takes up the doctrine of the sword, she may gain momentary victory. But then India will cease to be the pride of my heart. What policy the National Government will adopt, I cannot say. I may not even survive it, much as I would love to." This is, of course, just about nine months before he was assassinated. "If I do, I would advise the adoption of non-violence to the utmost extent possible, and that will be India's great contribution to the peace of the world and the establishment of the new world order." He added, "Democracies face a problem that obviously dictatorships do not. Violence and democracy do not co-exist well. When a democratic country takes to violence, it may undermine the very nature and fundamentals of that democratic polity. That, of course, is not the case with dictatorships."

He further said, "An India reduced in size but purged in spirit may still be the necessity of the non-violence of the brave." Finally, he averred: "If I can have nothing to do with the organised violence of the Government, I can have less to do with the unorganised violence of the people. For me, popular violence is as much an obstruction in our path as Government violence. Indeed, I can combat government violence more successfully than popular violence. For one thing, in combating the latter, I will not have the same support as in the former." This is, of course, something we know very well. Governments really look at the short end of the stick when it comes to the issues of violence. Mandela pointed out how valid Gandhi's ideas on the decentralised or the small-scale society were for today's globalised world. Again, I think that the point he made very strongly and earnestly was that centralisation as a system is inconsistent with the democratic and non-violent society. This, of course, is a great experiment for the European Union today, faced with the riddle of how to build a really democratic and non-violent Europe without appearing to be weak and divided as they were on the Iraq war.

Finally, this is what he said about terrorism: "I do not regard killing or assassination or terrorism as good in any circumstances whatsoever. This includes revolutionary terrorism. I do believe that ideas ripen quickly when nourished by the blood of martyrs." I would like to stress that sentence because it shows what clear political understanding Gandhi had of how mass ideologies and mass force works. "But a man who dies slowly of jungle fever in service, bleeds as certainly as the one on the gallows, and if the one who dies on the gallows is not innocent of another's blood, he never had ideas that deserve to ripen."

In conclusion, while talking about terrorism, he also says, "The only way to deal with violence is to understand what is the root cause of that violence. Trying to cut the hands that strike me is not going to help. It may only postpone violence to another day. But if I can understand why in the first place he was motivated or propelled to violence and I can deal with those causes, then perhaps I can indeed work towards a non-violent form of peace-building and, of course, ultimately a democratic society."

16

New Purpose of Leadership
Less to Rule, More to Educate

GEORGE PAPANDREOU

GANDHI has inspired my generation at a younger age and as Francesco Rutelli said, this was something which we thought about as his image loomed large in many instances. How we fight against the Vietnam War; how we fight in my country against the dictatorship; will it be through use of violence or would it be through use of non-violence? But I see that Gandhi's influence is now trickling down to the younger generation, and that is something we should be optimistic about. Before I received this invitation, my 16-year-old daughter came up to me and said: "Daddy, can you help me on a project that I want to write for my school?" I said: "Fine! What would you like to write about?" She said: "I want to write about Gandhi's non-violent movement and how it influenced Indian Independence." Thus, we spent a weekend researching and discussing about Gandhi. So, on return to Athens, she will certainly receive a Quit India T-shirt.

But today, as President of the Socialist International, I feel we owe a special debt to Mahatma Gandhi. His views are pertinent for the democratic and socialist movement I represent. Although his views developed in the context of the struggle of South Africa and India, they show an amazing insight into the problems of today's global economy and society. He spoke of poverty as dehumanising, causing loss of dignity, self-respect and human potential. Today, poverty remains a major issue for our movement. He felt that inequality destroyed the sense of community and solidarity between peoples. Today, we are in search of both universal solidarity and a sense of global community. He believed in full employment and work as means not only to satisfy basic needs but to develop each individual's necessary self-respect. Today, our movement is fighting for decent jobs for all around the world. He felt that over-industrialisation and consumerism would destroy the equilibrium between man and nature. Today, we have become concerned with climatic change and global warming. We are fighting for a new sustainable balance between human beings and nature.

His concept of non-violence was in no way a concept of passivity. On the contrary, it was a way to educate, to empower the citizen and allow him to discover new capacities and potential. He feared that technological progress could marginalise and disenfranchise large parts of the population. Today, while progress has been massive, so is the new digital divide we are witnessing. Our movement is experimenting with new forms of democratic participation from direct democracy to electronic democracy, to online communities, to decentralising political parties. In a sense, we have embarked on our own Satyagraha. We see active citizens' participation, civil society creating global network of citizens, as an antidote to global concentration of capital, media concentration, to alienation and marginalisation, to populisms and fundamentalisms.

I, however, would like to dwell on three points which I feel are especially important. First is the fact that Gandhi's stand was a moral one. He changed the framework of the colonial struggle. It was no longer a struggle between Indians and British. It was a struggle between values. On the one hand were the oppressors, cruel, authoritarian, and violent. On the other were the oppressed, humane, democratic, peace-loving, and proud. This stance has inspired many and I have been inspired by his wisdom. From 1977, I worked to revive an ancient Greek tradition, that of the Olympic Truce—a moment of tolerance and peaceful competition in our world.

On November 18, 2003, the United Nations General Assembly unanimously passed a resolution in support of the Olympic Truce, and during the August, 2004 Athens Olympics, North and South Korea marched under a single banner, a powerful moral victory for culture and athletics. To Gandhi, this moral world was based on truth. To him, violence arose out of ignorance; non-violence arose out of truth. Truth was to him an emancipating power. Truth, therefore, becomes intrinsic to peace. Thus, truth is a search, a life-long search. It is an ongoing dialogue. Dialogue, a Greek word—dia and logos—means true logic. So, Gandhi believed in the power of the mind, not in the power of violence, not in the power of terror, not in the domination of military or technological force. He could have told the US that in Iraq he who captures the hearts and minds will be the more powerful, not he who has the military strength.

This brings me to my second point. He understood the premises of a peaceful multicultural society, a common ethos, a common value system. Europe, as was mentioned, for example, is of a very diverse nature—different languages, religions, ethnicities and the history of wars. Yet today, because of the European Union, we share basic values, we can communicate, we discourse, we discuss, and it is based on basic principles, common principles and our differences have become a source of innovation, rather than of fear and violence. Is this not what Gandhi saw in a multicultural India, a common ethos which united this vast country and divergent groups? Is this not what our global community today is in search of, a global village which can share common values, yet revel in the beauty of the special identities we all have?

During my term as Foreign Minister, I was determined to challenge the image of Turkey as an eternal enemy of Greece. This was not an easy task. But in 1999, I worked with my counterpart Ismail Chem to turn a curse into a blessing. Devastating earthquakes hit both sides of Algeria. We left our differences behind and launched a policy of rapprochement. We initiated meetings between citizens, officials and business groups. Soon, Greece and Turkey had signed bilateral agreements after 40 years of isolation to boost trade and tourism. We signed environmental, cultural, energy-related, educational, civil emergency agreements. We discussed our history books. Our approach was pragmatic but was also a deep belief that non-violent methods could work.

Greece became a champion of Turkey's candidacy for membership in the European Union. Surely, if Turkey espoused the common values, undertook the necessary reforms to democratise its institutions and society, and curbed the power of military, this would benefit us all and reduce the possibility of violence. In this context, a dialogue between cultures was a reality. Ismail Chem and I represented two rival countries. However, we became in the Gandhian spirit close friends in our common cause for peace. This is why two days ago I was asked to place a shovel-full of soil over his grave and paid him my last respects.

Common ethos from human rights to tolerance, to non-violent resolution of conflicts, to the abolition of capital punishment, to democratic practice, to transparency, to fighting racism, to strengthening the rule of law rather than the law of the sword, this is what, as President of the Socialist International, we represent. I am confronted daily with the task of uniting the many voices of our diverse movements, over a hundred and sixty parties around the world into a single expression of solidarity, positive forces that can address very complex global challenges. We are committed to a global culture of peace. We continue to be active in the Middle-East, the Balkans, the Caucasus, Africa, Latin America and

Asia. Only a few days from now, we will be present in Nepal to support the formation of a democratic coalition Government following years of conflict.

India and Greece have also shared much in history even from ancient times. We share democratic traditions. In 1984, my father, Andreas Papendreou worked with Indira Gandhi and later Rajiv Gandhi to launch the initiative of the Six—a political alliance that lobbied for nuclear disarmament and peace. Others involved were Olof Palme, Julius Nyerere, Raoul Alphansin, Megale Dalamadrid. Today, I have found a friend in Sonia Gandhi. We share the common conviction to work for comprehensive nuclear disarmament.

And this brings me to the third and final point. How did Mahatma Gandhi's common ethos come about? He believed in empowering through education. But what could this education mean? It means many things. First, it is humanistic education. I would ask our friends, our outstanding intellectuals that we have with us today—if you were to develop a global curriculum for our citizens of the world today, who would you teach, what would you teach? Would Gandhi not be one of them? For sure. Mandela, Martin Luther King? Would it be Aristotle, Desmond Tutu or all our Nobel Prize winners? Would it be Joys of Courtesy or Kafka or Arundhati Roy or Dostoevsky? Who else? Should we not teach how people can deal with conflict? Should we not teach both our traditions as well as our neighbour's traditions and understand them? Should we not teach how to love, to learn, to search, to question, to analyse, to sift through a world of proliferating information? This education would in fact be deeply anti-dogmatic. No fundamentalisms, no absolutisms, no big impasse could fit into this education. The search for truth could only be the absolute value, and certainly this is what Gandhi believed in. Secondly, will this education not be empowering? Would we not need to inform, train all our citizens so that ignorance could not be weakness, a weakness to be exploited, so that the power of knowledge was not monopolised by the few, so that we had no digital divide? Thirdly, would knowledge not become our new commonwealth, a wealth shared by all, a wealth owned by none, a digital library, a social property, a source of everlasting discovery and creativity, a wealth accessible to all? Fourthly, will this knowledge not emancipate us—a process which means that the means of production, now highly dependent on knowledge of our brains, are ours, self-managed and collectively managed which free us rather than exploit us? And fifthly, will this knowledge not make us wise, wise enough to know our limits; wise enough to work together collectively; wise enough to stem our greed and respect our planet or environment, understand our responsibility to the generations who will inherit this world from us; wise enough to plan for tomorrow and not only today; to democratically design our future as we can today, wise enough to empower the poor, as Mohammad Yunus has accomplished, to create social businesses; wise enough to break down the walls of inequality between gender, races, nations, the poor and the rich; wise enough not only to break down psychological, religious, apartheid, racial walls, but also real walls, whether they are in Palestine or on the U.S. border to Mexico, or in Nicosia in Cyprus; wise enough to fight pandemics effectively, such as, President Kaunda mentioned, that of AIDS?

Inspired by Gandhi, education is in the forefront of my priorities in the Socialist International. My hope is to create an academy of fellows, an academy of progressive leaders and thinkers around the world who can highlight their best practices, relate their own experiences, and offer their knowledge in order to empower younger leaders in our global movement. I would very much like to invite you. I wish that you, the distinguished participants in this Congress, would be willing to participate in this exercise. For, in the end, it is Gandhi's life example as the life example of so many fighters for peace in this room that have educated our public; our people, our citizens. This is a new purpose of leadership today, less to rule, more to educate. And in a world where there are no simple recipes, we in leadership positions need to be humble enough as Gandhi, humble enough to be ready to be educated ourselves, to learn ourselves throughout our lives.

Mutual toleration is a necessity for
all time and for all races.
— M.K. Gandhi

17

Co-operation for Viable and Sustainable Social and Political Order

MAUMOON ABDUL GAYOOM

BY example, by effort and by precept, Mahatma Gandhi changed the course of history, not only in South Asia but also in many other parts of the world. Empires and ideologies have crumbled before ordinary people energised by the spirit of Satyagraha.

The presence today at this conference of leaders, teachers and activists from all corners of the earth and from diverse civilisational backgrounds is testimony to the abiding relevance of Mahatma Gandhi's vision and ideals. It was interesting to learn of the detailed operational plan developed by Dr. Sharp on Gandhi's Satyagraha principle.

Mahatma Gandhi was born at a time when imperialism was riding high, when oppression of peoples was a norm, when whole continents could be pillaged, and when prejudice and fear stood as the basis for authority and legitimacy. War and aggression were still legitimate instruments of relations between nations. He challenged the order of the day, not with war but with compassion, not with prejudice but with empathy, not with cowardice but with conviction, not with arrogance but with humility, not with bigotry but with tolerance.

Twice in his lifetime, the powers of the day chose not the path of Satyagraha but the Clausewitzian path of "politics by other means", and embroiled the whole world in total war. Their prescription for the so-called "20 years' crisis" between those two wars was more of the same, not appeasement, but being so-called realists, pursuing power that came from tank divisions and gun barrels. The upshot of all that was, the powers that be proudly articulated the comforts of "mutually assured destruction" or MAD. Of course to disguise our moral bankruptcy, we use nice words, such as deterrence, and when it fails, equally misleading words, such as smart weapons and collateral damage.

But the fact is, the so-called realist vision, with its focus on dominance and power, is unsustainable. Just as General Reginald Dyer's bullets at Jallianwala Bagh could not save the British Empire, there are clearly limitations to what is called "hard power". It can sometimes suppress a conflict, but more often than not, it would only aggravate a dispute. But surely, the use of violence can never resolve a conflict or establish durable peace. "Soft power", such as that of moral suasion, can establish the foundations of lasting peace. Mahatma Gandhi showed that power does not have to come from the barrel of a gun.

Our own experience in the Maldives and our predicament as a small state, demonstrates that peace does not equate with military ability. Our independence was secured without bloodshed, and it has been safeguarded through friendly relations with our neighbours and with the entire world.

The second half of the 20th century showed greater regard for Satyagraha. War did not bring lasting freedom. Freedom won by non-violent activism has proven to be more sustainable. No one would doubt the fundamental importance of the ideals propounded by Mahatma Gandhi, especially given the nature of the challenges that the world faces at present.

Mahatam Gandhi understood the fundamental importance of co-operation for viable and sustainable social and political order, co-operation achieved not through coercion or subjugation, as many of his more powerful contemporaries understood it, but through empathy and compassion, as all civilisations and religions have taught. Islam, for example, teaches us the importance of empathy. In the Holy Quran, the Almighty Allah says:

> O Mankind! We created you from a single (pair) of a male and a
> female, and made you into nations and tribes, that you may know
> each other (not that you may despise each other).

All the great religions of the world stress the importance of non-violence.

In recent decades, advances in technology have revolutionised the world and have accelerated the process of globalisation. There have been many benefits but also numerous problems, such as the rapid spread of disease, the rise of terrorism, the breakdown of nations, the degradation of the environment, and the proliferation of weapons of mass destruction. But it is evident that force is not the solution.

The European Union has shown that swords can indeed be turned into ploughshares. ASEAN is showing us that the same experiment can work very effectively even in other conditions. South Asia, the birthplace of Mahatma Gandhi, must demonstrate that it has the will to co-operate to achieve its vision of durable peace and dignity for the peoples of our region.

As Mahatma Gandhi observed, the worst form of violence is poverty. Eradicating poverty must remain a foremost goal of creating a world that is just and peaceful. I am confident that one of the outcomes of this memorable gathering would be to rededicate ourselves to the urgent tasks of eradicating poverty and the pursuit of the Millennium Development Goals. I also hope that this Conference would provide an impetus to the SAARC Summit that is to be convened here in two months' time. The vision of Mahatma Gandhi has direct relevance not only in matters of high politics, but also in inspiring us to work harder towards a just and equitable world. "Peace", he had said, "will not come out of a clash of arms but out of justice lived and done by unarmed nations in the face of odds."

Indeed, as Jawaharlal Nehru pointed out, peace is not merely the absence of war, but a condition of mind brought about by the serenity of the soul. Achieving that condition requires respect for human dignity and equality, freedom and compassion, justice and truth. Building peace requires promoting understanding and cooperation, and tolerance and dialogue.

The essence of Satyagraha is the power of the truth. It is about openness and fairness. Clearly, violence cannot be the answer to the world's woes. War has never been a solution. It is evident where the world is going wrong. But Satyagraha will triumph, as borne out by history. As Mahatma Gandhi observed, "When I despair, I remember that all through history, the ways of truth and love have always won. There have been tyrants and murderers, and for a time they can seem invincible, but in the end they always fall. Think of it always." The sooner the world accepts these truths the better.

Overwhelming participation of women in the Quit India Movement, 1942.

18

A New Satyagraha

JANEZ DRNOVŠEK

MAHATMA Gandhi gave us all great inspiration. But his messages and his example is not something that we can admire in the context of the history of the past century. It is something that should give us strength and inspiration to make the changes that humanity needs for the future.

Humanity today faces serious challenges, the most serious ever in history. We all know that imbalances of today's world are huge and that they do not diminish, but on the contrary, they get bigger and bigger. You can speak about poverty and huge differences that exist in the world. It gives the perception of injustice to the majority of people living today in the world. We can speak about the rule of the stronger and about the rule of wealthier. We can see that today's politics, business and media are too often influenced by, as I call it, a low level of consciousness coming out of selfishness—selfishness of individuals, of human beings, selfishness of nations. If we look at today's world institutions, including the United Nations, we can perceive that very often the members, especially those who have the decisive powers, pursue their own interests. They call them geopolitical interests, often these are economic interests. They have their own interests and the interests perhaps of their friends. But sometimes there is nobody, or very often there is nobody, who would defend the interests of humanity as a whole. That is why we cannot fight today the challenges that present the injustice in the world, the terrorism linked with this, the threats coming out of this, and which is even more threatening.

We cannot face the destruction of the earth, the destruction of our climate which is accelerating and the warnings of which we receive everyday. They are everyday more obvious but still those who can possibly to do something, to reverse the behaviour of institutions, of business, individuals and to do something to stop these developments, do not use their powers for that purpose. They do not look after the interests of humanity. Their consciousness is unfortunately too often reduced to selfishness, to power, to wealth, to profits and to destroy the earth and our climate for profits. And it is very obvious that with arms and the most modern technology following it, we cannot face the challenges of today.

The imbalances will continue to grow and at certain points they will destroy humanity. At certain points our climate will be destroyed so much that it will not be possible to do anything later; then just agony will follow. And we are still not capable today or conscious enough to face this challenge and to do something seriously about it. That is why I think that we need today a new Satyagraha, a new Gandhi; we need values, higher consciousness; we need people who can face these institutions of profit and power and defeat them, of course, without violence.

With violence we cannot achieve any sustainable change. History has proven that clearly. It can be achieved only without violence and only with higher consciousness of the majority of the people on the earth. This is the only way to raise the consciousness of people, to tell them the truth, to seek the truth. When we see the truth, then we will wake up, then we will start to move and try to change our behaviours, to influence our institutions—national and international institutions. This is the only way to go.

We are coming to a period where probably these efforts to raise the consciousness of the people of the world, especially politicians and business people, will be accompanied by catastrophes, mostly natural catastrophes coming out of the change of climates, probably some other kinds of catastrophes, too. And catastrophes usually have an effect of a shock, a shock that can wake up people, make them change their patterns of thinking and living, can be an additional impetus to raise consciousness of humanity as a whole. But we should not count on this only. It is very likely that this will happen. We have to do something ourselves—everybody in his surroundings, everywhere—so that more and more people will be conscious and more and more people will join the efforts to change the world for the better: to establish a more just world and to ensure a sustainable development of humanity.

What I have learnt from Gandhi and Satyagraha is that even if things look unchangeable, one can still change them provided one is convinced that the change being sought is based on truth and is being done to help others. Today it may seem impossible to change the institutions of the world, of power and of profit, but I think we will have to change them. If we do not succeed, then the world will collapse at a certain point and, I should say, in the foreseeable future. Once we realise this and become conscious of this fact, I think then we will act and we will make the impossible possible.

Mahatma Gandhi refusing to travel by rickshaw on his way to see the Viceroy in Simla, 1946.

19

Peaceful Resolution of Conflicts

JUSUF KALLA

9/11 is a very important date. It relates to two periods of modern history. One represents the struggle of non-violence and the other violence. Why is it so? I think as Gandhi said, if violence starts, another violence will follow. We are seeing this as a reality in the whole world. I think there are many reasons why violence is there. There are political reasons, economic reasons, social reasons and religious reasons. What is more dangerous is that there are combinations of political, economic and religious reasons.

If we look at Iraq, we see this combination but we do not know how to end this violence. In our country also, we are experiencing such a violence. Same is the case in other regions of South-East Asia and South Asia. It is happening mostly because of inequality, injustice and poverty. How do we solve this problem? I think we should be making principles and setting objectives, as how to achieve peace, justice, democracy and law enforcement, and how to combat poverty.

We all have our own experiences. We think about inequality and injustice from the political, economic and religious viewpoint. Politically, it is a combination of races and problems, and sometimes, due to the power of the post, it is very easy to do so. Economic causes include inequitable distribution of resources of a country, and also there are social factors. Then there are religious reasons. Religion is sometimes deceptively portrayed as a way to cheap salvation, making people believe that if you kill each other you will go to heaven. The fundamentals which will save the people from these misconceptions are education and ideas.

My country faces religious problems bred by politics. Why do they use religion? It is because it is very easy to bring solidarity through religion. So, how do we solve this problem? When five people had died in my country because of religious conflict, I said, "No, you would not be going to heaven because you have killed five people, you will go to hell because no religion preaches that you go to heaven if you kill each other." And when I said so, within one week the killings stopped and the negotiations started.

Same is the case with economic and political conflicts. We have a 30-year long conflict in Aceh because of inequality of resources. We have settled the problems of resources in a democratic manner through continuous negotiations. We thank the European countries for the support extended to us for these negotiations to stabilise the economy of the region and to bring equality and justice.

There are many reasons and many combinations due to which conflicts happen. The issue before us is how do we solve these conflicts with non-violence and how do we bring about peace. It is not so easy in a world where there is combination of politics, economics and religion. But I think through Gandhi's philosophy of non-violence we can find a way.

First, we should set an objective that we can do anything for the welfare of people. Secondly, the purpose for stopping the conflict through a peace process should not be to terminate the enemy but to terminate the conflict. If we were to terminate the enemy, the conflict will never end and we will never have peace.

We should also know the background of the problems and accordingly solve them. Sometimes we seek solution not according to the problem and thus face other problems. Therefore, there is no common solution but there are common principles. One such principle of non-violence is dialogue. The second is, maintaining the dignity of each other. Dignity means, of course, a win-win solution based on equality and justice. The last dictum is that peace can be achieved only if both sides love peace. If we do not have the will to have peace, we may make any number of efforts to find a solution, but we will not achieve it. That is why I say, love peace. Thus, Gandhian philosophy is very important in the present times.

20

Reviving the Gandhian Philosophy

ABUNE PAULOS

TODAY the whole world, more than ever before, is crying and striving for bringing peace and for avoiding violence, though it seems hard to obtain. Mahatma Gandhi's philosophy is widely exposed to research and deep analysis. It is ironic that after 100 years, we seem to realise that we have an urgent need for the philosophy of which he spoke a century ago. I am not pretending or intending to lecture about his philosophy. It is the work of great philosophers, economists and other deep thinkers and experts. But his philosophy is of special significance for religious people because we find God in the core of spiritual elements of Gandhi's teachings. The cardinal principles of Gandhi's thought are truth and non-violence. For Gandhi, truth is truthfulness in word and deed and absolute truth. Hence, ultimate truth is God. Non-violence or love is regarded as the highest law of humankind. To me, this is the fundamental truth that the world should understand and struggle for.

The teachings of Mahatma Gandhi were and are of universal significance and the commemoration should be shared by all the people of the world. Therefore, we can say, this is the time to revive the teachings of Mahatma Gandhi and use them in the present society where violence rules the lives and activities of all and where world peace is gravely threatened.

Though Mahatma Gandhi died 60 years ago, his ideas are immortal, growing afresh, especially in this epoch when the world has come to realise the need for an alternative after having passed through local national and international wars of destruction. His preaching about passive resistance, knowing that violence will provoke negative reaction and the concept of challenging a system without resorting to violence is ideal. It is really sad and unfortunate that such an ideal philosophy is not widely accepted and practised or has not dominated our world with many followers except, to my knowledge, a very few individuals such as the

Reverend Martin Luther King of the USA and some others like him. Yet, it is a living principle and remains ideal for people to adopt as their model, especially those who advocate peace, non-violence and those who have realised that violence has brought no benefit but disaster to human society. Gandhi's teaching cannot go contrary to any human philosophy because almost all genuine thoughts of different groups advocate peace and condemn violence.

As far as I am concerned, it is fair to say that all religious people give high value to the principles of Gandhian philosophy because the teaching of all religions stresses peace. We understand that peace is of ultimate value in human life, emanating from God. Our God is God of peace; to me God Himself is peace. In the same way, we find God in the core of the teachings of Mahatma Gandhi. Also, his teachings about patience and sympathy, implying endurance or sufferings as a means to an end; his belief that non-violence is an active force of the highest order, free from revenge have an important place in Christian tradition. Again, his definition of the word 'Satyagraha' given to the movement implies truth, openness, honesty and fairness, encompassing physical and mental non-violence and self-sacrifice, instead of inflicting suffering on the opponent. All these values indicate harmony with the teachings of the holy books. That is why, today all peace-loving and genuine nations, individuals or groups in the world, regardless of their religious or philosophical outlook, ethnic background, etc. give great value to the teachings of Mahatma Gandhi.

All in all, had the whole world accepted and followed God's commandment; had it also listened to God's messengers that arose at different times—including some special great philosophers like Gandhi—and applied it, no life would have perished unnecessarily. There would have been no conflict, war, displacement or destruction of property including that of civilisation, threat and fear that negatively characterise our world today.

21
World Voices

Liu Hongcai

Vice Minister, International Department of Central Committee, Communist Party of China

Mahatma Gandhi was an extraordinary political leader who continues to influence the modern world. One century ago, he launched Satyagraha or non-violent resistance movement against racial discrimination and unjust laws through peaceful means in South Africa. The movement greatly inspired the people in the colonial countries in their struggles for independence. He became the guiding force for the Indian people in their struggle for independence.

The values in Gandhian philosophy, that is, pursuing peace, justice, tolerance and defying violence had great impact on the democratic and progressive movement in many countries. The world today has completely changed from the world it was in Gandhi's time. Due to the struggles waged by the progressive forces, problems such as colonial rule and apartheid are no longer in existence. However, human society is still confronted with various challenges owing to local conflicts and unbalanced global economic growth. Mahatma Gandhi's ideals of peace and harmony among all human beings are yet to be fulfilled.

Mahatma Gandhi's doctrine of peace and non-violence is greatly enlightening for us today in handling international relations. We should encourage resolution of disputes and conflicts through peaceful means and discourage the use of threat or force. Efforts need to be made towards globalisation, balanced development, universal benefits and a 'win-win' outcome to bridge disparity in development and to eradicate poverty. We need to enhance regional and global economic cooperation and address the problems born out of economic disparity. Our ability to promote unhindered progress of all civilisations while maintaining the diversity of the world, would be our best tribute to him.

Pawel Zalewski
Chairman, Sejm Committee on Foreign Affairs in the Polish Parliament

Mahatma Gandhi was not just a great thinker, social reformer and politician but also a man who managed to preserve the most precious notion of humanity, creatively weaving it into the fabric of practical and successful politics. For me, the foremost lesson of Gandhiji's thinking is that losing nothing of its practicality, politics can be decent and honourable. And during the period of Communist Soviet oppression we all looked up to this very important lesson.

At the turn of the 19th century, when the demands for independence were becoming increasingly persistent in India, Gandhiji helped India choose a path of *ahimsa*—non-violence. It would however be wrong to say that Gandhi was ready to accept every humiliation simply to remain true to the idea of non-violence. For Gandhiji, non-violence was the ultimate weapon and yet he postulated that in choosing between cowardice and violence, one should rather choose violence than remain a helpless coward.

Gandhiji's greatness was not confined to practical politics. He was a social reformer, a person who perfected the use of a saintly language in order to modernise the traditional society and yet preserve its unique Indian identity because identity is what makes a nation. Gandhiji's deep desire to lessen the plight of the downtrodden and all those who suffered through ages of injustice was all a part of his great empowerment idea. It never ceased to generate respect and admiration in Poland too. The Solidarity Revolution was all about empowerment, empowerment of the State as a subject in relations with our neighbours, empowerment of the employees in relations with the employers, and finally, the empowerment of the people *versus* the State. Freedom, human rights, security, decent politics are the same all over the world. There is no better proof of it than the life and work of Mahatma Gandhi, a great, truly universal human being.

Lyonpo Khandu Wangchuk
Prime Minister, Royal Government of Bhutan

Mahatma Gandhi's philosophy of peace, tolerance and non-violence was a powerful instrument of social change. He pioneered the application of *ahimsa* or non-violence and peaceful protest as alternatives to violent revolution and led the movement to secure freedom for his country. At the same time, his philosophy inspired movements for civil rights and freedom across the world. His life and teachings inspired the lives of Dr. Martin Luther King Junior and Steve Biko, and through them there was emergence of civil rights movements and the freedom struggles in South Africa.

In a world beset with problems and challenges, the Gandhian philosophy of peace, tolerance and non-violence continues to be relevant and necessary. While the imperative of the human individual to exist amid peace, security and contentment cannot be over-stated, our world continues to be marred by violence, civil strife and protracted conflicts. In addition, new and emerging challenges continue to threaten the fabric of peace and security. In this regard, Lord Richard Attenborough stated: "The legacy of Mahatma Gandhi is not only vested in the independence of India and her position as one of the world's greatest democracies. His abiding greatness lies in the fact that the whole world needs Gandhian philosophy as much today as it did during his lifetime."

Today, as we endeavour to address the major challenges of the 21st century, let us commit ourselves to the principles and values that Mahatma Gandhi stood for. As we strive to contribute towards international peace and security, and to create an environment in which the hopes and aspirations of millions all over the world can be realised for a better future, let us emulate the path shown to us by Mahatma Gandhi and shun violence as a means to achieve our goals.

Ramesh Chennithala
President, Kerala Pradesh Congress Committee, India

Talking about Gandhi, non-violence is based on religious principles drawn from the diversity of scriptures, particularly the Bhagwat Gita, Bible and Quran. The Indian independence movement went on for three decades and involved thousands of Indians from all walks of life. Despite its size and duration, it remained almost uniformly non-violent. Gandhiji recognised the potentiality of various kinds of conflicts as an occasion to contemplate over the problems and also as an opportunity to search peaceful means to resolve them. He proposed and adopted Satyagraha as a moral equivalent to war and conflict.

Gandhiji recommended that politics should be a branch of ethics. Moral principles must be adhered to by politicians, ideologists, social activists as well as the ordinary citizen of the world, as there is no dividing line between private life and public life.

The need of the hour is to proclaim again and again the significance of Gandhian passivism to solve crucial problems of conflicts and violence. Gandhiji's approach had always been holistic and ethical as he believed that moral degeneration is the root cause of all evils, including conflicts. We must translate our own ways of thinking about the world in terms of mobs and markets. We should think in terms of men, women and children—the terms of Mahatma Gandhi's humankind.

To build a new world order and to achieve universal peace, it is imperative that we invest together and recapture the very spirit of Gandhian approach. The time has come to work towards a world free from nuclear and other weapons of mass destruction. For re-establishing trust, tranquility and peace and harmony in the world, the revival of the eternal principles of love, compassion and fellow-feeling are indispensable.

Farooq Sattar
Parliamentary leader, Mutahida Qaumi Movement, Pakistan

Till four years ago, it was not possible for the visitors of India and Pakistan to visit each other frequently. Today, thanks to bilateral efforts, social and cultural exchanges between the two countries have gained tremendous acceptability.

The India-Pakistan dialogue process needs the support of all the nation states. In fact, Mahatma Gandhi gave his life for bringing these two countries closer. The people of the two countries have great expectations from the process that is going on. They are desperate to see that the Satyagraha Centenary Declaration should send a very loud and clear message to those who are for war and not for peace, who are for violence and not for dialogue, who are not allowing this region to become durably and enduringly peaceful and non-violent. We need to continue with peace and dialogue process to send a strong message to all these people who are a stumbling block to the realisation of the dream of SAARC becoming a fraternity.

Navnit Dholakia
Member, House of Lords, Parliament of the United Kingdom

Discussion in relation to Mahatma Gandhi relates to freedom of India; discussion about Nelson Mandela is based on the freedom of South Africa; and discussion about Martin Luther King is based on the freedom of Black people in America. The discussion is relevant but I think what we need to ask ourselves is: how do we take these principles forward in the present century when the situations are no longer the same as they existed in those years when people were fighting for their freedom?

The question that is asked again and again is: if you want to resolve conflict, what are the essential elements, while dealing with different situations?

As an answer, let me just offer three steps based on the Gandhian philosophy. First, resolution of conflict can only be achieved when partners are equal. You cannot have unequal partners. You will then try to dictate the terms and that is unacceptable. The second is, resolution of conflict is best attained at the point at which it occurs. You cannot resolve conflicts of this nature standing miles away. You have got to be in the place where the conflict actually occurs and then try to sort it out.

The final and the most important thing is, it is the people, not the Government, who are correct in many of these countries, the countries which must be able to vouch that this is the type of peace they require. So, the big brother attitude of an imperial power is no longer relevant. What we need is what the world needs. We need better organisations based on economic parity and social condition within which there is give and take. No resolution is complete unless you are giving something up and also taking something in turn. The final thing is to make sure that there is an international dimension where we can resolve conflicts, and this is where we need to plan for peace, that is where we need to apply risk management. But above all, we need to do something more important, we need to develop a universal citizenship.

Sadok Fayala
Deputy Secretary General, Constitutional Democratic Rally, Tunisia

Gandhi does not belong to India alone, he is a world citizen. Prohibition of violence is very important because it not only affects India but it also affects the whole world at large. The world is facing more and more conflicts today. Terrorism, extremism and wars which are now raging in the world are all conflicts. Fanaticism is also showing its ugly head. So is ethnic and religious politics. These all are taking a toll on the world. We need to have interaction amongst all the people in all the areas and ensure that Gandhian philosophy is respected to ensure solidarity in the world.

We need to address these questions in a global manner. We have not been able to control the wars because we have been victims of certain historical circumstances.

The human spirit of hope however is the same all over the world. Therefore, we need to work on this human spirit as a human heritage. We need to create and innovate in such a way that we can bring the people of the world together. I would just like to stress upon what Mahatma Gandhi said. He underlined the importance of having interaction amongst people in a given context and in a complementary way. The philosophy of Mahatma Gandhi is a source of inspiration not only for human beings but also for the nations of the world and for the international community. He underlined that a human being is a social being therefore he needs to communicate with his brothers and sisters not only for his survival but also for the preservation of his race.

We therefore need to underline the necessity for a dialogue and cooperation amongst the people.

Mohamed Ali Rustam

Chief Minister of Malacca, Malaysia

It is the right time for all of us to reflect and ponder on a leader and a visionary who changed the course of history without using arms or violence but relying only on the basic concept of truth and peace—Satyagraha. It is the right time because we are witnessing conflicts in many part of the world. The international community must work towards reducing the gap in wealth, power and knowledge, in seeking enduring peace. Money spent on arms, for instance, should be channeled into activities that benefit humanity.

Mahatma Gandhi once said: "The world has enough for everybody's need but not for everybody's greed." The superpowers should be reminded of the ideology evolved by Mahatma Gandhi. Political instability occurs due to injustice being practised in certain quarters. We should develop understanding and empathy within the multi-cultural neighbourhood. All our religions and cultures encourage us to reach out to others; to share their joy as well as their opinion of philosophical tradition; to profoundly share our common humanity, the belief that Mahatma Gandhi held until the end of his life.

Pradip Giri

Member, Nepali Congress (Democratic)

Gandhi, the pioneer of peace, non-violence, truth-seeker and tower of moral power is always alive in our hearts. His teachings are even more relevant in the 21st century when violence, conflicts, stockpiling of arms, hatred and clashes are worldwide. He greatly inspired for our democratic movement and Nepali people accord great honour to him. People will always struggle for justice, equality and freedom but the means to achieve these goals must be peaceful. Violence is often used as a desperate reaction of helpless people but it cannot help achieve the goal because it creates counter-violence and helps the autocratic regime.

Karen Balcázar Cronenbold

Advisor for International Affairs, Santa Cruz Regional Government, Bolivia

We give honour and recognition to Gandhi's immortal memories. He made people aware of the eminent values of peace, non-violence, dialogue and reaching agreements as a solution to internal and international differences. For Gandhi, peace was not necessarily a state; it was a spirit, a legacy to which man has access when he meets his creator again, with whose love and in whose image and resemblance we were created. Gandhi dedicated his life to the humble, the forsaken, the poorest among the poor. He rejected any kind of discrimination, racial, ideological and religious, in the authoritarian dominion of the culture of one people over another.

India and Bolivia are countries which because of their diversity and ethnicity, language and culture have no similarities. Even so, both the countries strive for the Gandhian legacy of integration, civilised peaceful living, mutual respect, social inclusion and unity in diversity.

The world knows so little of how much my so-called greatness depends upon the incessant toil and drudgery of silent, devoted, able and pure workers, men as well as women.
— M.K. Gandhi

Lala Lajpat Rai

C.F. Andrews

Dr. S. Radhakrishnan

G.V. Mavalankar

Lal Bahadur Shastri

Kaka Kalelkar

B.C. Roy

Govind Ballabh Pant

Jayaprakash Narayan

Jamnalal Bajaj

Chittaranjan Das

Kamala Nehru

Kamala Devi Chattopadhyay

Srinivasa Sastri

Thakkar Bapa

Prabhavati Devi

Upendra Maharathi

T. Prakasham

Rafi Ahmed Kidwai

J.C. Kumarappa

Nandalal Bose

Ganesh Shankar Vidyarthi

Pandita Ramabai

Mahatma Gandhi with Dr. Rajendra Prasad

Mahadev Desai and Mahatma Gandhi

Mahatma Gandhi holding serious discussions with Maulana Azad and Sardar Patel

Manu and Rajkumari Amrit Kaur with Mahatma Gandhi

Mahatma Gandhi and Acharya Kripalani

Sucheta Kripalani

Madan Mohan Malviya

Mahatma Gandhi and Miraben

Mahatma Gandhi with Sarojini Naidu

Gandhiji with Vinoba Bhave

Abha, Sushila Nayar and Pyarelal

Section III Gandhian Philosophy for Poverty Eradication, Education and People's Empowerment

ASMA JAHANGIR

BHIKHU PAREKH

MARIANNE MIKKO

C.K. PRAHALAD

HAWA A. YOUSSOUF

E.S. MILIBAND

GIANNI VERNETTI

N. RAMGOOLAM

Section III

Gandhian Philosophy for Poverty Eradication, Education and People's Empowerment

This section corresponds to the Subject Session II of the international conference "Peace, Non-violence and Empowerment: Gandhian Philosophy in the 21st Century" held in New Delhi on January 29-30, 2007.

Chairperson: Chaiwat Satha-anand (Thailand)
Session Secretary: Jairam Ramesh (India)
Session Rapporteur: Pradeep Bhattacharya (India)
Paper Presenter: Bhikhu Parekh (United Kingdom)

Participants:

C.K. Prahalad (India), Navinchandra Ramgoolam (Mauritius), Edward Samuel Miliband (United Kingdom), Gianni Vernetti (Italy), Hawa Ahmed Youssouf (Djibouti), Asma Jahangir (Pakistan), Marianne Mikko (Estonia), Sergey Y. Glazyev (Russia), Conceita Xavier Sortane (Mozambique), Chaturon Chaisaeng (Thailand), Ken Nnamani (Nigeria), Kirti Menon (South Africa), Sunderlal Bahuguna (India), Sumitra Kulkarni (India), Rául Valdés Vivó (Cuba).

22

Gandhi on Poverty Eradication and People's Empowerment

BHIKHU PAREKH

> I do not know myself who is a Gandhian. Gandhism is a meaningless word for me. An ism follows the propounder of a system. I am not one; hence I cannot be the cause for an ism. If an ism is built up it will not endure, and if it does it will not be Gandhism. This deserves to be properly understood.[1]

A discussion of Gandhi is bedevilled by two difficulties. First, all his life he was preoccupied with the question of the best way to lead individual and collective lives. Dissatisfied with the moral and social ideas that he had inherited, he resolved to 'grow from truth to truth', and turned his life into a series of 'experiments with truth', as he suggestively called his *Autobiography*.[2] He made a close study of Christian, Buddhist, Islamic, Liberal, Socialist and other traditions of thought, tried out what he liked in them, and incorporated it into his ever-deepening system of thought. Not surprisingly, he set little store by consistency, and changed his views, sometimes radically, on a number of subjects. We cannot discuss him on the basis of views he might have held at one stage in his life but discarded later. I shall therefore concentrate on his mature writings or those he did not disown.

Secondly, Gandhi was not only a man of thought but also an activist who led one of the greatest anti-colonial struggles in history. He often had to make ideological and political compromises in order to hold the movement together. He sometimes went along with policies, and even lent them his explicit support, not because he agreed with them but because that was required by the exigencies and compulsions of political life. Since he spoke and wrote a great deal—so much so that even the collected works of a hundred hefty volumes are incomplete—he often said things that were not fully thought out or were meant only for a particular audience or context. Furthermore, Gandhi's views on the substantive issues of the day as well as policy prescriptions were conditioned by the world in which he lived, and that world has changed considerably. I shall therefore concentrate on his basic principles, his guiding vision, to see what, if anything, they have to say on the questions of poverty eradication and people's empowerment.

Poverty Eradication

Gandhi articulated a moral vision of human life and thought that the only thing that ultimately mattered was the kind of life human beings lived, the 'quality of their soul' and their social relations. Richness of individuals and society was to be judged by what they were and not what they had, by their virtues such as self-discipline, sense of dignity and pride, compassion, concern for others, integrity, spirit of non-violence, and openness to the world. Accumulation of material goods, endless multiplication of wants and constant titillation of increasingly jaded appetites not only did not raise human beings morally but invariably corrupted them and rendered their lives shallow and meaningless.

The point of economic life was to create the necessary material conditions of the good life. It should be firmly rooted in moral considerations, and should never be allowed to become a world of its own or to colonise other areas of human life. For Gandhi it needed to be organised in terms of the following basic principles.

First, a country's economy must be embedded in and go with the grain of its civilisation. Although Indian civilisation had much to be ashamed of, it also has cherished important values, and Indian people have developed certain qualities of character and temperament. While India should, of course, learn from the West, it should not mechanically copy its economic model. It should instead devise its own unique 'humane' economy that is best suited to its traditions, values and circumstances.

Second, poverty dehumanises human beings, undermines their sense of dignity and self-respect, wastes their potential and deprives their lives of all sense of meaning and purpose. It is one of the worst forms of violence that human beings can commit against other human beings. It is as bad as killing, and even worse for the fact that it is silent, slow, and invisible, arouses no anger, and is outside the purview of anyone's direct responsibility. As long as even one person is starved, is malnourished or lacks decent housing, the social order stands indicted lacking legitimacy. Basic human needs have the first claim on society's resources, and it has an obligation to arrange its economic affairs in a manner that the needs of all its members are met. As Gandhi observed:[3]

I will give you a talisman. Whenever you are in doubt, or when the
self becomes too much with you, apply the following test. Recall
the face of the poorest and the weakest man whom you may have
seen, and ask yourself if the step you contemplate is going to be of
any use to him. Will he gain anything by it? Will it restore him to a
control over his own life and destiny? In other words, will it lead to
Swaraj for the hungry and spiritually starving millions? Then you
will find your doubts and your self melt away.

Third, individuals should be able to satisfy their basic needs by means of work or
gainful employment. For Gandhi, work was a vital human need. It was by means of
work that we acquired self-discipline, self-restraint, capacity to plan our lives,
ability to relate to others, a sense of self-respect and a measure of social
recognition. Work was also a moral duty. Society was a system of cooperation, a
collective *yajna*, to which each of its members had a 'sacred' duty to bring their
distinct gifts and thereby contribute to common good. Work was a form of
participation in it, and to be denied was to be denied an opportunity to do one's
duty. Work was also a right because human dignity required that one should stand
on one's own feet and earn one's livelihood. Not the eradication of poverty *per se*
but full employment was, for Gandhi, the central social objective. Although welfare
payments by the state were sometimes necessary, they were no substitute for work.
They turned their recipients into social parasites, and denied them the
opportunities to develop their character and do their duty to society.

It was because, among other things, Gandhi placed such a great 'moral' value on
full employment that he was opposed to indiscriminate industrialisation and
urbanisation. He thought that 'industrialism', a self-propelling and an apparently
relentless technological domination of society, not only uprooted people from their
surroundings, exploited the villages, released the economic life from moral
constraints, and made pursuit of wealth the sole human goal but also led to the
unemployment of large sections of society. The only way it could avoid this was
either by colonising other societies and turning them into captive markets or by
encouraging domestic consumerism and planting ever new and largely unnecessary
wants, for neither of which he thought there was anything to be said.

Gandhi agreed that large-scale industrialisation produced cheap goods and brought
them within the reach of most but questioned its cost. It caused unemployment, was
ecologically unsustainable, disturbed the equilibrium between man and nature,

encouraged consumerism, and centralised economic and political power. Since human development had to be holistic, the benefits of large-scale industrialisation could not be considered in isolation. Gandhi therefore advocated minimisation of wants, small and medium scale industries, localised production of food and clothes, setting aside a share of their products for the market, limited and balanced industrialisation and agro-industrial units located in village communities. Some of these ideas do not make much economic or political sense in modern day India but their underlying principle is important and we need to devise appropriate ways for realising it.

Fourth, all forms of socially necessary labour are equally valuable. A sweeper or a coal miner makes as useful a contribution to society as a doctor or a professor, and the talents involved are equally precious.[4] Since some occupations require long training or involve rare talents, they need to be paid more, but not so much more that it leads to great inequalities of wealth, income, and power. The same principle applies to owners of industries. They have no natural right to their industries, for all rights are socially derived and conditional to the pursuit of common good. Furthermore their workers too contribute to their profit, and have as much right to it as their employers. As moral beings, the latter also have obligations to their fellow human being and hold their talents in trust for them. Like other socially valuable skills, that involved in accumulating wealth and successfully running an industry should be welcomed and encouraged.[5] But having made the money, one should know how to use it morally rather than remain its prisoner and be corrupted by it. Gandhi thought that just as people competed in making money, they should also compete in philanthropy.

Gandhi therefore insisted that while the talents of the industrialists should be welcomed and suitably rewarded, the rest of their profits belonged to society and should be used to develop their industries, provide welfare programmes for their employees, and contribute to the national exchequer for the promotion of collective well being. Gandhi knew that none of his industrialist friends, with the possible exception of Jamnalal Bajaj, saw or had any intention to see himself as a trustee of his industry. He argued that if popular pressure did not work, the state should intervene and impose trusteeship by law. This involved accepting the owners' formal right of ownership but laying down their maximum income and collecting a substantial part of the rest of their profits through taxation.

In his early years Gandhi was content to plead for the eradication of poverty and did not worry much about great economic inequalities. As long as no one was poor, it did not matter if some were rich, even very rich. Indeed, since wealth was a source of much evil and led to a shallow life, Gandhi even viewed the rich as objects of pity. As he grew older his views changed radically, partly in response to the growing working class unrest and the pressures of his socialist colleagues, and partly because of his reading of the dynamics of the capitalist economy. He argued that great economic inequalities were both the products and the causes of an exploitative economy. They produced anger and bitterness among the poor and the underprivileged, and provoked violence. They corrupted the moral tone of society, and channelled all ambition towards money making. They also concentrated economic power in the hands of a few, led to a corrupt alliance between the centres of economic and political power and undermined democracy.

Gandhi was particularly worried that inequality destroyed the spirit of community and mutual concern that every society required. The rich saw the poor as virtually a different species, an embarrassment and a threat. They held them in contempt, were indifferent to their needs and had no interest in distributive justice. This was repeatedly brought home to Gandhi by his futile appeals to the rich for help with his Constructive Programme. When he asked G.D. Birla to raise funds from his friends, Birla promised to do his best. A few days later, he wrote:[6]

> In Delhi, I walked from door to door for two days and I got only Rs. 1500 after great difficulty. One big contractor, who is supposed to be a great reformer and a Congressman.......promised to pay, but never paid. Ahmedabad is also helpless. In Bombay, four Marwari firms, after having promised subscription, are withholding payment. I do not think this is because people do not like the work. But everybody wants to evade payment, if it is at all possible...I confess that I cannot bring money from others.

Even Birla himself failed to live up to Gandhi's expectations. When Birla set up a mill in the princely state of Gwalior, the government obtained the land for him without paying adequate compensation to its poor owners. Gandhi pursued the matter with him in a series of letters and told him to drop the project rather than harm the 'just and legitimate interests of the poor'. When Gandhi received complaints about the working conditions in the mill, he asked Birla for an explanation. Birla blamed local 'agitators' for stirring up trouble. Gandhi wrote back, "The dispossessed class is today full of rancour. There is no denying the fact that they have been sinned against and as a class we have a lot to expiate for, not necessarily our sins but of system with which we are identified". The attempt to exonerate Birla as an individual but to inculpate him as a member of his class was typical of Gandhi. He asked Birla to show understanding and generosity "not in a spirit of virtue but as a simple discharge of debt overdue."

When Tata, Birla and Kasturbhai Lalbhai led an industrial delegation to Britain just before Independence, Gandhi feared, it would seem wrongly, that they might compromise India's vital interests by establishing unacceptable links with their British counterparts. He issued a public statement warning them against a 'shameful deal'. Birla was most upset, and cabled Gandhi from Cairo asking why his integrity and patriotism had been doubted. Gandhi reiterated his view in a telegram and, to rub salt in the wound, blessed him in the name of "famishing and naked India." He followed it up with a letter, saying that Birla and his associates had no reason to be upset "provided they were sincere in their protestations of injured innocence".[7]

Gandhi repeatedly warned the Indian bourgeoisie of the 'inevitable' violence of the workers and peasants. He announced that after Independence, he might himself lead Satyagrahas against vested interests and thought that they were likely to be 'more bitter' and protracted than those against the British. In 1942, he gave several important interviews to Louis Fischer in the course of which he argued that the landless peasantry would be right to refuse to cooperate with their masters and even to pay taxes in order to ensure an equitable distribution of land. He acknowledged that this might lead to violence by the landlords, but insisted that it was bound to be limited and could be easily brought under control.[8]

Professor Dantwala and others had a long discussion with Gandhi about the nature and implications of his critique of economic and other inequalities. They summed up his views in a draft which he endorsed after making a few changes, all designed to strengthen its egalitarian thrust. The final version reads as follows:[9]

1. Trusteeship provides a means of transforming the present capitalist order of society into an egalitarian one. It gives no quarter to capitalism but gives the present owning class a chance of reforming itself. It is based on the faith that human nature is never beyond redemption.

2. It does not recognise any rights of private ownership of property except in so far as it may be permitted by society for its own welfare.

3. It does not exclude legislative regulation of the ownership and use of wealth.

4. Thus under state regulated trusteeship, an individual will not be free to hold or use wealth for selfish satisfaction or in disregard of the interests of society.

5. Just as it is proposed to fix a decent minimum living wage, even so a limit should be fixed for the maximum income that would be allowed to any person in society. The difference between such minimum incomes should be reasonable and equitable and variable from time to time so much so that the tendency would be towards obliteration of the difference.

6. Under the Gandhian economic order, the character of production will be determined by social necessity and not by personal whim or greed.

Although Gandhi's egalitarian society has much to be said for it, and it was a great pity that his followers lost sight of it after Independence, it faces obvious difficulties. It rests on a particular vision of human life. Since that vision is not widely shared, it is difficult to see how it can be made the basis of public policy, especially in a democratic society. Globalisation further complicates the situation, for no country's economy can be planned in isolation as Gandhi assumes. The kind of trusteeship and the rate of taxation that he has in mind could lead to flight of capital or discourage industries. The ceiling on remuneration, when too low, could discourage or drive away talent. The kind of power that Gandhi is reluctantly prepared to give to the state presupposes that the latter is committed to collective well-being. This is not true of any state we know, and certainly not of contemporary India.

All this does not mean that Gandhi's vision of egalitarian society has no value or future, for its central insights are sound; rather it means that the vision needs to be made less extreme and more realistic and that we need to think of other kinds of policies than those he proposed. This is an intellectual challenge for Gandhians, who have a vital contribution to make to our current debate on the direction in which we need to go. In the light of their record so far, one could be forgiven for being pessimistic.[10]

Empowerment of People

For Gandhi, Swaraj was ultimately about power. It implied that society was in complete charge of its destiny and that every individual within it had both the confidence that he counted for something and the capacity to initiate and effect changes. For Gandhi every individual was a source of power. Power lay in the human will, which was within the reach of all. No one could compel others to do anything against their will. At best he might kill or torture them but he would not get them to do his bidding if they remained determined. The most important thing therefore was to ensure that individuals had a strong sense of dignity and self-respect, such that they would not allow themselves to be dictated to or manipulated by others. Power was not given by others; it was up to each individual to take and assert it.

Gandhi's lifelong struggles against injustices in South Africa and India convinced him that no system of oppression could come into being, let alone last, without the cooperation of its victims. When the Natal government passed discriminatory laws against Asians, they either acquiesced in them or resorted to devious ways of circumventing them. When Gandhi urged them to protest, they stayed quiet. Not surprisingly the government became bolder and passed even more discriminatory laws, including the Asian Licensing Act which made it difficult for Asians to obtain trading licenses. Once again, they did nothing and went about bribing the officials to get their way.

Gandhi analysed the British rule in India along similar lines. The British did not take India; Indians gave it to them through inaction and mutual rivalry. And the British consolidated their rule because Indians cooperated with it, supplied the necessary manpower including soldiers who used their weapons against their own countrymen and swallowed the self-justifying ideology of their rulers. As Gandhi often remarked, those who behaved like worms invited others to trample upon them, and it was the coward who created the bully. The victims of injustice were complicit in their oppression and never wholly innocent.

For Gandhi power was a highly complex relationship. Both the perpetrators and the victims of injustice believed that all power lay with the former. While this gave its perpetrators self-confidence and the courage to act decisively, it demoralised its victims and reduced them to supplicants begging for concessions. Each concession intensified their collaboration in their exploitation and reinforced their masters' power and prestige. Since victims of injustice believed themselves to be powerless, they fell into the habit of looking after themselves in devious ways or at the expense of each other and lacked the courage and the capacity to organise themselves. Their inability to act reinforced the existing system and perpetuated the climate of fear. The belief that the oppressor had all the power was, of course, an illusion. However, in so far as it was taken to be true by both the parties and formed the basis of their expectations and mutual responses, it became self-fulfilling.

It was, therefore, of utmost importance to demystify the system and expose the illusion. This could not be done by intellectual arguments alone, for the hold of illusion was too strong for that, especially when it was reinforced by habits built up over a lifetime and had its psychological attractions. In Gandhi's view, the answer lay in someone taking the lead in organising people, mounting campaigns and showing by example where power really lay. This was the purpose of his Satyagrahas, begun in South Africa in 1906 and subsequently continued in constantly revised forms in India. Each of them carefully selected a widely felt injustice, made demands that could be met, mobilised a particular constituency and was conducted in a manner that involved minimum reprisal. As it succeeded in achieving at least some of its objectives, it built up people's self-confidence, courage and capacity for organised action, gave them an insight into the nature of the prevailing system, weakened the morale and self-certainty of those in power and shifted the overall balance of power in favour of the people.

For Gandhi the power of dominant groups grew out of and was sustained by fear and was most effective when it generated a sense of powerlessness among its victims and paralysed them into inaction. This is precisely what the colonial rulers had done in India and they could not be removed until the fear was dispelled. Gandhi's greatness lay in setting himself the task of removing it, a point understood and expressed by no one as insightfully as Pandit Nehru, who deserves to be quoted in full.[11]

> And then Gandhi came. He was like a powerful current of fresh air
> that made us stretch ourselves and take deep breaths; like a
> beam of light that pierced the darkness and removed the scales
> from our eyes; like whirlwind that upset many things, but most
> of all the working of people's minds...The essence of his teaching
> was fearlessness and truth, and action allied to these, always
> keeping the welfare of the masses in view. The greatest gift for
> an individual or a nation, so we had been told in our ancient
> books, was *abhaya* (fearlessness), not merely bodily courage but
> the absence of fear from the mind. Janaka and Yajnavalkya had
> said, at the dawn of our history, that it was the function of the
> leaders of a people to make them fearless. But the dominant

impulse of India under British rule was that of fear, pervasive, oppressing, strangling fear; fear of the army, the police, the widespread secret service; fear of the political class; fear of laws meant to suppress and of prison; fear of the landlord's agent; fear of moneylender; fear of unemployment and starvation which were always on the threshold. It was against this all-pervading fear that Gandhi's quiet and determined voice was raised: 'Be not afraid'. Was it so simple as that? Not quite. And yet fear builds its phantoms which are more fearsome than reality itself, and reality, when calmly analysed and its consequences willingly accepted, loses much of its terror.

So, suddenly, as it were, that black pall of fear was lifted from the people's shoulders, not wholly of course, but to an amazing degree...It was a psychological change, almost as if some expert in psycho-analytical methods had probed deep into the patient's past, found out the origins of his complexes, exposed them to his view, and thus rid him of that burden.

There was that psychological reaction also, a feeling of shame at our long submission to an alien rule that had degraded and humiliated us and a desire to submit no longer whatever the consequences might be.

In a democracy political power was located in people's elected representatives including the government. Gandhi thought this was right, for people had other things to do, could not take the day-to-day decisions themselves and sometimes lacked the necessary political talents. This imposed two basic obligations on ordinary citizens. First, they must ensure that their representatives were men and women of integrity and honour, had the capacity for judgment and cared for national interest. They must therefore take great care about who they elected and keep a vigilant eye on them.

Second, since their representatives spoke and acted in their name and thus implicated them in their decisions, people must satisfy themselves that they were prepared to own, be held responsible for, and live with the actions of their representatives. Gandhi argued that they must take an active interest in political life and educate themselves about economic and political affairs. Every government was tempted to misuse its power and the democratic government was in that respect no different from the autocratic. What distinguished the two was the fact that one did and the other did not succumb to the temptation. And this was so because unlike the autocratic, a democratic government knew that if it did, its citizens would refuse to co-operate with it. Notwithstanding all its institutional checks and balances, a democratic government could easily turn evil if its citizens became apathetic or vulnerable to corruption and manipulation.

The virtues and vices of a government were not inherent in it but derived from those of its people. As Gandhi put it: [12]

> Real swaraj 'will' come not by the acquisition of authority by a few but by the acquisition of the capacity by all to resist authority when it is abused....by educating the masses to a sense of their capacity to regulate and control authority.

Until such time as the Indian people acquired the spirit and ethos needed to sustain Swaraj, they needed to be guided.[13] Gandhi thought that the best, indeed, the only way to do so was to build up a nationwide organisation of committed men and women who would do valuable constructive work among the people, understand their problems, build up their political capacities and educate and organise them against such injustices as might be done to them. This work could not be done by a political party both because it had its own interests and agenda and because it would be a divisive force. Gandhi wrestled with the question during the last few years of the Independence struggle and came up with an interesting proposal just before he died.

Gandhi thought that in the course of the struggle for Independence, the Congress had acquired moral authority equal, even superior, to that of the state, and trained an 'army' of workers whose morale, calibre and commitment were far superior to those of the civil servants. It was therefore uniquely equipped to lead the people, regenerate society and provide an effective moral and political counterweight to the state. Accordingly he proposed that now that the Congress had served its political purpose of attaining Independence, it should dissolve and reconstitute itself as Lok Sevak Sangh, a national organisation for the service of people. Its members were to settle in villages and become "Samagra Gram Sevaks," all purpose or comprehensive workers dedicated to their revitalisation. They were to increase people's awareness of their rights, sensitise them to the wrongs done to them, mediate between them and the official agencies of the state, help them fight against local injustices and when necessary, launch Satyagrahas. In these and other ways they were to win over the confidence and trust of the people, build up their strength and set up a structure of moral authority paralleling the legal authority of the 'official' state.

Gandhi was wrong to suggest dissolution of the Congress. Independent India badly needed a well-organised political party to hold the country together and run the government. The Congress not only had great organisational strength but also enjoyed considerable moral and political legitimacy which was passed on to the nascent state. Gandhi's idea of Lok Sevak Sangh or some such organisation, however, has its value. The task of regenerating India is too large to be left to the bureaucratic agencies of the state alone and needs the support of a grassroots-based organisation. The Sangh or some such body generates an alternative source of power to that of the state and holds it in check in a way that the organisational wing of a governing political party cannot. It can provide an alternative channel to those interested in political life and ensure that the state does not become their sole goal and politically overcrowded. It can check corrupt local officials, ensure that public funds reach their intended targets, act as an independent source of advice to the government based on its local experiences and organise people against local injustices. In short, it has the potential to act as the organised conscience of the people and a vital bridge between society and the state.

India has a vibrant but fragmented civil society. It has countless NGOs, some of which do excellent work, but others are poorly organised and run and are either too close or too hostile to state and central governments to be effective. Few of them enjoy the moral authority to speak in the name of the Indian people, or have the capacity to organise mass campaigns or Satyagrahas against ill-conceived government policies and the corruption and misuse of political power that scar our political system. Perhaps the time has come to experiment with a suitably revised non-partisan national body along the lines of Gandhi's Lok Sevak Sangh.

Notes

1. Cited in Raghavan Iyer (ed.) (1988). *The Moral and Political Writings of Mahatma Gandhi*, Vol. 1, p.64. New York and Delhi: Oxford.

2. Gandhi's Autobiography 'badly' needs retranslation. The existing text was prepared in a hurry, and is seriously defective. I first pointed this out in an article in *Indian Express* and *Gandhimarg* in 1986. Although it generated some public discussion, nothing happened. Perhaps this conference could be an occasion to start such a project. Gandhi knew that the translations of his works were faulty, and was so unhappy that at one point he wanted personally to supervise some of them. See *Collected Works*, Vol.79, p.36 and his "Just Two Complaints" in *Harijan Sevak,* 7.9.1940.

3. This was said in August, 1947.

4. *Harijan*, 25.8.1940, 12.4.1942 and 16.3.1947.

5. *Harijan*, 25.8.1940; *Young India*, 26.11.1931; *Harijan*, 31.7.1937.

6. G.D. Birla (1968). *In the Shadow of the Mahatma*, p.101. Bombay: Vakils, Feffer and Simons.

7. G.D. Birla (1977). *Bapu: A Unique Association*, pp.361-378. Bombay: Bharatiya Vidya Bhavan.

8. Louis Fischer (1950). *The Life of Mahatma Gandhi*, p.421.

9. *Young India*, 16.4.1931 and 17.3.1931.

10. For a pioneering recent attempt, see B.N. Ghosh (2007). *Gandhian Political Economy*. London: Ashgate.

11. J.L. Nehru (1982), *The Discovery of India*, p.358 f.

12. Anand Hingorani (ed.) *My Picture of Free India*, p.87.

13. For further discussions, see Bhiku Parekh (1989). *Gandhi's Political Philosophy*. London: Macmillan and Bhiku Parekh (1997). *Gandhi*. Oxford: Oxford University Press, 1997.

My mission is to teach by example and precept under severe restraint the use of the matchless weapon of Satyagraha, which is a direct corollary of non-violence and truth.

— M.K. Gandhi

23

The Next Big Social Innovation: Democratising Commerce

C.K. PRAHALAD

IN celebrating 100th anniversary of Satyagraha, we are not only celebrating Gandhi's legacy and its impact on the social consciousness of India in particular, we are also celebrating his commitment to the eradication of pervasive poverty. I have chosen for my remarks a somewhat difficult topic to explore. I thought it would be useful to look at Gandhi and globalisation. How do we re-contextualise his message and his method through the prism of poverty alleviation?

Mahatma Gandhi was deeply concerned about poverty. He called poverty the worst form of violence. Gandhian economics as a result is based on his abiding concern for the poor and the methods to alleviate poverty. But as poverty persists not only in India and around the world, it is legitimate for us to continue to examine his prescriptions. Gandhi in his own way gave us an implicit permission for this re-examination. He said, and I quote: "I would like to say to the diligent readers of my writings and others who are interested in them, that I am not at all concerned with appearing to be consistent. In my search after truth, I have discarded many ideas and learnt many new things." That was his greatness. He understood that his search was a continuous work in process and we have to start with respecting him for his extraordinary insight that the search for truth, search for poverty alleviation and search for progress of humankind is always a work in process. We can be sure that given the changes during the last 60 years, Gandhi would have done a lot of this re-examination himself. So, I want to start with the context of his message and the method.

In the context of British India it is important to understand that the socio-political context in which his prescriptions were born, India was a colony, Britain was a global power, India lived in its villages and often in very poor conditions. The poor were often illiterate, lacked specific skills and were mostly engaged in agriculture and agriculture-related activities. The landowners exploited them, industry was seen as using capital, equipment and machinery to take away jobs and further deprive the poor of employment and the source of livelihood. Gandhi's answer to this predicament of the poor, squeezed by the colonisers, the rich landowners and the industrialists, was to develop a set of prescriptions that allowed the poor to find a solution out of their misery. He came out with, I believe, one of the most radical ideas in human history. He believed that the poor ought to take charge and end their own poverty. That was the radical idea then and still is and that is what I want to talk about. How do we get the poor to solve their own problems rather than get someone else to solve the problem for them?

Gandhi's prescription for eradicating poverty starts with very simple and easily understood principles. I am just going to itemise some of them because in thinking about recontextualising, we have to start with not only the context in which these ideas were born but what the key ideas were. The first and the most important idea is: every individual has a right to a decent living. The focus must be on the mass of rural poor. The rural poor suffer from seasonal unemployment, low income levels and low consumption levels. Therefore, we must focus on village level production and consumption simultaneously to improve income and consumption. Low level of skills in rural India was a reality. Full employment is needed to alleviate poverty. Therefore, the *Khadi* movement or the *Khadi* economy was seen as the solution. And I think, it was totally characteristically Gandhi. With characteristic cunning, Gandhi not only created the concept of "consume only what you can produce" but went after the commercial interests of the British on the Manchester mills. And that was typically Gandhi, that he could accomplish both simultaneously. Further, since capital is scarce, a low capital-intensive, full employment-oriented industry had to be created. His solution was the handicraft economy that he proposed, that we adopt.

Next, the village must become self-sufficient in terms of both production and consumption. This is possible if the needs are kept in check. Gandhi was, therefore, a big advocate of restraints on consumption. We should consciously avoid machinery and capital-intensive businesses as they make very few rich and deprive the many poor of jobs. The key assumption here is that capital and labour could be in conflict. In his mind they were in conflict. Finally, this call for a highly decentralised economy centred in villages and he was very clear that India must develop her own solutions. Aping the West was not a way to get going and to get solutions that are consistent with India's problems and India's civilisation. He did not divorce, as others have said, his economics from his social, cultural and spiritual beliefs. Economics for him was an internal part of the total system of decent living and a concept of civilisation, not apart from it. So, I would say that Gandhi was oriented towards a decentralised market economy, primarily village-based but with no restrictions on trading. He was a great believer in entrepreneurship as an antidote to poverty. He believed in a self-regulating social system where equity and equality were paramount and the owners of wealth saw themselves as trustees. And this comes from his native Gujarat where *Nagarseths* and *Mahajans* had exactly the same idea that trusteeship is the privilege of the wealthy. He would have abhorred, and I state, he would have abhorred a highly regulated, centralised and a controlled economy. That was not his cup of tea.

I want to now take a few minutes to say, can we separate the message from the method? If we do not separate the message from the method, we cannot recontextualise Gandhi for the 21st century. I would like to pose four questions. Was Gandhi objecting to the use of machinery and capital or was his focus the provision of jobs to the poor? He believed that the use of machinery will reduce the need for large numbers of unskilled workers. Surprisingly, he approved of the Singer sewing machine. He thought that was okay because it reduced the drudgery of women. So, he was not consistent but he did not say he was going to be consistent. Did he, in fact, anticipate the possibility of what today in India we call jobless growth that we have in manufacture? He understood you could have jobless growth. Did he object to capitalism or the greed he saw in the capitalists? This is also what Lord Bhikhu mentioned in his remarks. Was he concerned about constraining consumption or the access to an equal distribution of natural resources to all people? Is the current debate about sustainable development just a modern variant of this concern? Did he want a decentralised, self-regulating market place centred on communities or did he want to avoid the tyranny of centralised bureaucracies and the influence of the elite on the lives of the poor? So, we could look at what he said but I think we need to separate what he said and what might have been the motivation.

There is no way we can be certain of his motivation. But we can extract the message from the methods he had advocated because of what we know of him as a social philosopher. I believe that he was concerned about minimum quality of life and I want to come back to it again, access to livelihoods, local determination of economic as well as social and cultural norms, personal choice, sustainable development and responsible use of natural resources, and finally, inclusion of all citizens in the economic and political processes. He was for democratising not just politics but commerce as well. His prescription assumed at its very core that every individual can be both a micro-producer and a micro-consumer. Our challenge is how to deliver on the values of the socio-political context that is very different today in India from the turn of the last century. Getting fixated on his methods without aspiring to deliver on his message is to me at best an intellectual compound.

The socio-political context of India in the year 2007, and looking at the next 10-20 years, is quite different. There are multiple dimensions and I am not going to go through all of them, but let me at least take a few. The Indian population in 1930 was about 280 million and a density of 90 people per sq. km. Today, the population is 1.1 billion—a four-fold increase. The density of population is similarly daunting. Looking forward, we may have 1.4 billion people in the year 2030. While the population and density have changed, India still lives in its villages. Close to 72 per cent of India is still in its villages in spite of the rapid increases in urbanisation. India has a very poor, a very young population. It is currently fashionable to call it a demographic dividend. A young population is a dividend only if they can all be consumers and producers. If a significant number of them are unemployed or unemployable, we will have a magnitude of poverty, both rural and urban, that Gandhi could never have imagined. Actually, today in India, there are more poor people than the entire population of India in 1930. That is a reality that we have to confront. The evils that Gandhi tried to eliminate—exploitation, needless deaths, lack of social mobility, illiteracy, suffering and abuses of power by the elite—continue to exist. In an interesting way the problems that Gandhi was addressing, have not changed in character. They have just assumed significantly larger proportions. There is a significant resource crisis in India. Water, energy, raw materials are all scarce. Water shortages are endemic. Simultaneously pollution, environmental degradation and deforestation have emerged as major issues.

For those of you, who know me in India, you will never see me being pessimistic. I had to say the negatives first. Now I can tell you the positives in India because there are lots of positives. India's circumstances have changed. India has emerged as a new and invigorated nation. Economic growth, confidence and prosperity in the cities are visible. India already is one of the largest economies in the world and one part of India is emerging as a modern, technologically savvy, globally competitive group. There is widespread use of technology in India even among the poor. For example, cell-phones have increasingly reduced the information asymmetry between the subsistence farmer, the middleman and the large firm. The expectation is that India will have a subscriber base of between 400 to 500 million cell-phone users by 2010. This change is the dynamic of the relationship between the poor and the rich, the rural and the urban. India has become an enduring democracy. Almost all Indians who are less than 55 years old have not experienced any method other than the ballot-box as a way to change their leaders. Peaceful national and regional elections have reinforced the belief in the electoral process. Yes, the poor have a voice. Even if it is episodic, they have a voice. India is lucky to have a very large and vibrant civil society which provides the social infrastructure focused on creative solutions to local and regional problems. Civil society has provided the much needed checks and balances to the behaviour of both the bureaucracy and industry. This contention often seen as unproductive between civil society, the Government and the large firm is a significant safeguard that was missing in the India of 1920s and 1930s. As always, India continues to be a country of contradictions. This paradox provides us a unique opportunity to keep the principal message of Gandhi and reformulate the methods that are consistent with the new context in India. World class and world scale capabilities with abject poverty and deprivation seem to coexist. Let us start with at least the few principles that I believe we are to keep and venerate.

The first is the dignity of the individual and the guarantee of a decent quality of life as the starting point. This we must hold valid. So is a decentralised, open, market-based, entrepreneurially-driven economy. Gandhi was not one for central planning and centralised regulation. India's own experience is, centralised planning has not delivered a decent living to the poor. After 60 years, we have more poor today than the entire population in 1930. The third critical principle we must continue to cherish is the respect for the use of resources and living in harmony with nature. We need to recognise, however, that a decent quality of life is a moving target. What will be considered reasonable today by a 50-year old even in a remote village in India would have been unthinkable in the 1930s. The skill levels needed to participate in most activities, be it agriculture or textiles, in connectivity or health, are considerably higher and different. We cannot assume an economy based on low, or no specialised skills. *Khadi* movement mobilised the country because it did not need a lot of capital or skills. Similarly, village level self-sufficiency was based on the need for improving the capacity to conceive and produce and improve livelihoods. But self-sufficiency in consumption and livelihood today for individuals and communities can be guaranteed by creating inter-dependencies across the economic units—regional, national and global.

Globalisation may create a new form of self-sufficiency in the communities to trade exchange of products and services and skills. The current view of a decent living, say, treating a cardiac patient in a village, cannot be based on self-sufficiency in that village but on access to high technology solutions such as tele-medicine. These services can be made available only through a system of inter-dependency. Therefore, we have to change our methods. I believe that the goal of democratising commerce is possible.

My own work over the last decade has demonstrated to me that it is possible to be true to Gandhi's message by changing his methods. Simply stated, the organising theme that can lead to the synthesis of Gandhi's message with a current context to Indian social transformation is to focus on democratising commerce. We must imagine India which combines in equal measure economic development and eradication of poverty, ecological stewardship and social justice. We must harness the forces of globalisation to create this outcome. We cannot extrapolate our past; we have to imagine this future I talk of. If we cannot imagine it, we cannot create it. Democratisation of commerce is built on a very simple premise. Every human being must have access to the benefits of globalisation, both as a consumer and as a producer. This is very consistent with Gandhi's philosophy. This is far from reality today. The bottom of the economic pyramid has been totally ignored and it is not in the purview of the organised sector. But considering an alternative to this neglect, we need to build a commerce focused on the majority. I started my work with a simple statement. If we stop thinking of the poor as victims or as a burden and start recognising them as resilient and creative entrepreneurs and value conscious consumers, a whole new world of opportunity will open up. The consumption side of democratising commerce is becoming obvious, whether it is ubiquitous cell-phones or two-wheelers or a TV set. That is not what I am going to focus on.

The second dimension of democratising commerce, to develop access to markets for goods and services that the poor can produce to improve their livelihood, is less well understood. How do we mobilise micro-producers? I want to take an experiment that is extraordinarily successful, from Gujarat from where Gandhi hailed. The Gujarat Cooperative Milk Marketing Federation, popularly known as Amul, is a case in point. Amul for over 50 years has been organising the poor subsistence farmers, mostly women, into a milk cooperative. The women still tend to their two or three buffaloes everyday. They bring their production to the village collection centres, both morning and evening. The milk is collected, weighted and paid for everyday. Milk is then transported to centralised modern processing centres, using refrigerated vans. Amul is a cooperative, has a membership of 2.2 million farmers, spread over 10,000 villages and 3,000 collection centres. They process about 6.4 to 7 million kilograms of milk per day. This is the largest milk processing facility in the world built on the backs of ordinary farmers, one-farmer-two-buffaloes at a time. The sales are currently pretty close to US $900 million. There is an emerging export market for their products. I can buy the products in Europe. Amul has, by effectively organising subsistence farmers, created a national powerhouse and competition for global companies, like Nestle and Unilever. The lessons from Amul and ITC e-choupal, a system that was started for accessing and aggregating soybeans from subsistence farmers are the same. About two million farmers are covered by the system. The logistics chain that they have created has created a system of inter-dependencies that creates both livelihood and consumption capacity at the village level.

So, the four big differences in the methods I envisaged for implementing Gandhi's message in the 21st century are the following:

- Re-define village self-sufficiency from a closed and independent system to an open inter-dependent system that openly trades with other economic entities outside the village for both improving consumption and livelihood patterns.

- Use advanced technology to eliminate asymmetry of information between the poor and the rich such that information-based arbitrage of opportunities, otherwise called exploitation, is brought down. Connectivity and access to the Internet become critical for reducing exploitation and so is the physical infrastructure.

- Allow the market to allocate resources in a transparent fashion such that resource-use is constrained. Eliminating energy subsidies, pricing water appropriately, pricing polluters are all part of promoting constraint consumption, one of Gandhiji's main platforms.

- Finally, provide checks and balances by encouraging civil society and the private sector to partner with each other to serve the common goal of improving the lives of the poor. This conversion can lead to a new form of governance of large corporations and NGOs and create a new social compact.

Like Gandhi, we have to start with principles, to pick the methods that are contextually relevant for India today. These principles are not hard to combine. Gandhi would have approved our focus on the inclusion of all in the economic, social, cultural and political life of the nation. Democratising commerce will accelerate the social and cultural integration and provide the multiplier needed to improve the political process.

Meritocracy and individual rights and not group rights. A focus on the rights of a group by definition reduces the importance and centrality of the individual in developing the new methods that re-contextualise Gandhi. Skill building at all levels is the key to alleviating poverty, and I want to say that India has trade to march into group rights rather than the rights of individuals. Gandhi would not approve of this because individual rights are important for dignity and meritocracy is one way of providing dignity. A focus on property rights such that those who were caught are able to keep the fruits of the labour. It is then up to them to use their labour wealth as steward and not as units. Wealth must be created first before trusteeship can happen.

Finally, individuals and communities are able to construct their own future and that there is no elitist imposition of a system on others. Choices are made in an open and transparent way. This is not the place to detail the process by which these principles can be operationalised. My task is to separate the core message of Gandhi that is more relevant today than 100 years ago, from his methods which need modification. I believe that there is enough evidence that these methods can work and a recontextualised approach is feasible. I also believe that the opportunities are immense. India has the opportunity to take the social and economic philosophy of Gandhi and use it as a platform for the next big social innovation, democratising commerce. The potential that is India was best captured by Jawaharlal Nehru almost 60 years ago, and I quote: "The service of India means the service of millions who suffer. It means ending poverty and ignorance and disease and inequality of opportunity. The ambition of the greatest man of our time has been to wipe every tear from every eye. Those dreams are for India, they are also for the world, for all nations, and people are too closely knit today for anyone of them to imagine that it can live apart. Peace has been said to be indivisible, so is freedom, so is prosperity now, and so is disaster in this one world that can no longer be split into isolated fragments." That was said 60 years ago and that is still true.

Indira Gandhi at eighteen with
Mahatma Gandhi, Shantiniketan, 1935.

Face to face with women power (Quit India, 1942).

24

Poverty Alleviation through Empowerment

NAVINCHANDRA RAMGOOLAM

BY seeking enlightenment from the Mahatma's thoughts and actions to address the present-day problem of poverty and the imperative need for access to education and people's empowerment, we are not only weaving a link between the past, the present and the future but also among the diverse cultures and traditions. These issues affect billions of people across the world. I myself am from a country whose history over the last century bears the imprint of the great Mahatma. It is not generally known but on his way from South Africa to India, Gandhi made a stopover at Mauritius. It was a stopover that was short in duration but momentous in importance and consequence. May I also recall that many Indo-Mauritians helped Gandhiji in his first campaign of Satyagraha in South Africa. One of them, Thambi Naidu, earned Gandhiji's glowing tribute in his book entitled: "Satyagraha in South Africa". He talked about his bravery and devotion, he was jailed with Gandhiji in South Africa and he was to Gandhiji and I quote: "the bravest and the most resolute of all the Indians jailed with him", and singled him out as the "most illustrious tower of the Indian community of the South African Union to whom he was a national hero."

During his stopover in Mauritius, Gandhiji found an entrenched plantation plutocracy and indifferent colonial administration and the toiling masses, many of whom were from India, living in conditions not dissimilar from those on the sub-continent of South Africa. The aspirations for dignity and emancipation of the people had as yet found but halting and uncertain expression. Even in his early days, he realised the importance of education and organisation. As Lord Bhikhu said, the answer lay in organising people so that the oppressed do not continue to be oppressed and that it should be conducted through non-cooperation. This is the message that he gave to Mauritians, especially the Indian community, in 1901 when he came to Mauritius. Gandhi's stay in England had given him an exposure to the intellectual form of a liberal democracy. He grew up at a time when memories of the Indian Mutiny of 1857 created a sense of outrage against imperial rule, and the personal indignities he suffered in South Africa and those to which he saw his people subjected, ignited in him a burning passion for freedom which was to guide his action for the rest of his life. I had the privilege to unveil in February, 1998, at the behest of President Nelson Mandela, a commemorative plaque at Pietermaritzburg Railway Station, where in 1893 Gandhiji was evicted from a whites-only compartment although he had a first-class ticket. This was a moving reminder of the humiliation meted out to Gandhiji.

During his stay in Mauritius, he demonstrated his total commitment to communal harmony and gave to the Indian immigrants a living example of secularism by staying with Muslim friends. To express his love for mankind, he stated: "I am a servant of Mussalmans, Christians, Parsees and Jews as I am of Hindus". He addressed several gatherings and the recurring themes of his speeches were the need for education and the importance of united action. What continues to impress me is his ability to live by example rather than by precept, and to practise in his daily life what he preached. It was part of his creed that faith in the abstracts without concrete expression would not work. He thus gave a new direction and impetus to the struggle of the dis-enfranchised for recognition of their values, their culture and their own world of human beings.

Empowerment indeed refers to increasing the social, political, cultural and economic strength of individuals and groups. It often involves empowering and developing confidence in the empowered, in their abilities and ideas. Gandhi's involvement with Mauritius and his interest in the country led him to delegate, after he left, to Manilal Maganlal Doctor, a lawyer and an active leader in his own country, to pursue the work of mobilisation and organisation. For Gandhiji, the political liberation of a country was a significant milestone to bring about necessary change in the social climate. The mission was later assumed by the Father of the Nation, Sir Seewoosagur Ramgoolam, who during his student days in London was the President of the London Branch of the Indian National Congress and was deeply influenced by all the leaders including Mahatma Gandhi for the struggle for independence. The date, 12th of March 1968, chosen for our independence was not fortuitous. It was chosen by Sir Seewoosagur Ramgoolam in remembrance of Gandhiji's Salt March. The party which he led and which I now lead and serve, has always been inspired by the Gandhian philosophy of focusing on people—putting people first, access to education for all, democratisation of economy and equipping people to stay out of poverty.

Personally, I joined politics in pursuit of well-defined social aims and I subscribe fully to Gandhiji's idea, and I quote "Man becomes great exactly in the degree in which he works for the welfare of his fellow men." In the early days of struggle for independence Mauritius Labour Party made the decision that our struggle would be democratic; it would be constitutional and non-violent. By the time Labour Party was founded in 1936, Mahatma Gandhi had already proved the potency of *ahimsa* in the struggle against imperial power. The party created since then has been based on the social, political, cultural and economic emancipation of the people and concurrently it has translated into the provision of education, social services and the promotion of ancestral cultures of the immigrants. It was through this kind of concerted effort to spread education and literacy that franchise was extended from some 11,800 people in 1946 to over 71,000 in 1948. This gave the working class a sane policy, leading to the legislation for the improvement of their working conditions. Mahatma Gandhi saw very clearly, at the beginning, that the majority were not involved. Not only were they not organised but they had no education. Therefore, he stressed on the need to organise them and to involve them in politics. The achievement of universal adult suffrage mobilised the energies required for the next struggle that is for the political independence of our country.

The road which was to follow our independence runs parallel with that of India, with many points of conjunction between them. After independence, to foster greater social justice, the welfare State was consolidated and although the Mauritius Labour Party, since its creation, was and remains today a Fabian Gandhian but neither the Fabianism of the Party nor its Gandhism is cast in stone. It devolves to take account of changing realities while being true to the creed of mass empowerment. An important plank of the empowerment platform was cultural. At a time when non-European mores and cultures ceased to be disdained and devalued, it was essential to create an awareness of the cultural, philosophical and artistic richness of the Asian heritage.

I believe that further democratisation of the economy will be achieved not by re-distribution of wealth or by confiscation but by giving free rein to ambition, to the intelligence and energy of our people. Again, I want to quote from the Mahatma who explained: "My humble occupation was to show people how they can solve their own difficulties." Gandhiji's emphasis on empowerment of the common man remains as relevant to the Mauritian people as people anywhere in the world. Personally, I have come to believe that the whole strength of Gandhian philosophy is its holistic approach to solving practical problems.

Poverty, he said, is the worst source of violence. Today in this era of unprecedented growth, abundance, accelerated technological progress in a world several times richer, the high level of poverty in sub-Saharan Africa and South Asia is a matter of great concern for the whole of mankind and I think that the ruling class, wherever they are, have to feel committed to achieving the Millennium Development Goals. If poverty alleviation remains the main thrust of our policy, if we focus on empowering the communities on piloting their way out of poverty, if we improve our relationship with nature, I am sure, we will solve a lot of other problems. Here, it is worth underlining Gandhiji's emphasis on the welfare of human beings and not on systems and institutions. A number of principles can be harnessed to address the issue of poverty, namely, education of the masses, practice of self-reliance by individuals, communities, villages and nations, prevention of massive concentration of economic power in the hands of a few, respect for the environment and ending of exploitation, especially of women and children. Let Gandhi's joyful steps be for ever hallowed in history.

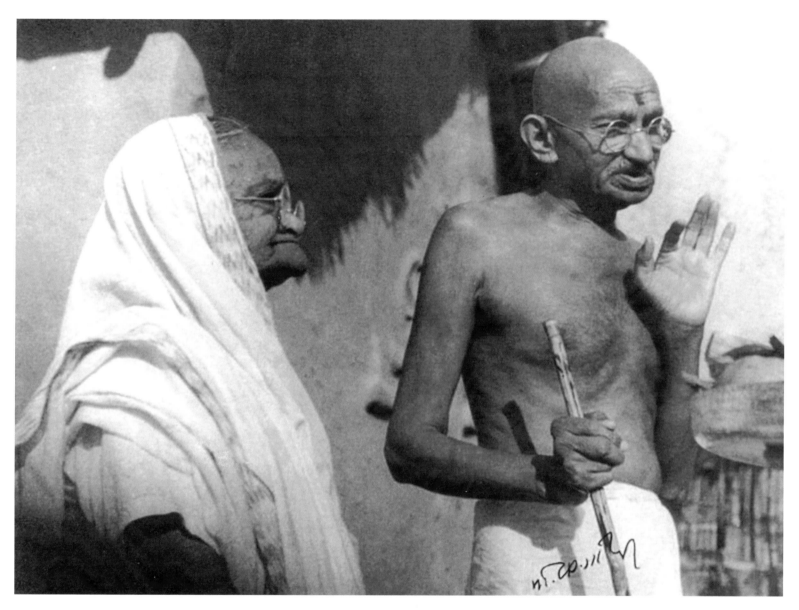

'Ba' and 'Bapu' (mother and father).
Mahatma Gandhi with wife Kasturba
at Sevagram Ashram, Gujarat, 1942.

To call woman the weaker sex is a libel; it is man's injustice to woman. If by
strength is meant brute strength, then, indeed, is woman less brute than man.
If by strength is meant moral power, then woman is immeasurably man's
superior. Has she not greater intuition, is she not more self-sacrificing, has she
not greater courage? Without her man could not be. If non-violence is the law
of our being, the future is with woman... Who can make a more effective
appeal to the heart than woman?

— M.K. Gandhi

A hug for Indira from Mahatma Gandhi
as Khan Abdul Ghaffar Khan looks on.

25

Equality of Empowerment

EDWARD SAMUEL MILIBAND

THIS year we mark the 60th year of Indian independence and I think there is much to celebrate now in this relationship of equals—links of family, links of travel, links of education, links of investment—both from India to the UK and the other way.

In this Conference, we are looking back to 1906 which was an important year for my party, the Labour Party. The Parliamentary Labour Party with 29 Labour MPs formed their first grouping in that year. And moreover, 1906 is the rooting of this Conference. In a way I think our task is to use that history, as the first three speakers have done, to look for that, and that is what I want to try and do.

We have already heard about Satyagraha as being about truth and non-violence but it is also about Gandhi's philosophy, about the ability of people to change their own lives and indeed the world around them, with the right ethics and the right movement. That is why the theme of empowerment is so important.

I want to talk about the relationship between the State, the individual and civil society in solving some of the problems that we face together. First of all, let me say something about the State. We know that the State taking its responsibility seriously is an essential part of meeting the challenges that we face today. In poverty reduction and development of a strong welfare State where they do not exist, and the maintenance of them where they do, seems to me to be essential for poverty reduction and poverty alleviation. We see this in Britain where one of our most treasured institutions is our National Health Service. This was referred to earlier by our obligation to tackle structural injustice at home and abroad, particularly for richer countries in the world, and it must be about meeting the 0.7 per cent of GNP target for development assistance. I am proud to say that the British Government has set a time-table for meeting that target.

Part of the welfare State, we are fortunate again that it has been referred to, is not just strong safety nets but also about education. We strongly admire the lead shown by India with the Primary Education For All programme—Sarva Shiksha Abhiyan—to which Britain has made a contribution. So, the State has to wake up to its responsibility. This is true and we find it in the United Kingdom also. If we take education as an example, education-for-all will not work unless we empower parents and empower people, making them partners in the process of learning. It will not work unless we address inequalities of power, inequalities of respect, inequalities of skills and resources which can shock parents out of learning. So, if we believe in equality of empowerment, we must show it not only in the services that are provided but the way they are provided. This came home to me yesterday on a visit I made in Delhi to a project which educates the street children and we were showed around by the guide who himself has been a street child. When I asked him what the biggest challenge for education of street children was, he said, it was persuading them that they are understood and not simply have their freedom taken away. In other words, it was about respect as a bridge to empowerment. I know, in Britain we used to think in terms of the delivery of public services in which we would see the individuals having the service delivered to them. I think we need to think much more about a collaborative model which understands the respect for and collaboration with the user, which is often the best way of ensuring the empowerment. Indeed Gandhi addressed this with a vision of a teacher, as a partner and as a companion on a learning journey.

We also know that the question of where political power lies, is often essential to whether problems can be solved or not, and this is true about the empowerment of the individual. I think what Gandhi taught us was that the extraordinary things could be achieved if the power is in the right hands. That is why India, I think, is to be congratulated on the integration of the *panchayati raj* system of local government in which there are now three million elected members and one million of them are women. I think this is the largest representation of women at elected level in the world. This kind of participation in democracy no doubt has impressed many colleagues here as well as in the United Kingdom. So, on the one hand, the State must take its responsibility seriously; it must not only do so in a partnership with the individual but also mobilise other partners. Here the social enterprise can play its role, which Muhammad Yunus has taught us. I know, in India experience with the new Right to Information Act, 2005 shows the valuable support that can be given to the individual by Third sector organisations to access their rights. In

Britain, increasingly we are seeing partnerships between the State and the Third sector organisations, sometimes with the State continuing to fund public services but the Third sector delivering them. And this is the recognition that no other State should abdicate its responsibilities for services and should continue to fund them where they can. But the recognition of the fact is that the State will find it harder to recharge and empower individuals, hard often than voluntary and the Third sector organisations. Of course, the Third sector plays a crucial role in making the State properly accountable to the people it is supposed to represent. And this was also a big theme of Gandhi. So, we believe that the State must play its role, the individuals must play theirs and civil society must play its part if we have to meet the challenges we face.

Let me end by recalling a great disciple of Gandhi—Martin Luther King Junior. He said that the philosophy of Satyagraha is eternal, it can be preached anywhere and can prevail everywhere. Dr. King often said, "The arch for the moral universe is long but it bends towards justice." This was not about historical determinism. It was part of an eternal optimism about human nature and about people's ability to solve problems and make the world a more just place.

A short time for me in India is most inspiring. Gandhi had great faith in his countrymen, he believed that the challenges they face can be overcome, and this optimism, I think, should give us great confidence about the future of this country.

A drop torn from the ocean perishes without doing any good. If it remains a part of the ocean, it shares the glory of carrying on its bosom a fleet of mighty ships.

— M.K. Gandhi

26

Peaceful Coexistence

GIANNI VERNETTI

DESPITE the radical changes that the world has witnessed since his times, Gandhi's philosophy and political ideology are still of crucial interest and relevance both in the Eastern and Western society, not only with regard to the universal value of non-violence but also for the eradication of poverty, education and people's empowerment. European culture first came to know and appreciate Mahatma Gandhi at a time when other continents were trying to overcome the destruction and the hatred spread by the First World War. To put it in the words of a great historian, "Europe was at that time turning to India in the quest for those eternal values that this country generated to elevate, counsel and save mankind." That quest became even more topical in the aftermath of the Second World War, not only for the opportunities it offered for the democratic reconstruction of the European post-war institution but also as a spiritual model for our affluent and fast-growing societies.

One of the most important lessons learnt by the great economic and technical improvement of the last decade is, in fact, that the global society we are living in, is suffering from lack of universal values which were at the core of Mahatma Gandhi's teachings. The unprecedented challenges of today's world lie in non-violence, in the peaceful coexistence of different cultures and religions, in the global respect and safeguard of environment and the new patterns of social and economic development which should be more and more based on simple and universal human values. Mahatma Gandhi used to say that the difference between what we do and what we could do would suffice to solve most of the world's problems. His tireless effort was based on ideas that would 'force' change by the example of 'good'. He says, "A leader is only a reflection of the peoples he leads." His renunciation of material wealth and his striving to satisfy human needs in the simplest manner, together with a communal life in which all labour was equally valuable, are today, as they were in his time, a lesson of paramount practical and spiritual importance. If you look at it from this particular angle, eradication of poverty, education and people's empowerment are strictly interconnected issues. Allow me in this regard to briefly touch upon the similarities between Mahatma's philosophy and that of Giuseppe Mazzini, the father of Italian independence and the Italian Republic. We have many other important Italian Gandhians and I think these are quite well-known. I would like to try to make this comparison to show their contribution.

Gandhi had the chance of reading Mazzini and he appreciated the solidarity Mazzini showed for India's freedom struggle. In 1908, in his book *Indian Self-Rule*, Gandhi quoted from Mazzini's writings that every man must learn how to rule himself. Then, with his non-violent philosophy, he added that Indians must not free their country by violent means since those who will rise to power by murder, will certainly not make the nation happy. What we need to do is to sacrifice ourselves. Not differently from Mazzini, Gandhi thought that the liberation and the development of the people start with its moral redemption, thus basing his political talk on the same ethos adopted by these great thinkers. We can see that spirituality has to be above materialism, altruism has to be above selfishness and national humanity above the individual.

Mazzini and Gandhi shared the awareness that the construction of society must be based on the education of its citizens and consequently on a vision where politics and moral values cannot be separated, thus coming to the conclusion that democracy is the only possible way of building a society based on justice and equality. These values stand today as the foundation of our democracy and remind us how India and Europe share so many common and basic values. "East is East and West is West, and they will never meet." This oldest and famous prophecy has fortunately proven wrong. The context, the intervention, the inter-dependency between our two ancient cultures, provides us with a very significant example in this regard. And in time of dangers and comparisons between different cultures, Europe, Italy and India share today, as in the past, a common effort to promote democracy. They also share a commitment to promote meeting and not clash of civilisations. Only mutual acknowledgement and respect of culture, religious differences, moderation, tolerance, respect of minorities and human rights can ensure peace and stability for the common benefit of all the countries. This is probably what Gandhi meant when he tried to explain his religious feelings and his inner quest: "I used to think that God is trust, now I would say that trust is God." I do not think much can be added to these words of supreme wisdom except to say that I am extremely thankful to all those who believe that the future of our planet lies in a peaceful, responsible and cooperative approach between all members of the international community. I feel that another lesson important at this moment and on which we have to work is that we have to communicate to the world that there also exists another September 11.

September 11 entered our homes with a horrifying act of terror, of people seeking clash of civilisations. And Gandhi's thinking really teaches us that it can be possible to expect another September 11.

My loin cloth is an organic
evolution in my life. It came
naturally, without effort, without
premeditation.

— M.K. Gandhi

A meeting of the Congress Working Committee held in the library of Anand Bhavan, Allahabad, 1931.
(From left: Acharya Kripalani, Sardar Patel, Mahatma Gandhi and Vijayalakshmi Pandit.

27

Keeping Non-violence Alive

HAWA AHMED YOUSSOUF

THE people of Djibouti are greatly attached to the values and the wise philosophy of Mahatma Gandhi—a heritage of values based on tolerance, solidarity and cultural diversity which are being recognised and acknowledged all over the world. In the current global context, the notions of peace and non-violence are facts which are dear to us as is the case in the many regions of the world. Our country is moving towards difficult times, as Africa for many decades has been riven with civil war and this brings in its wake a lot of sufferings. Unfortunately the spectre of violence is still looming large on our planet. But many people still cherish non-violence and peace and aspire for peace and concretising this ideal. My country shares this dynamic vision of peace and conflict resolution through peaceful means. Our aspirations feed on the heritage of Gandhi which is based on dialogue instead of confrontation.

Djibouti has always worked for contributing to pacify the war of the African region through several initiatives launched by the President of the Republic of Djibouti, H.E. Ismail Omar Guelleh. More than ever before, we are convinced that we shall not give in to fatalism but we shall focus on efforts and energies to consolidate and maintain good neighbourly relations and interactions among peoples. Without peace there can be no development because violence is always synonymous with polarisation of peoples. In the context of war it goes without saying that it is not possible for any government to federate the energies in an efficient enduring manner against poverty.

More than ever before, it is necessary to put all our bets on implementing social and educational policies which favour women and guarantee a better future for our future generations. This can be done through educational and awareness programmes that will enable us to inculcate in our people and youth this culture of peace and dialogue and give them the knowledge which is so necessary for understanding, acknowledging and respecting others. It is through knowledge that we will inculcate in our younger generation how to live and let live and bring out the best and keep non-violence alive.

28

Social and Economic Transparency

ASMA JAHANGIR

I come from Pakistan, a country where 33 per cent of the population lives below the poverty line, and there are probably more mosques than schools. But at the same time, we also very proudly have an atom bomb and spend enormous amounts on it. So, these are the contradictions we are faced with. It is amazing that we are sitting today in India, in this Plenary, making statements about having a nuclear-free world when Mahatma Gandhi spoke about it in August 1945 when he heard about the Hiroshima and Nagasaki bombing. He said, "I did not move a muscle when I first heard that the atom bomb had wiped out Hiroshima. On the contrary, I said to myself, 'Unless the world now adopts non-violence, it will spell certain suicide for mankind'."

One of the magnificent things that Mahatma Gandhi did was that he linked poverty to indignity of human beings. It was not simply deprivation; it was exploitation. It was not only that countries or fellow countrymen or human beings had to give charity to those who were poor but that the whole of mankind suffered because of the poverty. He went on to say that, "my notion of democracy is that under it the weakest should have the same opportunity as the strongest. That can never happen except through non-violence. No country in the world today shows any but patronising regard for the weak. The weakest you say go to the wall. Take your own case." He is talking about India. "Your land is owned by a few capitalist owners. These large landholdings cannot be sustained except by violence, veiled, if not open."

We see in many parts of the world today, that it is the accumulation of wealth that in fact is bringing in violence and is perpetuating poverty also. I know that poverty eradication or elimination is an extremely challenging job. But it is not an impossible job. Education, I believe, is only one of the tools and instruments of poverty eradication. But what we have experienced, particularly in the last two decades, is the emphasis on two types of education—poor education for the poor and quality education for the rich. This in turn is leading to creation of class-based society in our countries and also in the world at large. I think that it is not only education but it is the quality of education that is extremely essential for building not only a tolerant society but also empowering those who we are educating. It is obviously not just a privilege to be educated, we have to consider it as a right.

People's empowerment is another way through which poverty can be eliminated, gradually if not at once. I believe that when we talk about people's empowerment we have to link both civil and political rights to socioeconomic rights because if we are not going to link these together, we may try for one and may end up getting neither. We have, I think, since the middle of 1940s, talked about human rights. We have reached a point where we have to begin talking about implementation of these rights. There is awareness amongst people about their rights regardless of how disadvantaged they are. In fact, my experience has been that the more disadvantaged they are, the more aware they become about their rights. But they do not have the mechanisms to fight for these rights. Governments are not people-friendly and neither are the institutions that are being made. These institutions are being made at a very high level. They do not open their doors and windows to the people.

As a lawyer, I have had some very bitter experiences. I have also worked for the rights of bonded labour in my country. Early on, when I was much younger, I took these cases to the High Court and one of the judges told me: "Mrs. Jahangir, please can you take them out because it is very stifling. These people stink." When I turned around and said that the courts are for everyone, and if they are only for rich people, why do you not put a notice to the effect outside the courts. He thought that I was being very unreasonable by making such a statement and insisting that the bonded labour should be allowed to enter the court.

We talk about people's empowerment and social movements. We also need to address the question of discrimination and stigmatisation of people especially the poor. In the UN, we often time and again hear that the root cause of terrorism is poverty. In fact, this is stigmatisation of the poor. I think, they could be the victims of the terrorists' acts, they could be victims of terrorism recruitments but certainly not as authors of terrorism, people who have masterminded terrorist acts. There is this myth that is attached to poverty, and these are the myths that we need, as human rights activists and as political scientists, to address.

I have another problem with such myths. Wherever I have gone and talked about human rights violations in a country, Governments have always turned around and said: "But you see, we are faced with such a challenge because we have so much poverty, we have so much illiteracy." I think it is time for us now to bring home this message to Governments that poverty and illiteracy is not God-given, it is due to poor governance. Who is in-charge of governance? It is certainly not the poor people but the politicians and the Governments. We saw what happened when issues were identified under the UN Millennium Goals. This again became a blame game. On the one hand leaders of developed economies are not generous enough to the developing world. On the other, the leaders of developing world do not have proper governance. In both ways, we see that the leaders of developed worlds actually are quite happy and partner well with those in the developing world who are dictators and who do not have a system of transparent governance. And yet, they continue to ask that under the circumstances how they are expected to be generous. I think that it is something that we have to look at very carefully. We must insist and give examples, for instance, of Sierra Leone where you have unending resources, but it had poor governance—poor governance that was supported for a very long time by the international community—which led to unending conflict and extreme poverty. How is the international community using these early warning systems? These early warning systems are very important when we look at violence especially violence relating to poverty.

I think eventually in order to empower people, we have to insist on some new creative rights which are not just rhetoric rights but are dynamic rights. For example, under the right of transparent governance, it becomes the duty of the Government to not only provide its citizens all the information but also such institutions and mechanisms which will ensure this right to information.

Mahatma Gandhi and Netaji Subhash Chandra Bose.

Father of our Nation in this holy war for India's liberation, we ask
for your blessings and good wishes.

— Subhash Chandra Bose

Mahatma Gandhi with Rabindranath Tagore, Shantiniketan, 1940.

He stopped at the threshold of the huts of the thousands of dispossessed,
dressed like one of their own. He spoke to them in their own language.
Here was living truth at last, and not only quotation from books. For this
reason the Mahatma, the name given to him by the people of India, is
his real name.

— Rabindranath Tagore

Mahatma Gandhi in conversation with Jawaharlal Nehru at the All India Congress Committee meeting, Bombay, 1946.

When I am gone, Nehru will speak my language.

— M.K. Gandhi

29

Equality of Education

MARIANNE MIKKO

THE ideas of Mahatma Gandhi transcend time and place. They are as relevant today as they were at the time of their formulation. They are as true in the European Union as they are in India. For Gandhiji the key to freedom of India and its people was education in the broadest sense of the term. He recognised clearly that the Victorian education system imposed by the British was most of all an instrument of oppression.

Divide and conquer is a maxim followed by Empire builders throughout European history. A divided country is a weak country. In a country of such richness and diversity of cultures as India, education is most likely the common denominator. Therefore, it is very fitting and very gratifying that for the years 2007 to 2013, education remains one of the key areas for the EU-India Cooperation. Sarva Shiksha Abhiyan programme is fulfilling the goal Gandhiji set for India. Europe is proud to support it. India has been able to bring down the numbers of out of school children from 25 million to 12 million. This is probably the most impressive single step ever made in the world history of education. With the efforts of the Government of India and assistance of Europe, the ideas of Gandhi are coming to fruition.

For the universality of Mahatma's wisdom, we must thank among other factors his studies and work abroad. In this context, I have high hopes for the *Erasmus Mundus* India Window Project which saw its 137th beneficiary head to Europe in 2006. Gandhi learned from Europe and later Europe learned from him. I would like to discuss how the ideas of Gandhi worked in the educational system of Europe, particularly in Finland.

For a considerable number of years, Finland has been the world leader in secondary education along with Canada and Korea. The secret of Finland's success is the principle of equality which Gandhi regarded as the most fundamental while opposing the colonial rule. It is obvious that elitism has not done and cannot do much good. This is equally true for education also. Elite education can, by definition, be provided to the few only. But it is the majority that carries weight in a modern democratic society; enough weight to make its educational standards relevant. The central objective of the Finnish system is to overcome not only the obvious inequalities but the people who got it working have also undertaken to abolish the invisible injustice which emerges, to say naturally, based on family background and even the place of residence. A Finnish child from the remotest North is entitled to the same quality of education as a child from the best area in the Capital.

Throughout Mahatma's work, there is an underlying thought about education. This education is not just a thing in itself. Besides imparting skills, it imparts values. In building its education systems, society demonstrates what it considers important. More importantly, it invisibly but indelibly ingrains these values in its pupils as they progress through education. Finnish education is very inclusive in many senses. Pupils are not unnecessarily segregated according to their levels of talent; neither are there separate classes for most kinds of physically handicapped learners. Most importantly, learners are not divided along the lines of their religious and ethnic backgrounds. This Nordic system has been working for long along the Gandhian lines.

Finland has been emphasising technical education for some decades now. As a result, the majority of us present here today probably have Nokia cell phones in our pockets. Thinking ahead, even before the goals of Sarva Shiksha Abhiyan are achieved, new goals must be set. In most of Europe, only primary education is compulsory. But most countries regard secondary education as a norm. I am sure India will also set this goal for itself. India should set itself a goal of letting the local talent to flourish so that they can rival any talent in the world. There are only five million Finns but what a power: Nokia, connecting people. India with its billion people should be able to repeat that or even surpass that achievement. Gandhi has shown the way—proper free education for everyone.

Finally, I would like to emphasise that Mahatma Gandhi clearly saw that true equality between men and women is an integral path of freedom and prosperity of India. I am sure, you will all agree that everything must be done to ensure that India does not waste one-half of its great potential—women, more than half of them at the moment cannot read and write.

30
World Voices

Sergey Y. Glazyev
Member of the State Duma, Russia

After the disintegration of the socialist system, during the past 10-15 years, the world is passing through the process of globalisation which is based on liberal principles. This is leading to the erosion of national and state institutions including their mechanism of social partnerships, cooperation and social guarantees. States today have to compete with each other to invite international capital. It is done by refusing primary civic amenities to the people. The question here is, either the global capital will divide the world into different groups and create a big difference between the rich and the poor or we will be able to create a global mechanism for harmonising the entire world and creating national and social partnerships, increased respect and equal partnership among the nations.

Harmonisation can be achieved only through crucial fundamental values based on the principles and philosophy of Mahatma Gandhi—principle of non-discrimination, equality between people and love of human beings for each other. The realisation of these principles of Mahatma Gandhi might check the adverse effects of market forces and create positive opportunities for nations to realise their potential and achieve social welfare of their people. Many countries have reduced the funds allocated for the social welfare of their people at a time when need has arisen for larger allocation of funds for social welfare programmes. Differentiation among the income levels of the peoples of different countries is growing. To stop this we must create harmonious international systems and relations between capital and social interests.

We must also destroy the inequality based on monopoly; the growing disparity between the rich and the poor and monopoly by a number of countries in the international order—first of all being the monopoly of the United States of America and a number of developed countries having high technical potential. We must create a just system of trade in the world which will create conditions of harmony among the peoples.

Our financial systems without proper control are passing through a crisis. The American dollar is the primary currency and we should change over to a more just and transparent system which could exclude the monopoly forces from taking advantage, thus creating an international mechanism which ensures social equality and justice and welfare for all the citizens of the world. We must seek a different model of globalisation, a model where the collective vision of the people will ensure rights of each and every citizen. We should ensure synthesis between the philosophy and the policies of the political parties which should be directed towards the enhancement of welfare activities of the people. We should create conditions for healthy competition between developing countries with the use of modern technologies. We should also create a system of balance between different governments. We should create international standards and ensure social guarantee in the field of education and health. If we could establish harmony and create a just international mechanism then the ideas of Mahatma Gandhi can be realised in life.

Conceita Xavier Sortane
Frelimo Secretary for Cadres and Training, Mozambique

Mahatma Gandhi's philosophy is without doubt a great contribution to the struggle against poverty in the contemporary world.

Relations between India and Mozambique date back to many centuries. India and Mozambique share a common historical process of struggling against foreign colonisation. Independent India, the precursor of the Non-Aligned Movement, has given multifaceted support to Mozambique's struggle for independence and, in recent years, has become an important and strategic partner for Mozambique in our struggle against poverty, hunger and disease.

In today's globalised world, there thus exist great affinities between Mozambique and India that justify the establishment of a new strategic partnership in the struggle against poverty and for the promotion of sustainable development based on the promotion of mutual benefits, thus enabling the perpetuation of Mahatma Gandhi's life and philosophy.

Chaturon Chaisaeng
Acting Leader of Thai Rak Thai Party, Thailand

Gandhian philosophy—peace, non-violence and empowerment—is very relevant for the world.

Poverty eradication is one of the most important themes for any political party and subsequent governing bodies. As we all know, poverty leads to other major problems that we have been facing—family tension, children's malnutrition, crimes and other social violence, to name a few. We must stay focused on the matter and keep finding better ways to deal with it.

In *The Story of My Experiments with Truth*, Mahatma Gandhi wrote: "I do not want my house to be walled in on all sides, and my windows to be closed. Instead, I want the cultures of all lands to be blown about my house as freely as possible. But I refuse to be blown off my feet by any." I cannot think of a better grasp of the educational benchmark for today and tomorrow than that of Gandhi's. This policy guideline is universal. We all must open our hearts and minds to the reality of the changing environment and maximise our education as a major tool. Everything surrounding us must be built and encouraged to play a larger role in people's learning activities. The repeated emphasis should be on education for all and all for education. Education in this very definition is to give people courage to face the reality. What leads to hatred, conflict, selfishness and destructiveness of any kind should not be construed as education.

Ken Nnamani
Senate President, Federal Republic of Nigeria

Gandhi had the greatest influence on world history as a political activist who never occupied any political office. Gandhi was a highly disciplined person who led an austere lifestyle. The world cannot easily forget the saint in Calico dress, Mahatma Gandhi, who moved a whole nation to confront injustice and fought violence, fury and rage.

Today, one of the dominant issues in global politics is the issue of international terrorism. We know that terrorism has its roots in the feelings of exclusion and excruciating poverty. Perhaps persons who feel helpless and without opportunity for peaceful dialogue or resolution of issues are most likely to resort to the use of terror. Some scholars of international politics and peace studies established a relationship between the poverty trap and the incidences of terrorism. Both the

World Bank and UNDP are intensifying their efforts to reduce poverty and thereby minimising the incidences of people resorting to terrorism. However, poverty is not an excuse or justification for terrorism. It affects peace and can incite violence. We know the poverty trap has something to do with the elements of violence. Heavily indebted countries, especially in Sub-Saharan Africa, are prone to conflicts and wars. One way of ensuring global peace on a sustainable basis is to rigorously fight the global poverty trap. The challenge before the world is to create more wealth across the regions of the world so that massive poverty is reduced.

The growth in global economy has not positively impacted on all regions of the world, especially the so-called Third World countries. The difference in wealth has created two worlds, the haves and the have-nots. This division has further increased the propensity, the violence and acts of terrorism. The growth of world economy on an equitable basis would be the solution to poverty-induced violence and terrorism. Global economic growth with equity will help reduce conflicts. All over the world, many conflicts arise from competition of access to natural resources. The solution to conflict and access to resources and access to power is more inclusion in power and resource sharing. In other words, democracy appears to be the key to resolution. The philosophy of non-violence provides the method to confront the inequities and the inequalities of the world without miseries and poverty that result from violence. The way of non-violence is the way of human rights and human dignity. Most people, I think, tend to believe that it is a spiritual force that respects the integrity of life. Non-violence implies respect for human life and dignity. Non-violence will minimise the incidences of conflicts and save the world from wars that destroy the opportunities for equitable wealth creation. Again, one can easily say that non-violence by both the rich and poor countries will destroy the foundations of global terrorism. Non-violence is not peculiar only to poor countries. Rich countries can equally put it to significant use. But the rich can practice violence on poor countries by unfair trade policies and nefarious economic activities.

It is very necessary to add that for this philosophy to be very effective and to be helpful in reducing the human tragedy of wars and conflicts, a lot of patience is required to allow that philosophy to take ground.

Kirti Menon
Educationalist, great granddaughter of Mahatma Gandhi, Trustee of Tolstoy Farm, South Africa
It is very important for us to pause and remember the Tolstoy Farm, the site where

Gandhi began the first school for the children of passive resisters who were jailed. In the midst of all our discussion on Gandhian principles, I think there has been a fairly broad agreement that we all stand together raising the issues of equality, justice, fairness, transformation and redress; and the admission that we have limited resources and ways to deal with these issues. One of the most important lessons that began at Tolstoy Farm was Bapuji's experiments with multi-lingualism; fostering a communal spirit; developing values and issues which we are still talking about today, and how to develop critical citizens. These ideas and values are still very important and though we have a shared consensus about these values and ideas, we need to revive, translate and apply them in the present context.

The linkage between economics, education and political struggle has always been exemplified in different periods in Gandhi's life and we can learn from these lessons.

Sunderlal Bahuguna
Gandhian activist, eco-activist and philosopher, India

I had the good fortune of receiving a pat from Gandhi on this day, 59 years ago, on 29th January, 1948. I still remember that pat because it gives me the strength to act according to his prayers. Otherwise, I would have been lost in the power politics. Gandhi used to chant prayers from Muralidhar's scriptures, but his disciple Mira Ben asked him, "Bapu, is there any prayer which comes from the heart?" To which he said: "Oh, the Emperor of humility who dwells in the tattered hut of a scavenger, give me strength to be one with the common people of India." This is what Gandhi wanted. He aspired to be one with the common people of India.

Someone asked Gandhi for his message. He said, "My life is my message." He was a practical man. Today we have such big volumes on preaching. But Gandhi believed in practice. He said, a bit of practice is more effective than so much of preaching. We have to practise what we preach.

Gandhiji believed that we can meet all our requirements from our surroundings and that all human beings have equal right to these resources. His *Charkha* was not simply just a spinning yarn. Through his *Charkha* Gandhi gave us the message of self-sufficiency—fulfilling our basic needs and requirements from our surroundings.

Though born in India, Gandhi did not limit himself to India alone. He used to think about the whole humankind—not only the human beings but all living beings. It is this message of Gandhi which I hope you all will take from India.

Sumitra Kulkarni
Former, Member of Parliament (India) and Granddaughter of Mahatma Gandhi

All my countrymen and countrywomen are the granddaughters and the grandsons of Mahatma Gandhi. I don't claim any special privilege for this.

Mahatma Gandhi's idea behind trusteeship was that after you have met your own requirement, you hand over the surplus for the benefit of others. We should enjoy our wealth in a way as if it belongs to everybody else. But he never wanted that donations should be provided to remove poverty. Instead he wanted that jobs should be created. We should create circumstances which release the latent energy in human beings. Nobody is poor. It is only that some get limited opportunity to work. But it is also not about giving them an opportunity to work, it is about giving them dignity. When we give dignity to the poorest, they learn to uphold themselves, they rise up to be an element of divine and a divine element can never be defeated by anybody.

We want non-violence, not because we preach it, but because we cannot enjoy our lives unless we are at peace. If we respond to violence with violence, death is inevitable. Truth is important but the means to achieve truth are equally important. Nothing can be achieved, no matter, what the objective is or how lofty it might be. It is of no consequence if the means do not equally match the objective. In India we say that if one plants a thorny bush, one should not expect the thorny bush to bear sweet fruits. Similarly by following means which are in complete disregard to the basic values or the general well-being of the people, the desired end result can never be achieved. Therefore, truth is as essential as non-violence. Whether non-violence precedes or truth does, I cannot say easily. It is a matter of debate for all of us.

If we can give respect and dignity to the people, then I am sure, poverty can be eradicated, education can be brought to the people and the planet can be saved.

Rául Valdés Vivó
Member of the Central Committee of the Communist Party of Cuba

What Albert Einstein said about Mahatma Gandhi: "Generations to come will scarce believe that such a one as this ever in flesh and blood walked upon the earth." This explains the homage that today all nations pay to the father of the new India. Maybe one of the most important things to observe is that for the first time in history, the conditions are ripe for the ideas of Gandhi to advance in what we call our America. The process of integration and multilateralism is advancing in our lands, following the ideas of Simón Bolivar, a great liberator of human souls, as Gandhi was.

At the same time, we should not have the political blindness that Gandhi considered to be suicidal. We have to realise that it is also the moment of maximum danger for survival itself of human kind. The natural resources are being exploited and the great majority of people are poorer than in Gandhi's time. Another danger looming large over humankind is the threat of various kinds of conflicts globally.

In South Africa, non-violent progression and mass resistance were highly important in challenging the apartheid policy and European domination, especially between 1950 and 1990. Thus, a decisive factor for dismantling of apartheid was the heroic unarmed struggle of the African National Congress and other patriots from the rest of Africa.

We Cubans are very much in favour of non-violence in order to advance the objective of the people of the Third World. We do not send, anymore, international combats, but only physicians and literacy campaigners who can be termed an integral part of a human capital and whose job would have been applauded by the heart of Gandhi.

Section IV   Dialogue among Peoples and Cultures

MEWA RAMGOBIN

ESSOP PAHAD

MUSHIRUL HASAN

MAHDI AGHA ALIKHANI

RAJIV VORA

ASFANDYAR WALI KHAN

JOÃO CRAVINHO

Section IV

Dialogue among Peoples and Cultures

This section corresponds to the Subject Session III of the international conference "Peace, Non-violence and Empowerment: Gandhian Philosophy in the 21st Century" held in New Delhi on January 29-30, 2007.

Chairperson: Essop Pahad (South Africa)
Session Secretary: Salman Khurshid (India)
Session Rapporteur: Manish Tiwari (India)
Paper Presenter: Mushirul Hasan (India)

Participants:
Asfandyar Wali Khan (Pakistan), Rajiv Vora (India), Mewa Ramgobin (South Africa), Mahdi Agha Alikhani (Iran), João Cravinho (Portugal), Michael Sata (Zambia), Pradip Giri (Nepal), Samy Gemayel (Lebanon), Hilde Rapp (United Kingdom), Nouzha Chekrouni (Morocco), Anwar Fazal (Malaysia), Kirunda Kivejinja (Uganda), Salman Khurshid (India)

31

Dialogue between Cultures
Understanding the Contributions of India and South Africa

ESSOP PAHAD

DIALOGUE in the political, historico-spatial and cultural sense between Africa and India long predates the arrival of Mahatma Gandhi on South African soil. The trend actually spans over 700 years. In fact, there is evidence of long distance trade between Africa and India dating back to the 4th century CE—Aksumite coins of King Ezana from the year 320 have been found in Southern India.

In the case of India and South Africa, the 'dialogue' between our countries was in a sense strengthened in the period of British colonialism. It is illustrative to note that under British rule Indians were sent to South Africa and the Caribbean as indentured labourers and today there live large numbers of Indians and descendants of Indians in the diaspora. So, for us the ties have deep historical roots and the dialogue of culture, experience, identity, similarity, contrast and mutual sharing of forms of resistance spans over a century.

This dialogue is constructive and sustained as it remains rooted in our common struggle against colonialism. In our respective countries we consciously eschewed mobilising the anti-colonial struggles on narrow ethnic or racial grounds. Rather, we embraced a more universal concept of unity in diversity and mobilised on the principles of non-sectarianism and non-racialism. We also understood the importance of mobilising the broadest coalition of forces against colonialism and oppression, cutting across class, race and ethnicity. And emerging out of the principles of Satyagraha, our respective struggles embraced a set of values that embodied respect for human rights, the promotion of social justice and non-discrimination and the realisation of a just, caring and compassionate society.

In this sense, both India and South Africa can claim a moral high ground and we can and should use our considerable influence to open dialogic spaces internationally where we can use our experiences to influence the common global good.

The dialogue between cultures can take place in a number of ways and in a variety of forms. But the most productive is when there is dialogue around the achievement of common ends and there is a healthy and robust debate about the means to ends. Equally important, the dialogue that is most productive is the one that is premised on mutual respect and tolerance and acceptance of differences. Such a dialogue allows for healthy disagreement, free of the pejorative dimensions of cultural relativism and ethnocentrism. In avoiding the traps of cultural relativism and ethnocentrism, we need to develop a language of perspicuous contrasts where critical reflection, learning from others and debating differences in a non-judgmental way are based on principled positions and on the attainment of the ends of equality, freedom, democracy and social justice.

But more than sharing the history against colonialism, racism and tyranny, we share a commitment to democracy, to respecting the rule of law and to respecting our international obligations. We also share a commitment to promoting global peace and security, social justice and waging a war on poverty, unemployment and underdevelopment.

Both our countries are characterised by ethno-racial, linguistic, religious, regional and economic diversity and herein lies a very important basis for a dialogue between our respective societies. We are committed to nourishing and promoting diversity. We cherish this pluralism for we see tolerance and respect for fundamental human rights, the dignity of all as the hallmark of our mature democracies. We promote equality of opportunity and gender equality. We seek to accommodate the needs of people with disabilities so that they can be equal contributors to the well-being of our respective societies. This we do because of our mutual commitment to creating a socially just world, a non-racist, non-sexist world in which the fruits of our prosperity are shared more equitably between the rich and the poor.

We are also committed to countering xenophobia and the religious, racial and ethnic profiling that is extant in many parts of the world. It is also our responsibility to deal constructively with the major global issues of the day, and two of these include the struggle against terrorism and peace in the Middle East. We in South Africa continue to pledge to the people of Palestine our full support and solidarity in these very difficult times. We must give them our support so that they can achieve their national liberation from the occupying forces. We must continue to support the people of Palestine in their struggle for independence, justice, peace and security.

Mahatma's first meeting with Lord and Lady Mountbatten, Delhi, March 31, 1947.

I am not anti-English; I am not anti-British; I am not anti-any Government; but I am anti-untruth, anti-humbug, and anti-injustice. So long as the Government spells injustice, it may regard me as its enemy, implacable enemy.

No one will accuse me of any anti-English tendency. Indeed, I pride myself on my discrimination. I have thankfully copied many things from them. Punctuality, reticence, public hygiene, independent thinking and exercise of judgment and several other things I owe to my association with them.

— M.K. Gandhi

32

Dialogue among Peoples and Cultures

MUSHIRUL HASAN

ON 13 September 1931, two days before Mahatma Gandhi arrived in England, the Columbia Broadcasting System arranged for him to deliver a radio address to the American people. Gandhi approached the microphone with curiosity and asked, "Do I have to speak into that thing?" He was already on the air and these were the first words his listeners on the other side of the Atlantic heard. Three minutes before his time was to be up, a note was passed to him saying that his voice would be cut off in New York in three minutes. Unruffled, he began to bring his impromptu speech to a conclusion. After the engineer signaled him to stop, he commented, "Well, that's over." These words, too, were carried across the Atlantic.

In an article published in the mid-1990s, Nelson Mandela talked of his bond with Gandhiji, "in our shared experiences, our defiance of unjust laws and the fact that violence threatens our aspirations for peace and reconciliation." What would have the Mahatma said or done on this occasion, the centenary celebration of Satyagraha? For one, he would have deplored the perpetrators of violence, as he so often did. Throughout his public life, he had explored both the sources of and alternative to the dominant forms of violence in modern society. This had led him to conclude that non-violence consisted in refraining from exercising the power to hit back and was a virtue of the brave. Those lacking in courage and bravery could be no more non-violent than a mouse in its relation to the cat. In 1940, when he was asked about democracy in the United States, he replied:

> My notion of democracy is that under it the weakest should have the same opportunity as the strongest. That can never happen except through non-violence. No country in the world today shows any but patronizing regard for the weak. The weakest, you say, go to the wall. Take your own case. Your land is owned by a few capitalist owners...These large holdings cannot be sustained

except by violence, veiled if not open....*Your wars will never ensure safety for democracy* (emphasis added).

Gandhiji's method of dealing with individual and collective violence varied from time to time. After violence broke out in Chauri Chaura (1922), he called off civil disobedience. In September 1947, he went on a fast unto death in Calcutta to make the people 'purge themselves of the communal violence.' In Noakhali, he put to test his *ahimsa* (non-violence) by providing the healing touch to the victims of Hindu-Muslim riots. On 13 January, he began his fast in this city and I quote, "to find peace in the midst of turmoil, light in the midst of darkness, hope in despair." The inner peace was shattered as soon as the fast ended. "From calm, I have entered storm", he told a friend after the Delhi fast.

The Calcutta fast offers a lesson not in a clash of civilisations but of value systems between those who espouse religious tolerance, compassion and reverence for life, and those who do not. It is a point that Mrs. Gandhi so eloquently made yesterday. Gandhiji saw the clash in terms of contrasting views of truth, insisting that his approach to human relationships "excludes the use of violence because man is not capable of knowing absolute truth and, therefore, not competent to punish." Throughout his public life, Gandhiji displayed the creativity to unsettle traditional dividing lines and dichotomies. He believed in the process of conflict management that involved debate, argument, disagreement, compromise and cooperation, all within a system that permits opposing points of view to coexist fairly without recourse to violence. And this is the essence of, if you like, India's parliamentary democracy. Of course, he believed in reconciliation, a concept that went beyond the victim-perpetrator model. In fact, his constructive programme was both a process and a goal that aimed at overarching, recentring and rebuilding transformation. It was designed to promote handspun *khadi*, Hindu-Muslim unity, removal of social abuses, a programme of rural education, decentralisation of production and distribution, schemes for health, sanitation and diet.

Today in this world, as Archbishop Desmond Tutu had pointed out some years ago, there is no handy roadmap for reconciliation. There is no shortcut or simple prescription for healing the wounds and divisions of a society in the aftermath of sustained violence. It is, however, an essential point to address. Examining the painful past, acknowledging it and understanding it, and above all transcending it together, is the best guarantor to creating trust and understanding between the people. This, I presume, is the purpose of this exercise.

The concern to further a dialogue between cultures and civilisations has already been met by a well-considered and enthusiastic welcome in India. We have backed the UNESCO initiative, and we are well aware of the message that took shape in New Delhi on 9-10 July 2003.

Following the end of the Cold War, a strange and somewhat unreasonable argument came to be advanced that the grand conflicts of the future would centre on issues established by civilisational factors and the identities associated with them. Little has been said that was convincing about why this should suddenly become the order of the day once the grander animosities of the Cold War had apparently receded. But we have become more sensitive in the world about our differences, and the unscrupulous actions of terrorists of different religions have accentuated such worries.

Is there anything that one can add, though, to what has been said concerning the dialogue in the past, and what practical steps can be taken to advance it? Certainly, one can restate one's enthusiasm. And India has already expressed strong views on how this dialogue could proceed. But perhaps I can also append a note to what has been said—an appeal of sorts, for acknowledgement of the foundations that we are working with, and a request that such foundations should not go unnoticed. That this should be said here, in New Delhi, I think, is important. For so much has India sacrificed to develop its own sense of the world and its own right to establish a dialogue with the globe on its own terms that it would be a major injustice to let this opportunity go without recognition of the significance of what this involved. My point, in fact, is this. With due acknowledgement of the differences of our time, the notion of the dialogue seems to me to echo the principles we associate with the spirit of our early nation-building. And as a student of history, I would like to briefly reflect on that.

In the years immediately after 1947, guided by Jawaharlal Nehru's vision of the new international order, the early cultural and foreign policies were formed with a specific set of ideas in mind—ideas which are the very foundations of any dialogue of civilisations. At Nehru's behest in 1952, some of you would recall, the Indian National Congress supported Satyagraha against racialism in South Africa. Again, in 1955, he made a plea for understanding South Africa. "Now", he had said, "how does one understand a people? You have to understand not only their minds, what is moving in their minds, but their hearts. What are their urges? What are the big forces that are driving them and in what direction are they being driven?"

Guided by such ideas, important institutions were founded in India and major assemblies and conferences were put together. As India decides how she should contribute to this process, those who take part in the venture must have a keen eye on this legacy. And as any such dialogue proceeds, the initiators should consider the resources we have already built up and devise ways and means to give them both a regional and an international dimension. And it is in this context that I regard it as a major global initiative.

The early statesmen of post-1947 India, together with likeminded public figures from Asia and Africa, emerged from colonial rule to establish a firm commitment to define and advance their own cultures within the framework of an imperial aegis. In India certainly, but also in other cases, it was clear that such definitions were to be framed and evolved with a sense of the global environment with which they were interconnected. For us, this meant close attention to Iran and Turkey's cultures, the rich and varied environment of South-East Asia, and due attention to China and Japan. It also meant a keen interest in the way these regions had interacted with nations further afield—especially in Africa and in Europe. Elsewhere in East and South-East Asia, this meant similar though varied activities.

Indian statesmen, together with many others, sought to send out a message that it was at the cultural as well as the political and economic level that India and other newly independent states sought to break with colonialism. Our priorities and the terms that described our nationhood and our identities would and must cease to be tinged by the colours that infused it as a consequence of imperial governance. We were determined to take stock of ourselves in a manner that such governance inhibited and we were determined to frame our own sense of the world and the future of our cultural environment.

As Nehru had made clear in his book *The Discovery of India*, for instance, India's civilisation was not limited by the boundaries of the sub-continent. It had evolved within the ambit of a broader compass. And South-East Asia, Central Asia and West Asia were crucial to that compass. We would inevitably have an eye to these areas—for our past as well as our destiny was inextricably connected with them.

In all of this, we could not compete with the enormous expertise on various subjects that the US or the countries of Western Europe had been able to evolve. After all, we did not have the powerful machinery of imperial control to establish the grand libraries and museums of London, Paris or Berlin. Nor did we have the wealth of America to copy and buy what we did not possess. We also had development problems of a major order on which our resources had to be spent. I consider the world and our fellow-civilisations to give sufficient importance to us to demand that we take an interest in them at a professional level, and so that we may develop that expertise. We were guided by passion and commitment nonetheless. And in some cases, we had a gut sense of the meaning of the world around us that all the wealth of the world could not easily replicate. Our contributions to the excavations in Cambodia were the consequence of the expertise we developed as a result of such interests.

The result of such a perspective was a regular interest in maintaining a lively exchange with the regions that had been crucial to India's civilisational experience; a concern with how they had developed and how we had remained connected or how we had diverged. The consequence in due course was that our early nation-building was deeply involved in an intercultural dialogue at a global level, as well as the sturdy development of our own self-awareness. I think this holds true for other nations of the Asia-Pacific region as well—though political circumstances have changed, as have the terms on which imperial authority came to be displaced.

In India, the consequence of this perspective was the construction of a number of major institutions. The Asian Studies Conference was an indication of our intentions. The formation of the Indian Council for World Affairs, and, later, the School of International Studies in Delhi, the School of Foreign Languages, as well as the evolution of a host of Area Studies Programmes were the mark of India's interest. Our major museums and universities developed exchange programmes with the broader world around us.

I do not deny that there is much that is new in the world around us. There is urgency about the dialogue with the people and with civilisations because the frictions that the spread of globalisation has thrown up are intense. There is also genuine fear among us that commercialisation and globalisation will rapidly lead to the disintegration of much that constitutes our cultures—that much in culture will be unable to keep up in the far-ranging hurly-burly of today. A genuine dialogue will, perhaps, enable us to preserve some sense of priority and scale in what takes place.

Significantly also, the end of the Cold War has opened up opportunities for interaction as never before in the 21st century. Borders have become weak, and the movement of peoples allows for real inter-penetration and mutual assessment of civilisations. Technological change has enhanced such opportunities and has quickly overcome limits placed by language and custom on global understanding.

Our own encounter with the dialogue between cultures and civilisations must take these matters into consideration. We must proceed, encouraged by the opportunities of today and driven by the worry of what may occur if we fail to take them. But as we do so, let me exhort you not to forget what we have already set in motion in another time—often prompted by nation-builders and system-builders who were visionaries in their own right. We have foundations upon which we should build. Should we choose to lose sight of them, we would be doing a grave injustice to them.

"We may not have it in our power," Thomas Paine had proclaimed in 1776, "to begin the world again." But we can provide an adequate language to not only comprehend the 21st century but to decide for ourselves the importance of living together, understanding each other, and interpreting each other's lifestyle and value systems.

Arnold Toynbee had summed up this message candidly in the following words:

> In order to save mankind we have to learn to live together in concord in spite of traditional differences of religion, civilization, nationality, class and race. In order to live together in concord successfully, we have to know each other's past, since human life, like the rest of the phenomenal universe, can be observed by human minds only as it presents itself to them on the move through time...For our now urgent common purpose of self-preservation, it will not be enough to explore our common underlying human nature. The psychologist's work needs to be supplemented by the archaeologist's, the anthropologist's and the sociologist's. We must learn to recognize, and as far as possible, to understand, the different cultural configurations in which our common human nature has expressed itself in the different religions, civilizations, and nationalities into which human culture has come to be articulated in the course of its history. We shall, however, have to do more than just understand each others' cultural heritages, and more even than appreciate them. We shall have to value them and love them as being parts

of mankind's common treasure and therefore being ours too, as truly as the heirlooms that we ourselves shall be contributing to the common stock.

Gandhiji, the Father of the Nation, once told a correspondent why he had stopped talking of aspiring to the age of 125: "I have lost the hope because of the terrible happenings in the world. I don't want to live in darkness", he had said. One hopes that today the war clouds will disperse and the sane voices of restraint and moderation will be heard across the globe. Maybe then, we, Indians, Afghans, Arabs, Pakistanis and Americans, can aspire to live for another 125 years! Only if we accept that people can be 'conscious creators of their own history' will we be able to instil hope and optimism in ourselves without which there can be no change. The fact is that we cannot give up. Remember the poem by Ben Okri:

> They are only the exhausted who think
> That they have arrived
> At the final destination
> The end of their road
> With all their dreams achieved
> And no new dream to hold.

Experience has taught me that silence is a part of the spiritual discipline of a votary of truth. Proneness to exaggerate, to suppress or modify the truth, wittingly or unwittingly, is a natural weakness of man, and silence is necessary in order to surmount it. A man of few words will rarely be thoughtless in his speech; he will measure every word.

— M.K. Gandhi

33

Overcoming the New Face of Violence

ASFANDYAR WALI KHAN

I come here from a land that has been steeped in violence since the late seventies, the land of the Pakhtuns, the land of the Afghans.

In every political decision, a lot depends on the timing of the decision and I feel that the decision to hold this conference is most appropriate. Looking at the stature of the people who have come to attend the gathering gives people like us a great hope.

My grandfather, Khan Abdul Ghaffar Khan, Badshah Khan, was a very, very close associate of Gandhiji, to the extent that he came to be known as the Frontier Gandhi. The borders that we are talking of crossing today—the borders of culture, the borders of religion—were crossed by Badshah Khan a long time back. In spite of the fact that today I am the third generation of Badshah Khan, I am still called a Hindu by certain people in Pakistan. Not that I regret it.

I thought we were the only people who were fighting against violence. I have to thank the Indian National Congress for giving us this opportunity to realise that there are millions out there who are fighting for non-violence. So the basic question is, can those millions be galvanised and channelised? I use the word channelise because today, 99 per cent of the violence that is taking place is state-sponsored violence.

Today dialogue has transcended the boundaries of peoples and cultures, it is more of dialogue among peoples, cultures and 'religions'. Because today if you look at the world, every person who is advocating violence says it is a clash of religions; it is a clash of Islam *versus* Christianity. Islam is a religion of love, understanding, tolerance. Only, certain bigoted Muslims will define Islam as nothing but Jehad.

With the end of the Second World War, the United Nations was formed giving people a hope that it would be able to solve the problems. But with the advent of the Cold War, the United Nations was not, and is not, in a position to play the role that it should play. For a big part of the world, the end of the Cold War signified the end of violence. But for us, Pakhtoons and Afghans, the end of the Cold War meant the beginning of a new phenomenon known as the Jehad where you had suicide bombers. The whole concept of violence has changed. Violence before was violence of one state against another, one army fighting another. The person who went to war knew that he could be killed but he had the weapons to defend himself. What is happening today is that the targets do not know that they are the targets. The people who die never even imagined that they would be targets of violence. The days when events in Mysore would not affect the people of Peshawar, or events in Calcutta will not have an effect on Kabul, are over. Today destabilisation and violence in one region affects the world as a whole. It was that destabilisation in Afghanistan and the Pakhtun belt of Pakistan that resulted in 9/11. So where does our responsibility lie?

Today, I am not a pessimist. Living in a state like Pakistan, being in the Opposition for 50-52 years of my life, we cannot afford to be pessimistic. One has to be an optimist to survive in a state like Pakistan and being in opposition for such a long period. But let me tell you, belonging to that area, this region is sitting on a powder keg. It can explode any time. Unimaginable amounts of arms and ammunition have come into that area and the terrain is such that it is very difficult to control these activities.

I will give you my own example. Along with our friends, the people here from India and Bangladesh know that in the border region between Afghanistan and Pakistan known as Bajore, a lot of violence was taking place and we, the disciples of Badshah Khan, decided to go to Bajore. When we reached the border with white flags, saying that we were going to Bajore for peace, the administrative forces first resorted to *lathi* charges. When we did not move back, they resorted to tear gas and when that also did not deter us, they resorted to firing. But we kept on going, we did not retaliate, because we have learnt from Badshah Khan and we have learnt from Gandhiji that if you retaliate, then the principle of non-violence that you preach is finished. You then don't have the moral authority to ask others to accept non-violence if you don't accept it yourself.

I remember one phrase that Badshah Khan always used to tell us, that violence breeds hatred, non-violence breeds love. And let me tell you that the Pakhtoon you see today is the picture of the Afghan that is given to you, it is the same Afghan, more than a hundred thousand of them, who at that time took an oath of non-violence. Their children still stand by that oath, "We stand by non-violence." Non-violence means not only that we will not pick our gun but that we will work towards dialogue. At the height of the Afghan crisis, we were the only people who were saying, "Let us go in for a dialogue, go in for a Loya Jirga." They went in for the Loya Jirga only after 2.3 million Afghans' blood had been spilled. Even today, I as President of the Awami National Party which is the successor of the Khudai Khidmatgar of Badshah Khan say that, we did our bit among Jirgas in Peshawar. People stand for peace; we have to force the states to stand for peace. I have just one last appeal to make: If in our hearts, we decide sincerely that there is to be no violence in the world and we get up together hand in hand, do any of you doubt the fact that violence will not end? But, let us now transform this from just an exhortation to action.

French writer and poet Romain Rolland played host to Mahatma Gandhi during his visit to Switzerland in December 1931. Rolland had earlier authored the book *Mahatma Gandhi* which discussed Gandhi's ideas at length. The two friends would spend hours together discussing important themes, including the worsening situation in Europe and the hope that lay in non-violence.

34

Gandhi's Dialogue on Civilisation

RAJIV VORA

AS Mahatma Gandhi gave a weapon of truth, Satyagraha, on 11th September 1906, he also, in the course of his struggle, entered into a dialogue with the extremists, the school of violence, and with the imperial rulers—the mediators of Western civilisation in India—about the cultural difference in the meaning of freedom, progress, governance, and civilisation. As he unfurled his epic war against the colonial rule, he wrote his manifesto or the root text, namely *Hind Swaraj* (Indian Home Rule) in 1909. I was pleasantly surprised when the Deputy Prime Minister of Italy referred to this seminal text of our times. This is the guide for those who want to transcend the limitations that modern rationalism, secular ideologies and irreligion in the name of religiosity put on us, and who want to pursue the path of truth, justice and freedom. Gandhi pointed out: "Swaraj is a sacred word meaning self-rule and self-restraint, and not freedom from all restraint which 'independence' often means."

Mahatma Gandhi conducted his dialogue mainly on three planes. At a political plane he dialogued with extremism and imperialism—so very much today's scenario. At a cultural plane, at the plane of our intellect, our reason, he conducted dialogue on the very nature of civilisation. He does not recognise modern civilisation as "civilisation" at all. He calls it Satanic. That is why it clashes with whoever is unlike it and does not conform with it. Gandhi defines civilisation as "that mode of conduct which points out to man the path of duty. Performance of duty and observance of morality are convertible terms. To observe morality is to attain mastery over our mind and our passions. So doing we know ourselves. The Gujarati equivalent for civilisation is 'good conduct'." At that time it was Western, now it is ours too! As the attributes of the goodness are universal, similarly the other attributes also are universal. At the spiritual plane he raised the dialogue on truth, sovereignty of all as all is pervaded by divinity, and true religiosity. All these planes for him were one and not separated. He taught us to value our own identity—each individual's sovereign identity—as well as the larger national and universal. These two must harmoniously reconcile because every individual has an inner quest to transcend one's self interest, self identity and unite with the entire humanity. That is the spiritual self of an individual and this is also equally universal. Modern civilisation is grappling with one very intrinsic problem—the inability to reconcile justice and freedom—the two governed by political and spiritual needs of human beings. In Swaraj he showed how these harmonise. When Western civilisation upholds freedom, it brutally violates justice; and when from its own womb socialism came up with promise of justice, it brutally violated human freedom.

Every human being, of whatever colour, creed, class or nationality, is naturally born with two most fundamental quests. One is the quest for freedom. We can see that most of human history is replete with wars for freedom. Another similar quest which is more powerfully explosive is the quest to be loved and to love someone, to be selfless, to make sacrifice. The quest for justice is only the other side of the same coin of the quest for love and sacrifice. These are the two quests and in modern times we do see that when some nations have tried to maximise freedom, they did it through employing human reason to its best ability. The West did this. The Western civilisation, the modern civilisation is one of the best examples probably in the human history of exhausting human reason in order to find the truth about the material world. Right in the beginning, perhaps during the ancient Greek times, they decided that they cannot find the truth about who is behind the creation but can at least look into the material truth of the creation. What the West has achieved since is a marvel. They have finally reached the ultimate indivisible constituent of matter. Human reason thus employed only looked at the material side of the world and not at the spiritual side. So the spiritual side, the other truth of human existence, was unknown to Western civilisation because the Western civilisation was born out of this quest of reason in the middle centuries when the liberation of intellect demanded that everything that could put shackles on human reason must be rejected. So they rejected God, divinity, they rejected sacredness; they rejected everything that could not be perceived by the human senses. All those things which could not be perceived by human senses were thus declared untruth and all those things which could be perceived only by human senses, which today we call the 'infrastructure of modern science' were the only truth in the terms of modern civilisation.

Mahatma Gandhi dialogued on the true spiritual culture of human beings. Spirituality to him does not have a separate compartment of its own. What is a human being? Human being by nature is non-violent. Non-violence is a human being's culture. There are different stimulants and therefore our other attributes are conflagrated and the attributes of non-violence are repressed. But in the most violent cultures, in the most violent person, if the right attributes are stimulated, you can grow non-violence in them. Mahatma Gandhi proved it and Badshah Khan is the greatest example. Pathans are known to be aggressive people, but what must be the great magic of that man who turned this most violent race into the best soldiers of non-violence. Similarly in Africa, this was proved, where manhood was attained only when one killed a lion. That Africa also showed us the great example of non-violence. I am therefore hopeful.

Our problem in India, with Hinduism and with Islam is that we have lost the track of reasoned faith. Godless reason and reasonless religion are two curses of modern times.

It would be very interesting to know that in 1942, somebody asked Mahatma Gandhi, "What are you talking about? Why don't you talk about socialism? Look at what is happening in the Soviet Union. It would be good if you look at the socialist experiment and talk about socialism rather than what you are talking about." This was in 1942. And he said, "'Let the Soviet example live at least 50 years. If it survives 50 years, then we must give a thought to it, then we will think about it." Now look at the fate. Almost to prove Mahatma Gandhi right, exactly after 50th year of this statement, the Soviet empire collapsed. So, how do we reconcile justice and freedom? This is what Mahatma Gandhi wrote. This is his dialogue on Swaraj: "Where truth is not only the truth of the material self but truth also of the spiritual self of an individual."

Mahatma Gandhi's dialogue acquires a very great significance in today's times because those who have mastered human reason were earlier driven by the quest of freedom. They put human reason and rationality to the service of seeking freedom. But after 9/11 things have changed radically. The West is now driven, not by the quest for freedom. It is driven by fear. It has become fearful out of its own deeds. The same excellence of human reason is no more in the service of refining the meaning of human freedom. It is now hinged to fear, it is now employed entirely in the service of fear Do we realise that this is the most deadly combination! Do we understand the meaning of this radical shift that the world has arrived at today? There can be no deadlier combination than the most excellent human reason being in the service of fear. And it has happened after 9/11. Where is a dialogue on human culture and civilisation that can match this challenge? This 'is' the time therefore for a serious global dialogue on the paradigm Swaraj, the culture of non-violence.

When somebody asked Mahatma Gandhi the reason why he was talking about God and spirituality, he said: "Look, reason is like King of England, guided and controlled solely by its council of ministers, the senses." Our human reason is not pure. It is impure because it is captive of our self-interest, of our desires, of our ego, our fears therefore. How to liberate human reason so that reason becomes purer and it does not become the weapon of exploitation, domination and of violence is the problem all peoples, cultures and nations have to face.

The force of love, the force of truth exists everywhere. Somewhere it manifests in certain higher levels, somewhere it manifests in certain lower levels, but it is never absent. Therefore, to paint anyone as just dark or to paint someone else as just the enlightened would be very wrong on the anvil of truth. Therefore, Gandhi's dialogue is on truth, the truth that combines the reason of the spiritual self and reason of the secular self.

I would certainly suggest to all to look at this very small booklet of Mahatma Gandhi, *Hind Swaraj*, which is the text of our times. Once you read it, you will certainly realise that you find many answers for your questions. It will also raise questions. And particularly to the people belonging to, let me say, non-Western traditions, for them this would appeal the most and within the West it will appeal the most to those who have become aware of the inner violence of modern civilisation.

35

Global Coexistence
Development Leading to Freedom and Peace

MEWA RAMGOBIN

SOUTH Africa and India have enjoyed civilisational links and synergies and I believe that integral to this is the life and work of Mahatma Gandhi. But what I am going to do, rather cursorily, is to present the perspective of the Phoenix Settlement Trust which was established by Gandhiji in South Africa.

Under the aegis of the Phoenix Settlement Trust and supported by the South African Government, we have just emerged from a year-long celebration of Satyagraha, which was born in my country. For us at Phoenix, Satyagraha is a proud heritage of the human race. And in this context, it is my respectful suggestion on behalf of the Phoenix Settlement that people all over the world, especially in India, must resist the temptation to Indianise Satyagraha.

For us, this celebration was not just an event. It was so designed to be a call of duty, to engender among us real, active and visible ways to realise a better life for all. The Trust deliberately chose to conduct the first leg of the celebrations, in pursuance of dialogue among our culturally diverse peoples, on dates of historical importance for the entire nation. To have launched the celebration on South Africa's Human Rights Day was a humble proclamation by us that human rights as enshrined in our secular constitution are the cornerstone in determining our policy options for governance. Peace and non-violence, we say, will remain superfluities as long as human rights are violated. On the other hand, human rights too will remain debilitated without economic rights for the poorest of the poor. Who better than the people of India can understand this. We are indeed happy to be identified with all and any initiative to renew and reinforce human efforts and commitment to Gandhiji's noble mission of building a world that is at peace with itself.

Thus on South Africa's Freedom Day and Labour Day, through the dialogue to celebrate Satyagraha in the context of the Gandhian Trinity and *Ubuntu*, we reflected unambiguously on the concept of freedom and peace. I will come back to the concept of *Ubuntu* and Trinity at the end. Was it and is it enough to invoke non-violence towards 'peace'? What of our liberation from poverty, hunger, disease and homelessness? Do we not seek liberation from Xenophobic tendencies, religious and ideological bigotries, and fundamentalism, no matter where they come from? Is peace possible without these aspects, which we at Phoenix call, "in our state of unfreedom."

In this context we need to challenge why the Millennium Development Goals are, for all intents and purposes, shelved. Why the World Trade Organization, a multilateral system, ostensibly fair and rules-based, continues to have preferential trade practices and why the International Monetary Fund and the World Bank lack adequate representation of the developing countries? And, lastly, why is the reform of the United Nations Security Council so vehemently resisted by those in whom the veto is reposed? This we asked at Phoenix in the context of our commitment that Satyagraha has to be celebrated in the spirit of the Gandhian Trinity, rooted in *Ubuntu*, directed towards the African renaissance for global coexistence.

On global issues, the leadership of IBSA reaffirmed their commitment to the promotion of peace, security and sustainable economic and social development. They reaffirmed their commitment to multilateralism and the pre-eminent role of the United Nations. These are excellent positions because they more than anything else recognise the need to develop global partnerships for development leading to freedom and peace.

It is against this background that I read President Thabo Mbeki's injunction: "I believe that for us to ensure that things do not fall apart, we must, in the first instance, never allow that the market should be the principal determinant of the nature of our society." He goes on to say: "We should firmly oppose the 'market fundamentalism' which no other than George Soros has denounced—I repeat the word 'denounced'—as the force that has led society to lose its anchor." He further goes on to say: "Instead, we must place at the centre of our daily activities the pursuit of the goals of social cohesion and human solidarity...We must therefore strive to integrate into the national consciousness the value system, contained in the world outlook, described as 'Ubuntu' " and so well reiterated in the concept of Gandhian Trinity.

How much of this injunction is within the grasp of our youth today, across the spectrum, I don't know. But there is no gainsaying the fact that it is absolutely essential for social cohesion and human solidarity, which is why Phoenix, amongst other reasons, conducted the third leg of the Satyagraha '100' Celebrations on Youth Day. This was celebrated by us to salute the youth who sacrificed their lives, their limbs and their freedom to live in South Africa, the youth who refused to acquiesce in apartheid. This for us was another form of Satyagraha. Those of us, who were in dialogue about the choices our youth have to make, were formidable representatives from all political parties and different religious formations. And in unison, they reflected on the ills they faced, the aspirations they had, the responsibilities they would have to shoulder and the kind of society they would have to create for themselves.

The concept of the Gandhian Trinity in the context of *Ubuntu*, they felt, should be included in the curriculum of schools. It was, and is, very special for us at Phoenix to have the reaffirmation by President Mbeki of our position that "Human life is about more than the economy, and therefore material considerations." He goes on to say: "That as a nation we must make a special effort to understand and act on this—that personal pursuit of personal gain, as the beginning and end of our life's purpose, is already beginning to corrode our social and national cohesion."

Whilst Phoenix pioneered the Satyagraha '100' Celebrations and continues to address the challenges confronting us, we in no way assume that we are anywhere near the ideal. But it will be less than honest if we denied our joy when President Mbeki again remarked at Phoenix some years ago that "Phoenix belongs to you, it belongs to me, it belongs to our children and it belongs to our children's children and all the children yet to come, cherish it and nourish it."

In this context, the resurrection of Phoenix from its destruction in 1985 by the forces of apartheid should, perhaps be a lesson in domination, alienation, introspection and liberation. And for the African Renaissance to have meaningful proportions, the question of women and their rightful place in society is vital. For Phoenix to hold a discourse on Women's Day to celebrate Satyagraha '100' was to face a challenging reality where our women are concerned. In the words of Stephen Lewis, the UN special envoy for AIDS in Africa, "What has happened to our sense of international values? How dare the leaders of the G-8 crow about progress on aid and debt while continuing to watch the economic, social, physical and psychological decimation of so many of the world's women?" He continues to say: "How in heaven's name can they be sanguine about the catastrophic loss of so much human potential?"

Dialogues among peoples and cultures, as part of the Satyagraha '100', are not mere events for us at Phoenix. They are of vital importance to us. In the spirit of the Gandhian Trinity—towards the African Renaissance and Global Peaceful coexistence—we held our last discourse, symbolically on Robben Island to coincide with our National Day of Reconciliation. This day demonstrates a fundamental aspect of Satyagraha towards reconciliation and harmony in South Africa for all our people regardless of their affiliations, political or otherwise.

As I have just mentioned, the second leg of our celebrations has begun, wherein we seek not only the Reconstruction and Development Program in physical and material ways but it is also directed to what Comrade Nelson Mandela calls, "the RDP of the soul." For this purpose I would like to suggest "Reconstruction and Development Program of the Mind."

In conclusion, we have said and done what we have said and done on the premise that South Africa belongs to all who live in it. We have assumed the duty to make South Africa livable for all who live in it. The celebration is directed towards African renaissance, towards global coexistence and that Satyagraha cannot be viewed in isolation from the context of Gandhian Trinity.

Every moment of my life
I realise that God is
putting me on my trial.

— M.K. Gandhi

At Noakhali, East Bengal, 1946.

Mahatma Gandhi taking a walk with his granddaughter
Manu and Khan Abdul Ghaffar Khan, Sadaqat Ashram,
Patna, 1947.

36

Time for Peace and Dialogue

MAHDI AGHA ALIKHANI

THE evolution of human society has witnessed abundant conflicts and mutual mistrust over long centuries before realising that dialogue is the very essence of survival. Dialogue has two distinguishable bases, *viz.*, equality of parties and an intent of give and take. Nowadays human societies are seeking equality, justice, freedom, human rights, mutual respect towards religions, traditions and inter-self relations and enrichment. I do believe that through dialogue all these demands can be satisfied.

Why do we need international and intercultural dialogue? Mohammad Khatami, former President of the Islamic Republic of Iran, in his speech at the United Nations, proposed that the year 2001 be named: "The year of dialogue among civilisations". This idea was welcomed globally and it also received the General Assembly's approval. But what do we demand from 'dialogue among civilisations'?

The first outcome of accepting dialogue is accepting equality among nations and cultures, negating domination and discrimination and laying emphasis on respecting the nations' freedom and independence. Common basis among nations and cultures can be found through dialogue and by avoiding giving priority to differentiation points. Further, we have to be hopeful for negation of violence and a future devoid of arms in nations' endeavour towards their security.

In recent years, in spite of emphasis on dialogue, misinterpretation among religions has managed to provoke discrepancies particularly among Islam, Christianity and Judaism more than ever before. The majority of Muslims are talking about peace and friendship. The idea of dialogue among civilisations came from an Iranian Muslim religious intellectual. In ancient Iran, tolerance and dialogue have always been the basis of civilisations. All saints and religious heads preached in favour of adopting a humanistic attitude. Saadi, one of the most renowned Persian poets, appealed against inimical approach and advocated rapprochement amongst adversaries. He considered human ethos as the very essence of unity. There is no doubt that his great spirit entered Mahatma Gandhi's body. Gandhi was against the idea that violence is the only answer to violence. Gandhi was aware of the two fundamental elements of human embroilment in violence—lack of religious tolerance and regional inequalities. This is why he emphasised spirituality without religious fanaticism. Mahatma Gandhi pronounced that: "Intolerance is the worst kind of violence." Today we have to attempt to keep ourselves away from these two unpleasant factors which are the most important barriers to peace and dialogue among civilisations. India, Iran and other cultures and civilisations, with Asian cultural backing, could expand this dialogue.

Accepting and welcoming dialogue among nations and various societies has inclined the trend towards peace, justice and lack of discrimination in human society, proving the necessity of dialogue among nations and various cultures to be true.

Thus, we could be hopeful of the realisation of fruitful dialogue when we witness social development and promotion of civil rights within our society and at the international level; better regulation of international rights and charter of the United Nations; justice observation at the international level and nations' non-deprivation of their own rights and letting them participate in the decision-making especially in situations of dialogue substantiation. Economic poverty at the domestic level is a barrier to formation of a civil society and at the international level it provokes conflict. So one of the most important aspects of providing dialogue is poverty elimination in the societies. Lastly, we have to consider dialogue among nations and cultures without the mental unrest activities of civil and non-governmental institutions at the national and international levels. Till then, we should work towards tolerance and dialogue under the shadow of cultural and intercultural communication in a non-formal and non-governmental atmosphere.

This is time for peace and dialogue instead of conflict, violence and war. I do believe that the philosophy of Gandhi will lead us to this way.

37

True Dialogue
Acceptance of Universal and Local Values

JOÃO CRAVINHO

NONE of us bears comparison to Gandhi. But I would argue that the most pertinent litmus test of the validity of political participation is the desire to somehow move the world, albeit in its most minute manner, through personal commitment, sound reflection and sacrificing love for others. That is what Gandhi's practical idealism was all about and it constitutes, I believe, one of Gandhi's enduring legacies to politics in the 21st century and beyond.

To enact any sort of change in this world, one must start from an understanding of others. And there is no better path to understanding than listening. Allow me then to start with a few considerations about the role of dialogue among peoples and cultures with a view to moving towards our ideals, Gandhi's ideals and the ideals that we today hold dear—ideals of peace, non-violence and empowerment.

Listening to others can help us develop an understanding of the aspirations and concerns of other people, people who live far from us, people who live in different countries and have different cultural heritages. And when we listen to others, we are struck by the fact that their aspirations and concerns always contain an element of universality, side by side with elements of their local and cultural circumstances. I believe that in our understanding of others, it is a particularly important challenge to find an appropriate balance between the universal and the local.

Globalisation has done nothing to reduce the relevance of this quest for balance. We should not imagine that the existence of cheap air travel or e-mail is going to eradicate the deeply rooted cultural heritages that each of us possesses. Just as it would be foolish to think that the values of freedom and tolerance, for example, were invented on the internet.

When Gandhi created the National University of Gujarat in Ahmedabad in 1920, he did so in order to allow Indians to understand their own cultural heritages—and I stress the plural of that word "heritages"—in response to the marginalising pressure of British rule. But while stimulating the study of Hindi or Sanskrit or Urdu, he did not forbid the use of English, for he understood that diversity in itself should be cherished, for in diversity we find the richness of our common humanity.

Peace, non-violence and empowerment—these key elements that are present in the Satyagraha movement require us to establish and practise particular forms of international dialogue in current times. I would like to explain briefly some of the aspects that I believe to be pertinent today in the way we approach dialogue.

The doctrine of Satyagraha means to combine the ideal of truth and firmness. It is the very opposite of fanaticism. Only dialogue can overcome difference of understanding through persuasion and demonstration and not by imposition. It should not be a condition that differences disappear. Indeed quite the contrary. Differences are healthy, differences reflect a richness if they are matched by the vital qualities of tolerance and respect.

When we establish processes of dialogue, we must commit ourselves to ensuring that it does not turn into a monologue, that the content is not just another empty shell but rather that it contributes generally to our goals. It should be about finding the right balance and understanding between the universal and the local values. We cannot presume that our values are universal. Even universal values, such as freedom and tolerance, require understanding of local conditions and traditions, if they are to flourish. Too often in the past, we have seen true dialogue being replaced by imposition of the point of views of those who are stronger. Such a forced dialogue invariably fails, whether or not it is backed by military strength. It is my great hope that we have sufficient wisdom to learn the lessons of past mistakes.

Of course, the practise of international politics offers us some good examples of lost opportunities for dialogue or a forced dialogue. But it is also the case that in some situations there comes a time when dialogue is no longer useful in furthering the causes of peace and empowerment of the weaker. Gandhi at various moments was quite explicit in saying that there are extreme circumstances in which the use of force is justified and he even participated personally in two war efforts of the British—the Anglo-Boer War in South Africa and the First World War in which he organised an Indian Red Cross. So dialogue cannot be thought of as an infinite or unproductive process but in the current world, in which the capacity for destruction is so great, it is essential that dialogue should prevail over violent solutions whenever it is possible. Unfortunately, we see too many occasions in which dialogue is placed aside in preference to violence, in preference to a shortcut which turns out to be a very long way around.

Earlier, I mentioned how Gandhi had established the National University of Gujarat based on the principle that diversity reflected the richness behind our common humanity. Very recently, in 2005, over a hundred nations signed the UNESCO convention on cultural diversity which corresponds faithfully albeit with some 70 or 80 years behind time to the same idea. We can take this as an example of Gandhi's foresight. But it is also true that the current world is faced with very specific challenges, in some ways challenges that are even more deeply entrenched in those that faced Gandhi, when we seek to overcome issues relating to cultural diversity. Whereas for Gandhi, respect for diversity went hand in hand with the culture of tolerance, today we find that some political movements manipulate national, ethnic or religious identities in order to use them for short-term political gains. Invariably we find that these manipulations involve a recreation of the past in which examples of tolerance in the historical past of a particular community are swept under the carpet in favour of a new interpretation or a new writing of history which presents that given community as a victim of oppression that must now seek revenge. This is not the way Gandhi thought of cultural diversity.

At the Durban conference last year on Satyagraha, this issue was quite rightly identified as a matter of growing concern. Our role is not to downplay the relevance of cultural diversity that is a factor of richness amongst us but instead to emphasise the vital connection between such diversity and the values of tolerance and respect for others. In the European Union, having learnt from our very considerable mistakes in the 20th century, we strongly believe in the international initiative that seeks to promote a dialogue of civilisations. And we need this because it is an increasingly important element in the promotion of global peace and security.

Turning for a moment to the question of empowerment, another key element in Gandhian thought, I think it is a paradox that increasing communication possibilities in today's world may have led to less real dialogue. Technology depends on the uses that are assigned to it. It is not in itself good or bad. In the present world, the possibility of dialogue presupposes the notion of equality, at least equality of respect between the two parties. And hence empowerment of those who have few advantages at the outset is a vital element for the promotion of dialogue.

An essential part of such empowerment is education as the instrument that gives us all the capacity to make decisions, to have opinions, to participate actively in dialogue. Education is, of course, a vital factor for reducing differences in power and it is only right that the issue of education, both at the basic level and higher levels, should have come to the forefront of development discussions over the past few years. Gandhi not only understood the importance of education but also knew that education had to have a strong element of citizenship. 'Citizenship' is not a Gandhian term. But the idea is Gandhian enough, the idea that people should be educated to believe in themselves, to believe in the importance of playing their rightful role in society, to believe in the importance of demanding their rights and above all to believe in the importance of respecting their duties. All of the revolutionary power of the Satyagraha movement came from an interpretation of this belief and this is a lesson that the contemporary world could well afford to learn once more. Since Gandhi's time, this insight has been less present than we would have liked it to be. And it constitutes, I believe, one of his greatest legacies. Gandhi was an exception. We cannot expect the world to be constantly illuminated by Gandhi. But we owe it to tomorrow to seek and to grow from his teachings.

It is time for Gandhi to visit many more countries around the world. I don't doubt that the world would be much richer and more peaceful if that was the case.

38
World Voices

Michael Chilufaya Sata

Zambian politician and former chief executive of the ruling Movement for Multiparty Democracy

The Centenary celebrations of Satyagraha movement could not have come at a more appropriate time as we seem to live in a world in which pursuit of individual self-interest has become the norm. The idea of putting others before self, looking out for justice and fair play for the least able, all seem to have been sacrificed at the altar of self-interest and greed. In consequence, the first few years of the 21st century have been a time of self-doubt for all the people of goodwill who subscribe to the values of freedom, social justice, international solidarity and peace.

We now live in a world in which there is hardly any country still under colonial oppression. Yet many countries that won self-determination as an aftermath of the Second World War especially in the African continent, the cradle of humanity and the birthplace of the Satyagraha movement, can hardly decide anything for themselves. We also live in a world in which enormous scientific and technological advances have created many opportunities. It is a whole new world in terms of its productive capacity. It produces enough food to feed everyone. Yet we still lose lives to hunger, malnutrition, not only in poor African and South Asian countries but even in the more affluent and so-called developed and newly industrialised countries. Humanity has found solutions to most of the problems that confront us. But the solutions never reach the poor, weak and vulnerable, the very people who need them most.

Many countries that seem to have escaped open conflict often describe themselves as peaceful and even peace-loving. However, absence of open conflicts or war does not necessarily mean that they have peace or are at peace. There can be no peace where there is injustice and absence of fair play. Thus in the Gandhian philosophy of non-violence, the struggle for social justice, fair play and preservation of human dignity is still relevant.

With the economy of so many emerging super powers growing rapidly, there is no guarantee that the emerging super powers, like the old imperial powers, will not seek global domination to prevent another global war like the Second World War. We must begin to actively promote the Gandhian philosophy of peaceful co-existence and the resolution of conflicts without resorting to violence. It is therefore incumbent upon all of us to begin constructing a more peaceful world through adhering to non-violence in resolution of problems. To do that effectively, however, we must take stock of the present situation and reassess our commitment to the proven Gandhian ideal of promoting world peace through non-violent collective action. Those of us who have abandoned or failed to uphold similar principles that could help promote world peace should recommit ourselves to those ideals.

Pradip Giri
Member, Nepali Congress (Democratic)

It was loudly argued that after the Cold War and after the downfall of the Soviet Union model of communism, a new world order will be established and it will give equal opportunity to all. Arguments were repeatedly cited that globalisation is the *Ramban* (panacea) for all the ailments. But after two decades, the contrary situation is before us where the gap between 'haves' and 'have-nots' is increasing. Globalisation has put forward some opportunities but the capacity to utilise the opportunities by the vast number of marginalised people is becoming more narrow. Globalisation has posed a serious threat to the cultural, linguistic minorities. They are facing the threat of losing their identity. I do not want to generalise the post-Cold War situation as an era of clash of civilisations, but it is obvious that through globalisation the 'haves' are trying to impose their values, culture and ideology upon rest of the world through their military strength and economic and technological supremacy. Capitalism, globalisation and consumerism are the main challenges to a harmonious, tolerant and orchestral world cultural order. Yes, we want a global and universal cultures, such a global culture which can incorporate all the diversities, identities and uniqueness. We want a rainbow culture. But some forces are trying to impose unitary, white collar culture upon the world. Democracy and access to information have created great consciousness and awareness in humans, Dalits, ethnic groups and the marginalised strata of the society. They want to discard the unjustified history and start a new era of justice, equality and coexistence.

If we fail to address these problems it could create a feeling of dissatisfaction, arrogance and revolt that would eventually degenerate in violence, clash and secessionism. And feeling of desperation can lead to terrorism. Time has come to end the centralised, hegemonic and undemocratic structures and restructure itself on the basis of pluralism, diversity, coexistence, equality, mutual tolerance and respect. Here lies the relevance of Gandhian philosophy of Ahimsa, Satyagraha, Sarvodaya and empowerment.

Samy Gemayel
Political activist and lawyer, Lebanon

Lebanon is formed by 18 communities. The people of Lebanon are pluralist and it is one of the best examples of dialogue between cultures.

On March 14, 2005, Lebanon liberated itself from a 30-year long Syrian occupation through Gandhian way without shedding a drop of blood. But the problem that Lebanon faced after liberation was that it did not base its dialogue on truth. Without truth, we fall into lies and hypocrisy and are unable to build a real dialogue, a real and lasting peace as was done in South Africa and was called 'truth and reconciliation'. Truth is very important to dialogue because when we do not base the dialogue on truth, we build false peace. This is what happened in my country also. A year ago we did not have true dialogue/peace therefore we are once again countering violence and disrespect for each other.

Dialogue should also be based on respecting differences. We cannot impose anything on anyone anymore. There is no nation-state any more, all the nations are multicultural. No state can claim to be monocultural. Each state is formed by multicultural people and pluralism should be respected and granted by all international laws. If we do not respect the differences, we fall into dictatorship, we fall into tyranny and that is what we saw in the past and are still seeing. For the growth of humankind, it is important we accept and respect differences and avoid tyranny and dictatorship.

Hilde Rapp
Co-Director of the Centre for International Peacebuilding, England

What I would like to reiterate is that if we find in ourselves the strength to align our minds and hearts with the spirit of truth, we may find that we can let go some of our fears of each other. And we all have them. We all had them as children and we are taught to deny their existence. So what we tend to do is, we deny that we are afraid and then we try to bristle. If we can let go of our fear and can cling to the truth, we might start walking on the road to freedom and peace and to do the very thing that Gandhiji always started with—a very, very sincere self-examination where we look for the roots of violence within ourselves before we look for them in others.

I also think that we are often too ambitious in our attempts to engage in dialogue with one another. Often, in my experience, a conversation turning towards each other rather than a dialogue, which is setting out differences, is the beginning that builds trust and relationship where we enter into friendship with one another at a personal level. This then leads to the possibility of building platforms for dialogue where we can then indeed find the strength and the courage to honestly look at significant and important differences between values and not necessarily between values of East and West but between values which we all respect. This is often avoided in inter-faith dialogue in which I am very much involved.

So, let us create the conditions for that true dialogue which is not afraid of differences, not afraid of conflict so that we can tackle the challenges that we heard about this morning, the challenges of the 21st century—how we can work together, all of us and for each other, to tackle the challenges of war, famine, environmental destruction, the dying of hope and the scourge of AIDS. Let us work together in friendship.

Nouzha Chekrouni
Moroccan Minister-Delegate in charge of Moroccans Living Abroad

It is true that Gandhi is one of the great philosophers of our time. He was one of the first to have thought that he could conquer a country without lifting a single arm. I think it is best explained by the fact that Gandhi aligned his philosophy with his political combat. The alliance between wisdom and his actions and policies is an excellent combination. This method based on non-violence came into being in the beginning of the 20th century. Gandhi's philosophy has been the source of inspiration and respect the world over and has become a political strategy for fighting against injustice.

Satyagraha is not just a refusal to accept violent means. It goes beyond that, it takes the sentiments of the oppressed into account. When we speak of Gandhi, we talk about his applied wisdom, his efficiency in the field, his political success. The application of the principles of non-violence helped to liberate his country from colonial power.

Gandhi was the first leader who thought of non-violence as a political strategy. We need to understand and experiment with this non-violent strategy. But at the same time, we must be careful about certain visions, about certain stereotypes about Gandhism which present itself as a complete doctrine in itself. He encourages us to ask essential questions concerning the very meaning of our existence, the meaning of our history, and as he himself has said, it is for us to invent the best possible responses to the situations that face us today.

The teachings of Gandhi, the originality of his methods are very relevant today when we are haunted by a wide range of problems—territorial conflicts, conflicts relating to governance, scandalous inequality, the condition of women, the arms race for nuclear weapons and so on.

Anwar Fazal
International Activist, health environmentalist and human rights crusader, Malaysia

We abound not only in weapons of mass destruction but also weapons of mass deception where people who can control media, control the influences and the way in which we proceed in the world. We are also prone to such weapons of mass addiction in terms of products and consumption patterns against which Gandhi told us to be extremely careful.

What can we do? I think one of the most important things is how we can harness all the different kinds of diverse energies and come up with some format that links all these initiatives. One of the suggestions I would like to make is that on this hundredth year, we actually set up a world-wide institute that could perhaps be the Satyagraha International Institute, much like the French have the Alliance Française, the British have the British Council and the Chinese have the Confucius Institute. And this institution can help move forward the agenda of information, capacity building, creating leaders, not just followers and advocacy of non-violence throughout the world.

The second initiative is for us to take inspiration from September 11, the one that Gandhiji told us about. We make September 11 the start for ten days of action throughout the world ending with September 21, which is the International Day of Peace.

The third is the power of information. Now that we have the internet, we can globally link different kinds of ideas through a website. Through this portal we can bring together the goodness and the information linking all of us together the world over.

And finally the power of success. Let us share and let us celebrate even a small positive step that has been taken anywhere in the world. Let us celebrate, share, remember, record every single success that we have achieved. Because such celebration gives us more optimism and more courage to move forward. Little things done by little people in little places have changed the world and we want that to continue to happen.

Kirunda Kivejinja
Third Deputy Prime Minister and Minister of Disaster Prepararedness, Uganda

The contribution of Gandhiji to human freedom continues to be an epic in the history of mankind that has inspired many of us. On a personal note it has been the guiding principle in the four decades of my personal participation in our struggle for freedom.

Although it was India that gave Gandhism to the world, it was Africa which gave Gandhi to India. Africa after being repressed for so long is now on the rise and it should not be taken lightly. There are many lessons to be learned from Africa as we are the most culturally diverse. According to Nehru, there is not a single race in the whole of the world that has suffered like Africa. We, however, don't have the history of recrimination. Otherwise, we would not be in dialogue with certain groups, groups which have again introduced differences amongst us leading us to genocide. So, while contributing to this Gandhism, the study of Africans needs to be ever strengthened.

When we attained our independence there were a lot of underdogs in the world. It was the clarity of the leaders who said that they were not going to chug behind the powers that were determining the fate of the world. And the Non-aligned Movement was born, in conjunction, of course, with Nkrumah, Nasser and Tito. And it saved us at that time. It saved mankind from polarising and colliding with each other. Now years later, the world is again going berserk. We want to kill each other. We seem to have forgotten that part of history where some human beings were not considered to be human; a time when Gandhi came to lead them and exert the power of the people.

We live in a world where might is controlled by fear, with the powers of destruction. This conference is very unique and it should not just end here. With 50 years of India's development, we expect that within a few years, the intellect and the financial muscle, for the first time, will be democratically in the hands of the majority of the world humanity. So it is our duty that we should not end this conference without trying to start another Non-aligned Movement, a movement which should cater to the under-developed in terms of poverty alleviation, in terms of understanding that variety and diversity is actually the essence of our world. Through inter-cultural dialogue we should start a movement, again, to influence humankind in the next decades.

Salman Khurshid
Educationist, social reformer, political thinker and Member, Indian National Congress

The challenges facing us are indeed big. And I think that the talisman that Mahatma Gandhi gave to us, "whatever you do, please ask yourself, does it help the poorest man in his worst situation" needs to be adopted again as a fresh talisman. As we go ahead in our modern lives with all its complexities we should ask ourselves: what would have Mahatma Gandhi done in these trying circumstances?

सत्याग्रहाश्रम
साबरमती

Satyagrahashram,
Sabarmati
B. B. C. I. Ry.

मिति _____ १९८ .

Date _____ 192

My dear Jawahar,

my love to you. It was all done bravely. You have braver things to do. May God spare you for many a long year to come and make you His chosen instrument for freeing India from the yoke —

Wardha
3 12 28

Yours
Bapu

Jawaharlal Nehru presenting the
National Flag to the Constituent Assembly,
July 22, 1947.

Section V Towards a Nuclear Weapons-Free and Non-violent World Order

JOHAN GALTUNG

CHAIWAT SATHA-ANAND

MANI SHANKAR AIYAR

JOS CHABERT

PAUL VAN TONGEREN

TZANNIS TZANNETAKIS

Section V

Towards a Nuclear Weapons-Free and Non-violent World Order

This section corresponds to the Subject Session IV of the international conference "Peace, Non-violence and Empowerment: Gandhian Philosophy in the 21st Century" held in New Delhi on January 29-30, 2007.

Chairperson: Johan Galtung (Norway)
Session Secretary: B.K. Hariprasad (India)
Session Rapporteur: Bhubaneswar Kalita (India)
Paper Presenter: Mani Shankar Aiyar (India)

Participants:

Chaiwat Satha-anand (Thailand), Tzannis Tzannetakis (Greece), Paul van Tongeren (Netherlands), Jos Chabert (Belgium), Mosiuoa Gerard Patrick Lekota (South Africa), Jürgen Störk (Switzerland), Antonio Marques Porto e Santos (Brazil), Kenneth Kaunda (Zambia), Kefenste Mzwinila (Botswana), George Khutsishvili (Georgia), Charles Namoloh (Namibia)

39

Non-violent World Order

JOHAN GALTUNG

THIS is a momentous day for us all. Fifty-nine years ago, that great light was extinguished and it is our task to keep the light shining not only inside us but for the world. I was a little boy at that time and I remember myself weeping, which I don't usually do. I had a feeling of something spiritually incredible that had happened. And I became a Gandhian.

Having initiated Satyagraha on 9/11/1906, how Mahatma Gandhi would have reacted to 9/11/2001 and its horrifying aftermath is a hypothetical, but an extremely pertinent question. Possibly he would have encouraged Muslims/Arabs with very legitimate concerns about the 1945 Treaty between Franklin Roosevelt and Abdul Aziz Ibn Saud, to non-violently encircle all the embassies of the US around the world, demanding a dialogue saying, "We will not touch a hair of your head, but we have something to talk about. Come out. Dialogue is the essence of democracy and let us practise it." He would have definitely rejected the violence of that 9/11 and the violence that followed.

I am mentioning that because the twin issues of nuclear weapons-free and non-violent world order are being brought together in the high-end unfortunate politics of the Anglo-American reign. I think he would have followed the way he did with the British Empire. An absolutely ingenious combination of changing acts of commission to acts of omission. You don't cooperate with the system, you don't even drink a bottle of Coca Cola and you don't travel by Boeing if there is some other aircraft available. And he would have combined that with dialogue.

We have had countries in the past defying world opinion to make a world community. Today is no different. Our task now is to ask, is there a non-violent peace order that we can talk about? This non-violent peace order presupposes, among other things, a nuclear-free world.

The Times of India

ESTABLISHED 1838

NO. 193. VOL. CIX.   BOMBAY: FRIDAY, AUGUST 15, 1947   PRICE TWO ANNAS   DO NOT PAY MORE

BIRTH OF INDIA'S FREEDOM

NATION WAKES TO NEW LIFE

Mr. Nehru Calls For Big Effort From People

"INCESSANT STRIVING TASK OF FUTURE"

Assembly Members Take Solemn Pledge

Pandit Nehru

NEW CABINET OF INDIA

Fourteen Members

PANDIT NEHRU TO BE PREMIER

NEW DELHI, August 14.
The new Cabinet of India, which will function from August 15, announced tonight, will consist of the following:

Pandit Jawaharlal Nehru—Prime Minister, External and Commonwealth Relations and Scientific Researches.

Sardar Vallabhbhai Patel—Home, Information and Broadcasting.

Dr. Rajendra Prasad—Food and Agriculture.

Maulana Abul Kalam Azad—Education.

Dr. John Matthai—Railways and Transport.

Sardar Baldev Singh—Defence.

Mr. Jagjivan Ram—Labour.

Mr. C. H. Bhabha—Commerce.

Mr. Rafi Ahmed Kidwai—Communications.

Rajkumari Amrit Kaur—Health.

Dr. B. R. Ambedkar—Law.

Mr. R. K. Shanmukham Chetty—Finance.

Dr. Syama Prasad Mookerjee—Industries and Supplies.

Mr. N. V. Gadgil—Works, Mines and Power.—A.P.I.

Mrs. Naidu's Message

NEW DELHI, August 14: Mrs. Sarojini Naidu, in a message on Luck-now Day, says: "O, lovely natal day of new-born India, the ancient capital of Prithviraj splendid flag of new-born India to be unfurled on the ramparts over the Red Fort of Shahjahan! We pay you the homage of our dedicated hearts and souls and pledge ourselves to renew the rich glories despite the dreams that were our share and inspiration in the long darkness of our bondage.
—P.I.

The Arab support of Jaffa is to be inspired, re-planned and modernised within the next 30 years at a cost of two million pounds. Dr. Yusuf Haikal, Mayor of Jaffa, told Reuter in London.

STATE VISIT TO KARACHI

Their Excellencies ... Service ...

FRENZIED ENTHUSIASM IN BOMBAY

Crowds In Festive Mood

THE national flag was hoisted over the ... of Bombay Civil Secretariat at midnight ... of Bombay greeted the dawn of independence ... vocation and frenzied rejoicing.

"Citizens of free India ... are now free",—said ... Minister, Mr. ... raising th... cere...

WILD SCENES OF JUBILATION IN DELHI

From Our Special Representative

NEW DELHI, AUGUST ...

ENTIRE DELHI KEPT AWAKE ... NESS THE HISTOR ... USHERING IN THE FREE ... AT THE HOUR OF MIDNIGHT ...

Unprecedented scenes of enthu... ed both inside and outside the Con... Chamber, where seething, swaying ... cheered the momentous event, heralded ... ing of conches.

Raising to the height of the occasion, Pan... speech in the Assembly which was at once notab... piece of literature.

"Years ago we made a tryst with destin... "and now the time comes when we shall redeem ... not wholly or in full measure, but very substan... the stroke of the midnight hour, when the ... India will awake to life and freedom".

"With becoming humility, Pandit Nehru reminded ... that freedom and power bring responsibility and ... future is not one of ease or rest but of incessant ... so that we may fulfil the pledges we have so often ta... the one we shall take today.

Choudhry Khaliquzzaman, leader of the Muslim League group, in a brief speech, whole-heartedly supported the motion moved by Pandit Nehru for the adoption of the pledge and assured "faithful and loyal" co-operation of the Muslims of India in implementing the pledge of dedication.

Dr. S. Radhakrishnan, the noted philosopher, supporting Pandit Nehru's motion, pointed out the cores in the Indian body politic and urged that every Indian at this hour should pledge himself to purge the society of corruption and intolerance, and took the occasion to pay a sincere tribute to the rule of British and British statesmen in bringing to ...

(Continued on page 15)

MR. GANDHI'S FAST TODAY

Also League Leaders

CALCUTTA, August 14: The ex-rajah observance of Independence tomorrow by the Gandhi will mortar a 24-hour fast. He will spend the whole day in wrapping and holding special prayers.

Mr. H. S. Suhrawardy, the retiring Premier of Bengal, and Mr. N. N. Sircar, ex-Mayor of Calcutta and Secretary of the Calcutta District Muslim League, will also fast along with Mr. Gandhi.—A.P.I.

(See Page 15)

'Go Forward In Tranquillity And Prosperity'

MR. ATTLEE'S MESSAGE TO FREE INDIA

NEW DELHI August 14.
"My colleagues in the United Kingdom Government join with me in sending on this historic day greetings and good wishes to the Government and the people of India," says Mr. Attlee, Prime Minister, in a message to Pandit Nehru.

"It is our earnest wish that India may go forward in tranquillity and prosperity and in so ...

UNION JACK HAULED DOWN

Lucknow Residency

LUCKNOW, August 14: The same flag as the British Crown which was never hauled down since 1857 the Union Jack was flying on Lucknow Residency was hauled down last night almost 21 hrs before to the transfer of power from Britain to the Indian house. The morning ceremony this legal day polite and quiet in the Indian authorities.

The Union Jack hauled down remained Honour Karachi, now independent the important town of this era of the British Governor of the United Provin...

The famous "National Flag will be hoisted on Government House in Mar... Saturday Nable announcement something.—A.P.I.

The Hindustan Times

DELHI EDITION

LARGEST CIRCULATION IN NORTHERN, NORTH-WESTERN AND CENTRAL INDIA

NEW DELHI, SATURDAY, JULY 19, 1947   PRICE TWO ANNAS

VOL. XXIV, NO. 193.

END OF 200-YEAR-OLD BRITISH RULE IN INDIA

ROYAL ASSENT TO INDEPENDENCE BILL

BRIEF BUT COLOURFUL CEREMONY IN LORDS

Two Dominions Created

LONDON, July 18: Precisely at 10.16 a.m. G.M.T. today (1.40 p.m. I.S.T.) the great new Dominions of India and Pakistan were born and the Indian freedom, when it came into their inheritance of full political freedom with ceremony at the Bar of the House of Lords, a Royal Commission of Peers gave the Royal Assent to the Indian Independence Bill among other measures.

To Both Houses, in the House of Lords, in the classic formula Assent was signified to William Cecil Dunn...

King George VI

FREE INDIA FLAG

Provisional Govt. For Burma

ANNOUNCEMENT LIKELY NEXT WEEK

RANGOON, July 18—A Provisional Government for Burma from ...

Return Of Bollaert To Viet-Nam Welcomed

SAIGON, July 18 ...

FRONTIER REFERENDUM ENDS

TRAVANCORE WILL BE INDEPENDENT ON AUG. 15

Ruler's Announcement

TRIVANDRUM ...

Indonesia's Rice Offer Holds

BATAVIA, July 18 ...

Gandhiji's Visitors

UNION'S RELATIONSHIP WITH RULERS

PROVISION FOR PROVINCES' JURISDICTION IN STATES

(By Our Special Representative)

NEW DELHI, Friday—An important provision to produce exercising jurisdiction in the Indian ... Give or judicial sphere in the territory of the Indian ... an agreement supported by the Federal Gov... adopted by the Constituent Assembly today ...

The sub-committee consists of Sir B. L. ... for A. Ramaswami Mudaliar, Dr. B. R. Am...

ATTLEE

MESSAGE FROM PREMIER

Equality Of Status With Britain

VICEROY TO VISIT LAHORE

40

Towards a Nuclear Weapons-Free and Non-violent World Order

MANI SHANKAR AIYAR

I think I can do no better than to remind you of what President Kaunda told us in his address: "To save humanity from destruction in the 21st century, the world must be armed not with weapons of mass destruction but with the values and wisdom espoused by Gandhi and embodied by the Satyagraha movement." And it is to address ourselves to this call for saving humanity in the 21st century that we are gathered in this session today. As Mr. Galtung, our Chairman, also emphasised, there is an indissoluble connection between the abolition of nuclear weapons and the establishment of a non-violent world order. For even if it is possible for us to conceive of a world without nuclear weapons, such a world cannot be sustained unless the world order itself is based on non-violence. And this proposition derives from the incontrovertible fact that the technology for the manufacture of nuclear weapons is now a part of the human heritage. You can abolish nuclear weapons but you cannot abolish the knowledge of how to make them. And the only way of allowing us to coexist with the knowledge of nuclear weapons and yet not have them is to ensure that the world order is not based on injustice and inequality, as at present, but is linked to the essential values espoused by Mahatma Gandhi and which are resumed in the expression 'a non-violent world order'. And it was to attain such a state of affairs, a world without nuclear weapons but one based on non-violence that on the 9th of June, 1988, the Prime Minister of India, Shri Rajiv Gandhi, presented to the Third Special Session on Disarmament of the United Nations an Action Plan for Nuclear Weapons-Free and Non-violent World Order.

I think the essence of the Gandhian system of struggle against injustice was to recognise that in a world of asymmetric power, it is only an asymmetric response that can enable right to prevail over might. This is because if one party is well armed and the other party is not at all armed or only partially armed, then any attempt by the latter to enter the struggle on a field where the former has already established one's dominance will lead only to disaster. That if armed might of the mighty is met by the armed might of those who do not have that might, then inevitably in the clash of arms, it is the superior might that will prevail. However, it is far from necessary to pit violence against violence, or hatred against hatred, or prejudice against prejudice. If the weaker party were to choose the asymmetric response and say, "I desire nothing of what you desire and if my weapons will never be your weapons and if the goal that you seek is not the goal that I want, then in this new paradox, it is the weaker power that sets the terms of the engagement." Therefore, when confronted with the mightiest armed empire that the world had ever known, the British empire, whose jewel in the crown was India but which extended so far across the globe that the British could say with justice that the sun never sets on the British empire, to which, of course, one of our freedom fighters gave the response, that it is because even God wouldn't trust the British in the dark, we were able to not only secure freedom of India, but also secure the freedom of a large swathe of humanity by means that until Mahatma Gandhi belonged to the realm of ethics and not to the realm of politics. And what Gandhiji did was to pick up ethical values, that were certainly not originating in him but which were in fact part of the human heritage from the Buddha and Jesus Christ and Hazrat Mohammad onwards, and bring them into a framework of political action that was designed to pit an asymmetric response to the existence of an empire based on force and violence.

We find in terrorism, that we are familiar with today, a similar attempt to devise an asymmetric response, that instead of trying to convey an army to the shores of Manhattan, to just identify two aircraft with two hijackers on it and create a response thereof. Thus, we have an interesting and ironic paradox of what 9/11 stands for. 9/11/1906 was the date on which the movement of Satyagraha or truth force was launched as asymmetric response to overwhelming power, and 9/11 at the beginning of this millennium was the violent asymmetric response launched in order to meet with overwhelming force. And the one prevailed and the other must not be allowed to prevail. In these circumstances, we have to ask ourselves in the context that we have got now, here in this session, whether a world in which some have nuclear weapons and others don't, is a world order that is in fact sustainable. For the knowledge that was the preserve of a few when the atomic bomb was first invented some 60 years ago is no longer the preserve of a few. There is a large number, or at least a considerable number of nuclear weapon-states, in which the latest additions are India and Pakistan. It is a knowledge that is available to so many other countries that there is a whole swathe of nations that are trembling as it were at the brink of becoming nuclear weapon-states. And the solution that is proposed through the non-proliferation treaty is that the non-nuclear weapon states undertake an immediate and binding commitment which will be enforced by force by the nuclear weapon-states, if necessary, to not acquire nuclear weapons while those who possess nuclear weapons, the recognised NWS, make a general commitment towards eliminating nuclear weapons but are not required by the treaty in any way to take practical steps in that direction. And it is this asymmetry in the treaty arrangements of 1967 which has led India to reject the NPT route as the acceptance of an unequal treaty. As we have seen over the last 40 years, since that agreement was arrived at, there are a certain number of countries that have crossed the nuclear threshold and several others which are in danger of doing so. And if the nuclear weapon-states insist that nuclear weapons are essential for their security, then how can it be indefinitely denied to others that they too begin to regard the nuclear weapons as essential for their security. If, as the nuclear weapon-states maintain that nuclear weapons are an important currency of power, then how is this currency of power to be denied to others who also wish to exercise power in a world of unequal power. And while conceding all this, one cannot forget that nuclear weapons are like no other weapons ever invented before. For one thing, all previous weapons, including weapons to end all weapons, such as the crossbow of Switzerland many many centuries ago which was regarded as the ultimate weapon in its day could only destroy the enemy in a limited geographical area, in a limited period of time and a limited number of people. But the nuclear holocaust is one which does not take place only in a flash of a second but continues its effects all over the world depending on the way in which winds take radiation and entering the very genes of the human being and other life forms. It goes on indefinitely for generations to wreck even that which succeeds in surviving. Moreover, it is the only weapon in the world ever invented that not only destroys the party that is attacked but also eventually destroys the attacker. It is a truly insane weapon because it can never bring victory. It can only bring utter destruction involving eventually the destruction of he who uses it. And yet the curious thing is that nuclear weapons not only continue to exist in the stockpiles of the nuclear weapon-states but with increasing sophistication, with increasing destructive power, and with increasing numbers. But, they pose increasingly a threat to whom? Obviously the biggest threat before us today is terrorism. But terrorists by definition are non-state actors and nuclear weapons can only be used, if ever they are to be used, only against hostile people or a state. They can hardly be used against a state or a people where these individual terrorists happen to be hiding. Moreover, so long as there are stockpiles of nuclear weapons, that is the treasure-trove from rogue states and rogue terrorists will be able to access these weapons and eventually use them against all of us. Nuclear disarmament is therefore an imperative that brooks no further delay. Yet, does it behove a country like India which when it was a passionate advocate of nuclear disarmament, to continue campaigning for nuclear disarmament after it has itself become a nuclear weapon state? I say this because when Shri Rajiv Gandhi presented the Action Plan, we were a threshold nuclear weapon-state, we are now, even if the other nuclear weapon-states won't recognise us as such, as much a nuclear weapon state as the United States or the Russian Federation. How can I then without hypocrisy pouring out of my mouth stand here in the name of Mahatma Gandhi and plead as a Government Minister for nuclear disarmament?

I think the answer to that lies in the fact that we have been in the last 60 years through three phases of our nuclear weapons status. For 27 years, from 1947 to 1974, India was a non-nuclear weapon state. In 1974, we had our first nuclear explosion at Pokharan and became a threshold nuclear weapon state because at that time we established that we could become a nuclear weapon power at the turn of the screw as it were, if we so wished, but that deliberately we were refraining from crossing the threshold in the interest of trying to persuade the world to come to the path of Mahatma Gandhi. Then in 1998, there was a second explosion. At this point, India became a nuclear weapon state and it has been the stated policy of the government to continue to have a credible, minimum nuclear deterrent, but also to never resort to the first use of nuclear weapons. In both these respects— refusing to resort to nuclear weapons for first use and in insisting that we will not join the nuclear arms race by maintaining no more than a minimum credible nuclear deterrent—we are distinguished from the other nuclear powers who have not undertaken similar commitments. In other words, while we have crossed the threshold, we continue to be a threshold NWS on the other side of the threshold.

Now in doing so, we have, in all the three phases—when we were definitively not a nuclear weapon state, after we became a threshold nuclear weapon state and then later we became a full-fledged nuclear weapon state—been very very consistent in asking for universal nuclear disarmament, but subject to two conditions. One, that the process of nuclear disarmament must be non-discriminatory, that it must involve not only the states that haven't become nuclear weapon powers and the states which could if they wished to become nuclear weapons powers but also the states which have become nuclear weapons powers. That an unequal treaty cannot be sustained; that a treaty, if it is going to be sustained, has to be non-discriminatory, must involve all. And in that sense it has to be comprehensive. And furthermore, that the goal must be set as the first step in a time-bound manner. There is little point in talking about an eventual elimination of nuclear weapons if a time frame is not set within which that goal is to be achieved. For unless you know where exactly you are going to reach and by when, the steps taken in the direction of disarmament could lead to discriminatory disarmament, as, for example, having regional pacts for 'no nuclear weapons' which might prevent those regions from having nuclear weapons but would not stop those regions from becoming the victims of nuclear weapons, were they to be used in other regions. Or to suggest that there are partial disarmament measures that would work for the nuclear weapons states but there has to be an absolute cap on everybody else. What is more, in a world where nuclear weapons powers or non-nuclear weapons powers are threatened with the use of weapons of non-mass destruction or of destruction, there is a tendency to push those who feel threatened over the brink.

That is why in 1988, Prime Minister Rajiv Gandhi, when we were non-nuclear weapons power, we were a threshold nuclear weapons-state at that time, presented a proposal to the United Nations in which having announced that within 22 years, which at that time was the year 2010, there would be a complete elimination of all nuclear weapons was based on three stages. In stage I, which was to last for 6 years, there would be several measures to be taken for nuclear disarmament and measures collateral to nuclear disarmament as well as dealing with other weapons of mass destruction, conventional forces and then measures collateral to nuclear disarmament etc., including verification, which was very important, until we went to Stage II. Where again there would be further measures and that would last till the year 2000 and finally Stage III stage when by 2010 there would be elimination of all nuclear weapons in the world, the establishment of a single integrated multilateral comprehensive verification system which would ensure that no nuclear weapons are produced, where all conventional forces would be reduced to minimum defensive levels, where steps should be taken to prevent the emergence of new arms race, where there would be universal adherence to a comprehensive global security system and so on and so forth. But above all, to end this dangerous militarisation of international relations, we must build a structure firmly based on non-violence.

In the last 18 years that have passed since the presentation of this Action Plan, the rest of the world has produced nothing comparable; and most of the world, or almost all the states of the world, have simply put this one on the back burner. In the meanwhile there has been a dramatic change. At the time the action plan was presented, there was a Cold War on with two major powers locked in eyeball to eyeball confrontation. The end of the Cold War, one would have imagined, would have singled out a world without enemies and therefore a world in conjunction in which this action plan could have been taken up. Yet the sad fact is that it hasn't been taken up. But there is a voice of sanity which is rising even in the hardest of hearts and that is, what is the most hopeful sign for this conference—that if we continue to talk of time-bound, non-discriminatory, universal abolition of nuclear weapons, then ours are not the voices in the wilderness. There are many people who are realising that if there is ever a conjuncture in which this could be attained, it is now.

I draw your attention to an article by Robert S. McNamara, the US Defense Secretary who was Defense Secretary during the worst phases of the Vietnam War, in *Foreign Policy* where he has first informed us of how again and again the world almost came to nuclear war during the Cold War. And he cites the Cuban example in particular but there are others that he mentions. He also says how much is the tendency to use a weapon which is in your armoury is a temptation so long as it is there and he draws attention to "the bizarre situation" in which the President of the United States of America who has with him all the time a little bag in which there is a button to press to start a nuclear holocaust has only 20 minutes within which to make the decision as to whether to press that button or not.

I also draw your attention to an article which has come out at the most appropriate time, on the 4th of January 2007, i.e., just 3 to 4 weeks ago. It is an article jointly written by two former US Secretaries of State, one is a name renowned in academic and political circles, Henry Kissinger, and the other is George Shultz, and two former US Defense Secretaries who are Sam Nunn and William Perry. These four highly distinguished cold warriors, people of whom as the Chairperson of our conference reminded us yesterday, had dismissed what Rajiv Gandhi had said in 1988 as "not worthy of further comment" and are now citing him in this very same article. I want to quote a few lines from this article because of its importance. It says:

> Apart from the terrorist threat, the US will soon be compelled to
> enter a new nuclear era that will be more precarious,

psychologically disorienting and economically even more costly
than was Cold War deterrence.

They argue that the deterrence had a validity in their view during the time when
the US and USSR were confronting each other. But now the US and USSR are not in
confrontation with each other, and that USSR has in fact ceased to exist, and that
all the nuclear weapon states who recognise themselves have the best of relations
among themselves because of which there is no problem among the nuclear
weapon states. Theories of deterrence thus are no longer of relevance to the
contemporary international world and in this situation, they ask for a return of the
US administration, and by implication of all nuclear weapon states, to the dreams
of Eisenhower in 1953 who expressed America's determination to help solve the
fearful atomic dilemma to John F. Kennedy. Kennedy said that: "The world was not
meant to be a prison in which man awaits his execution." And the aim as they
have stated of President Reagan and General Secretary Gorbachev at Reykjavik
where according to this article Reagan and General Secretary Gorbachev aspired to
accomplish more than what they did at their meeting in Reykjavik 20 years ago,
their aim being to secure "the elimination of nuclear weapons altogether." This
was not vouchsafed to us at that time. But if today, two former Secretaries of State
of the United States, two former Defense Secretaries of the United States, recall
and bring to mankind's attention what would have been determined at the height
of the Cold War, at some of the worst periods of Cold War, as the need for the
elimination of nuclear weapons altogether following which Rajiv Gandhi's Action
Plan becomes an agenda not for yesterday but for today. With this in mind, there is
another provision in the article by Kissinger *et al*. They say that the immediate
requirement is intensive work with leaders of the countries in possession of nuclear
weapons (that would include India and Pakistan) to turn the goal of a world
without nuclear weapons into a joint enterprise.

So we are not alone and we are not eccentric and we are not on the margin of
humanity. What we have gathered here in the context of the centenary of the
Satyagraha, to work towards a nuclear-weapons-free world based on the non-
violent world order is in fact the agenda being urged by some of the most
distinguished cold warriors of the past and who are at present advocates of a
certain present. To do this requires specific steps. It is not enough for us to beat
our breast and say, that this is the way forward. What we need is an action plan.
And we have an Action Plan. The Action Plan is of course 18 years old. So there are

many things said in this which require updating. Furthermore, Action Plan is not a treaty. And so we need to render the Action Plan into legal language. That is exactly what the President of the Indian National Congress, Shrimati Sonia Gandhi, did a few years ago when this document was updated, rendered into treaty language, and was presented by her to the UN Secretary General. But even that was several years ago. And there have been further developments since then. So we need to work further on it. And in order to work further on it, the Indian delegation to the first committee of the UN General Assembly in October, 2006, circulated a working paper aimed at the commencement of negotiations on the subject of a nuclear weapons-free and non-violent world order. We have taken this initiative. We need to push it forward. In order to push it forward, we need, above all, public opinion before we turn to the government. Public opinion on the subject is represented by those of you who have taken the trouble to come from all continents of the world to join us here to commemorate the centenary of Mahatma Gandhi starting the movement of "Truth Force" or Satyagraha. I am sure it is more of what you say and do than what the aide memoirs that governments exchange among one another that will determine the course of future action. Mr. Galtung reminded us of 16th of February 2003 when 15 million people gathered in 600 sites around the world to protest the use of force against a power which eventually turned out to have no weapons of mass destruction at all. So that is the kind of force that we want to go back to. Meanwhile if there is such a groundswell of Gandhian opinion, perhaps we can get back to the world which Gandhiji envisaged at the end of the day, as he said, "The bomb will not be beaten by counter bombs, violence will not end with counter violence." He said that the only thing that the atomic bomb, as it was then called, showed to him was that for the survival of humanity, non-violence is essential. And the Rajiv Gandhi Action Plan which combines a nuclear-weapons-free world with a world order which is based on non-violence is the Gandhian way forward and we invite you to please endorse it.

Painting by Upendra Maharathi.

I am not aching for martyrdom, but if it comes in my way in the prosecution of what I consider to be the supreme duty in defence of the faith I hold. . . I shall have earned it.

— M.K. Gandhi

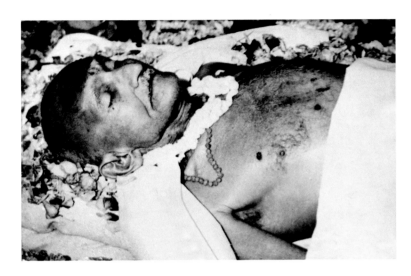

Indira Gandhi on the train which took the ashes of Mahatma Gandhi, 1948.

41

Countering Hatred and Violence through *Shanti Sena*

CHAIWAT SATHA-ANAND

A hundred years ago, on September 11, 1906, the powerful Indian non-violent movement was born in South Africa. Four decades later, this movement led by Gandhi known as Satyagraha went on not only to free 300 million people from the power of the British *raj*, but also inspired if not shaped a century of non-violent struggle around the world.

In December 1938, a member of the International Muslims Conference at Tambaram in Madras met Gandhi and asked him how humanity can be saved from the impending international crisis that threatens to plunge it into an orgy of hate and violence. The issues raised at that meeting included: how non-violence would work in the cases of a minority (meaning the Jews), international warfare (meaning China's ordeal against the Japanese) and the nature of modern warfare that had become mechanical, and the ruthless dictatorships such as Hitler's and Mussolini's?

I would formulate Gandhi's answer into four concepts: avoid passivity, courageous non-cooperation with the invaders, importance of human heart and redemption. With regards to human heart I would like to quote what Gandhiji said: "Behind the death-dealing bombs, there is the human hand that releases it, and behind that still is the human heart that sets the hand in motion. One of the problems with violence is that sometimes it prevents us from seeing the heart that lies behind the hands."

Now the question is, in facing the problem of hatred and violence around the world, what would be Gandhi's answer? Would he give similar answers to the malady of the world as he once did in 1938? Would these answers of his continue to be valid in a world gone mad with hatred and violence at the advent of the 21st century?

I am not interested in the first question since I am not trying to imitate Gandhi and I doubt if anyone should or could. But there is a way to deal with the second question through an experiment already attempted in Thailand. In the southern part of Thailand, for three years already, there has been ethnic violence between the minority Muslims and the State as well as others. There have been almost 6,000 violent incidents resulting in more than 4,800 casualties of which about 2,000 have been killed. There have been attempts to explain and contain the recent phenomenon of violence. In April of 2005, the previous Government and the former Prime Minister who was ousted, Thaksin Shinawatra, established a most unique commission called the National Reconciliation Commission. Their task was "to find a long-term solution to the problem of violence in the South in order to bring about, through reconciliation, peace and justice." The Commission's report is now ready and one of the most controversial recommendations is to set up an unarmed army unit called "Shanti Sena." Imagine we are now fighting insurgency in the South, we are talking about State violence against the people, about daily conflicts and here the report is suggesting that we have a *Shanti Sena* to serve as an immediate measure of reconciliation aiming at solving violence. The report suggests the formation of a peace unit; confronting violence with the aim to combat it with a political victory through the reconciliation approach. No doubt it requires a willingness to accept risk and the use of non-violent actions to resolve the conflict. The idea of *Shanti Sena*, or unarmed peace unit, is an innovation in conflict transformation. The core missions of *Shanti Sena* are: to perform a peace building operation in the event of a conflict between the people and the state. Instead of using violence, we come in as an unarmed unit; undertake a peace building operation in the event of people to people conflict; regularly educating local government officials and residents on the skills to face violence with non-violent actions; organise dialogues between one another and between the people and officials to foster better understanding and non-violence; and to inculcate in government officials integrity and raise their working morale through the use of religious principles.

Gandhi actually thought about the idea of *Shanti Sena* shortly before his death but he did not see it into fruition during his lifetime.

The *Shanti Sena* proposed by the National Reconciliation Commission is different from the Peace Brigade International and the bodyguards' notion that has been used in Central America and the Middle East and in the Philippines, for example. This is different from other initiatives because it is not a substitute for military training for students, as was the case in India, nor is it a set of actions for the people in the fight against the repressive state or its agents. On the contrary, it is proposed "as an additional weapon for the military in the context of heightened deadly conflicts between the local people who are Malay Muslims and the government officials who are mostly Thai Buddhists." This weapon is not designed to protect either side of the conflict—ordinary people or government officials—but protect both by preventing a conflict situation from sliding into violence. Inspired by Galtung's idea that conflict can be transformed, the proposed *Shanti Sena*'s main function is to non-violently intervene in a potentially violent conflict between the demonstrators who are by and large non-violent and state security forces, the police and the military, who are normally with arms almost without exception.

Inspired by Gandhi's answer outlined above, I would argue that to some degree the idea of *Shanti Sena* proposed by the National Reconciliation Commission reflects Gandhian insights on dealing with hatred and violence. Because first, the proposal is far from passive. It urges to initiate an active response to deadly conflict situations by using non-violent actions instead of allowing the absence of violence to emerge accidentally. It insists on understanding the principles and practices of non-violent actions, preparation and training as pre-requisites for such a unit. It doesn't come automatically. Second, the element of courage is extremely significant in this proposal. Courage here has a double meaning because it requires more than courage of those who are physically armed to lay down their arms by choice. It also means that policy makers, both military and civilian, have to have the courage to explore non-violent alternatives. And that I think is much more important.

This brings us to Gandhi's perception on the role and significance of the human heart. The place of heart in the analysis of conflict is profound. When one walks unarmed into a conflict with the potential for violence, one is taking a risk. Taking a risk is not only a manifestation of courage but also points towards one's willingness to trust. Risk-taking is a manifestation of trust and therefore absolutely important for any reconciliation measure. Soldiers who decide to walk into a town known for violence have to have some faith either in God or in the cause. But extremely important is that they have to believe in the human heart. This belief must be strong enough for them to trust the strangers with their lives.

I am not certain if in proposing the *Shanti Sena* to the Thai Military, with its record of violence, the National Reconciliation Commission was thinking about the possibility of redemption. But if a proposal like this is indeed picked up by the State, it will open up a space for thinking about some possibility in confronting violence including that committed by the state itself because *Shanti Sena* is designed to prevent the state itself from committing further violence against its own people. Perhaps here lies the Gandhian possibility of redemption.

On January 30, 1948, Gandhi's life was taken away by the bullets of an assassin in Delhi. Six decades later, the relevance of a composition by one of Siam's greatest contemporary poets assumes significance. It is a conversation between a father and his daughter and it is called "Dew Drops".

"Father" said his daughter, "What are dew drops"?

"Dew drops are the tears of time".

Daughter asked the father: "Why does time weep, papa? Is time so sad, papa?"

Father answered:

"Time weeps because it has to leave us to a far away land in the waves of irreversible wheel of time. But the time cries and it is not only due to sorrow. Because dew drops are also pleased to pay respect to the sun to be able to mirror the true value of all seven rays of sunlight as that gift to the world. Yet dew drops grieve since in their immediate evaporation, they have to bid farewell to us. They cannot remain to polish our glances so that we can profoundly appreciate rainbows and other beauties. Thus, with glee or in grief dew drops are the tears of time."

Can there be a better way to remember Gandhi and everything that happened in the past 100 years? Through beauty truth can be seen, truth seen through the eyes of beauty will allow us to continue to live as Gandhi did, as human beings in reality do with the strength to believe in the idea of the good.

42

Creating a World Free of Nuclear Weapons

TZANNIS TZANNETAKIS

THE 20th century was the bloodiest century in human history. Over 90 per cent of the casualties of the wars were civilians. In the later half of the century, the threat of nuclear annihilation hung over all humanity. The United States and the former Soviet Union engaged in an arms race in which they developed the capacity to destroy humanity many times over. Somehow, the world survived the insanity of nuclear arms race but we are not yet safe. There are still far too many nuclear weapons in the world, over 30,000. And even today, a surprisingly large number of them, some 4,500, remain on a trigger alert.

Nuclear weapons are morally and legally unjustifiable. They destroy indiscriminately soldiers and civilians, men, women and children, the aged and the newly born, the healthy and the infirm. Nuclear weapons are profoundly undemocratic. They concentrate power and take it away from the people.

Nuclear weapons were born in secrecy and have always been surrounded in secrecy. The decisions to develop, deploy and use these weapons have always been in the hands of only a small number of individuals. Even today, a single leader, or at the most a small group of individuals could envelop the world in nuclear conflagration.

Our goal is to create a world free of nuclear weapons. The long-term aim is a new world order. In this new world, no man is foolish enough to kill or be killed to defend his master's word or ego. We must seek a world in which no man, woman or child goes to bed wondering whether he or she will live through the hunger, pestilence or violence of the next day. A world in which, we look around this room, we don't see murdering, thieving enemies against whom we have to defend ourselves but brothers and sisters on whom our own safety, security, survival and enjoyment depends.

Nuclear states are continuing to spend tens of billions of dollars per year on maintaining their nuclear arsenal. That means some tens of millions per day. At the same time some 30,000 children under the age of five are dying daily of starvation and preventable diseases. Relatively small amounts of food and inexpensive adaptation could save these children. The world continues to squander resources on nuclear arsenals that have virtually no military utility while children go hungry and without adequate nutrition, healthcare and education. Justice Morton once said, "Military expenditure would provide clean water, adequate food and shelter and primary education for all the people on our planet." The potential is there to turn our planet into a paradise for all of its inhabitants. But to do so, we must break out of the world cultures that militarise and poison this planet.

Disarmament, unfortunately, is not an automatic process. It requires sustained human attention and action by all sectors of society from the most powerful leaders to the average citizen. It requires an end to the cycle of violence and building a culture of peace. Disarmament also means seeking non-violent means to resolve conflicts and working actively to prevent wars by creating the condition of peace. But disarmament must be combined with active engagement in ending poverty and starvation. Disarmament to be effective must be, in my opinion, concentrating on three main targets.

The first is abolition of nuclear weapons. Elimination of nuclear weapons is essential to ensure a human future. The second is international law and institutions. I believe that the international law must be strengthened and the United Nations and its specialised agencies must be empowered to do their jobs effectively. Without universal respect for enforcement of international law, it will not be possible to effectively stop human rights abuses, destruction of the environment and weaponisation of the planet and outer space. Legally binding instruments should be developed with respect to enjoying 'no first use' undertaking between the nuclear weapon states and as regards non-use or threat of use of nuclear weapons against the non-nuclear weapon states, the so-called 'negative security assurances'. The final target is to succeed in using science and technology for constructive rather than destructive purposes.

The terrorist attack on the United States soil of September 11, taught us that even the most powerful nation in the world is vulnerable to terrorism. The strongest military in the world with its blooded nuclear arsenal could not protect against a small band of terrorists propelled by hatred and committed to violence. Military force is largely impotent against those who hate and are willing to die in acts of violence.

Spiritual dimension of non-violence as lived by Gandhi is to me most important. Gandhi firmly believed that non-violence is more natural to man and woman than violence. His notions were built upon his confidence in humankind's natural disposition to love. He said: "Democracy can only be saved through non-violence, democracy so long as it is sustained by violence cannot provide for or protect the weak. My notion of democracy is that under it the weakest should have the same opportunity as the strongest. This can never happen except through non-violence. Non-violence cannot be preached; it has to be practised." A thought of Mahatma Gandhi that relates so directly to our nuclear age and which provides an answer is: "In this age of the atom bomb, non-violence is the only force that can confound all the tricks of violence put together."

Jawaharlal Nehru paying homage to Mahatma Gandhi at Rajghat, New Delhi.
Also in the picture: Indira Gandhi with young Sanjay and Rajiv Gandhi.

43

Cooperation and Dialogue

JOS CHABERT

"BE the change you want to see in the world, that you be the change." This is one of the most famous quotations of Mahatma Gandhi which can inspire us as responsible politicians to give examples of change, when we talk of the values of dialogue to resolve contentious issues. To change attitudes in peoples's minds, more dialogues are a real necessity, especially for people like me living in a big city in Brussels, capital of Europe, where our differences—ethnic, linguistic, religious, philosophical—are part of our daily life. Dialogue is an attitude by which one can make room for others. However much are they different from you, you find that they have a bit of truth that you are missing.

An example of best practice for dialogue is in the Brussels capital region, where we live together, with more than 140 nationalities, peacefully, in harmony. I took the initiative to create an inter-religious and philosophical platform—Hope for Brussels, a meeting place of leaders from different religions; philosophical traditions were established in the belief that multi-culturism is for the benefit of society rather than the cause for division.

The platform tries to bring about cooperation and dialogue between the highest representatives of the various religions and philosophical traditions, allowing them to exercise their moral authority as well as carrying out their values of tolerance and mutual respect. Hope for Brussels wants to be an organisation which through means and actions in concert with various representatives can call for calmness, reflection and respect in case of crisis or cultural tension. And with the creation of this platform by the Brussels authorities, religions and philosophies of life underline the fact that they share a number of goals, values and convictions and that those common values constitute the basis of their cooperation.

Approximately 45 per cent of the Brussels population is of foreign origin. Moreover, natality is evolving in such a way that within a couple of decades Brussels will truly be a city where the majority is comprised of minority. Each group has its own history, culture, religion, philosophy of life and view of the world. And migrant flows as well as secularisation process force the religious monopoly which in the past was characteristic of our country, Belgium and Europe, to make way for religious and philosophical pluralism, producing a radical change in the relations between the Christian faith and other religions and philosophies of life.

Brussels representatives of different religions and philosophies of life share the government's belief that a dialogue between all these communities should be started. Using this dialogue, they want to play their part in the realisation of reconciliation, mutual understanding and peace and through this inter-religious and philosophical platform, the various representatives enter into conversation with one another. We meet every month, so that knowledge and respect for each other will increase. So that they know each other better and in case of conflict or possible tension, which has a direct or indirect effect on the Brussels' population, the religious and philosophical leaders come out together and use their moral authority to call upon people to maintain peace and calm. We are all for reconciliation, understanding and cooperation.

This is the beginning of a structural consideration. We want to contribute to a peaceful and harmonious society all over the Brussels capital region, all over Belgium, and further on all over Europe. This platform brings together the most important leaders of the Catholic, Protestant, Anglican, Orthodox Church as well as the highest representatives of Judaism, Islam, Buddhism and those of the free thinking philosophy. Also likely to join in the near future are the new members of the Hindu community. So we share together the same values towards a non-violent world order. Let us all be extremists, extremists of tolerance and mutual respect.

44

Investing in Peace

PAUL VAN TONGEREN

THE immediate need in today's world is to create a non-violent world order. In doing so we need to create a coalition of consciousness between governments and civil society to fight against violence and poverty.

In this context, I would like to mention two things which have already been done. In June last year, in Geneva some 50 countries convened and drafted a Geneva Declaration on Armed Violence and Development. It is a very good declaration but totally unknown. I think this is a declaration which we should perhaps keep in mind. Secondly, the former Secretary-General of the United Nations, Kofi Annan, in his latest progress report on prevention of armed conflicts, called for strengthening coalitions for peace and enhancing infrastructure for peace. Not only just coalitions of governments but also of UN and civil societies. I think we need to convert these thoughts into action and work towards such coalitions. We have to invest in peace-building like we invest in development, like we invest in health or environment. There is an urgent need that we work a shift from reaction to prevention as there is not much that we do to prevent the escalation of conflicts.

A few years ago, in Ghana, one of the kings and his 40 followers were killed and the Government of Ghana was fully aware that they really needed to work on a long-term solution to transform conflict. And they decided in Ghana to build an infrastructure for peace and to have a National Peace Council with eminent people from Ghana in the Council. Such structures were also created at the district level and also at the local level to train and involve the people towards further peace enhancement.

I think this is what is really needed globally. But we cannot do that alone. We have to form and establish partnerships to work together between governments and civil society for long-term solutions.

Rajiv Gandhi paying homage to Mahatma Gandhi at Rajghat, New Delhi.

45

World Voices

Mosiuoa Gerard Patrick Lekota

Minister of Defence, South Africa

I think everybody will be aware that South Africa has already got rid of its nuclear capacity and we have been participating in international debates on this issue in order to assist and support the drive for disarmament or nuclear disarmament. We do not oppose the decision that India took to proceed in this direction at the present time. But we hold the view that it is and it will always be wrong that a huge majority of humankind lives under the threat of nuclear weapons by nations far smaller in numbers. This of course, doesn't justify our moving in the direction of armament. The question for me is: what is the practical action that can be taken in the various theatres of conflict? Because if the smaller conflict is a conflict such as in Iraq, the clashing interests in the situation could easily escalate the situation so that the resulting conflict could become out of control. The question that we should really be answering is, that in the globalised world how to provide guidance to nations and to people that find themselves in theatres of conflict to undertake practical actions that will help ease tensions before they reach such proportions that we cannot take control of them. Because if we are not able to contain or ease these limited conflicts, they could become a danger in the same way as the limited tensions which led to the world wars. And the challenge for the non-violent practitioner is how to deal with this issue.

I think we increasingly need a situation in which while we accept that some will lose their temper and run out of control, we must nurture the majority of humankind on Gandhian thought and solve the problem not out of anger but in a way that everyone is accommodated in the outcome. This is the challenge what we face today in the various theatres of conflict that are arising in Somalia, Darfur, Duraysah. We have moved forward in some way in Africa, but we need to be doing much more for these various theatres of conflict.

Jürgen Störk

Member, Peace Brigade International's International Council, Switzerland

In the early 20th century, Gandhi firmly confronted colonialism, apartheid and taught the world such effective non-violent tools that gave the assurance that the blight would not revisit us at the end of the century.

How can we apply Satyagraha, the force of truth, today? It is my belief that in our days, at the dawn of this 21st century, we have to confront and overcome an even mightier blight of mankind—the cancer of militarism. There are about 180 nations spending every year hundreds of billions of dollars on weaponry and military. They employ thousands of highly skilled scientists thinking about nothing else but how men can kill each other more effectively, or how to defend oneself from the sophisticated weapons of the others. Almost all nations do have a Defence Ministry. But there is not even a single nation which has a Ministry for Peace. We all know that we are in desperate need of these wasted resources to tackle the real problems of the world—poverty, disease, hunger, inequality, discrimination and so on. Yet, besides the calls of a few peaceniks, never taken seriously in this so-called realpolitik, there is nothing or little done to end this madness. On the contrary, instead of any serious onslaught, we witness steady proliferation, both in amounts and kinds. So where is that famous turning point of history? When do we cry out, enough is enough? Where is truth? What does Satyagraha mean in today's struggle so that our children's children might be able to state at the end of our century that mankind was able to remedy militarism?

If we want to follow and use Gandhi's teachings today and as a guide for the future, our demands must go far beyond. To establish a non-violent world order, we must indeed aim for the abolition of all arms of all national armies. The question is, how can we convince the nations to accept the truth that a world without armies is not only perfectly viable but indeed profitable to everyone and ultimately nothing more than a simple, sheer necessity for survival.

A call for total demilitarisation may sound too radical to be acceptable. The same goes probably for an appeal to all citizens of the world to follow Gandhi's much cherished civil disobedience. Instead, let us call on all nations to voluntarily apply a year's moratorium of arms and defence expenditure—of course, extendable. Such an experiment with truth, as Gandhi would call it, will help us take the first step towards halting the world's biggest and most useless waste of resources and freeing them to be used for peace building, poverty eradication and trust-building between nations for real demilitarisation.

Antonio Marques Porto e Santos

Special Envoy to Foreign Minister, Brazil

The world has taken a step forward recently with the creation of a Peace Commission in the United Nations with a new focus. The focus is no longer on ending the conflict but on preventing it as well as peace-building by addressing the causes of the conflict. Because it is not just a question of stopping conflict, it is a question of preventing it and when it occurs, of fighting the causes of conflict. This focus is very Gandhian because you have to understand what the aggressor's motives are to be able to be non-violent.

It is very difficult to have a clear-cut, solid, concrete and monolithic approach to nuclearisation. What is needed is the abolition of weapons, reform of international law and international institutions and the proper use of technology. With these three things in mind, we might be able to advance. But, to be candid, when I look around myself, I do not see much hope except in hope itself.

Kenneth Kaunda

Former President, Zambia

I am grateful for these wonderful contributions made by my brothers and sisters. I feel that out of the proposals which have been made, we need to leave something solid behind so that these ideas of Peace, Non-violence, Empowerment—Gandhian Philosophy—can move forward. Let me put forth my proposal which takes into account all that my colleagues have said. We should think of the big powers, violent powers, and have an organisation which will move us towards the Gandhian way of thought and further action. How do we do that?

I propose that before we leave this place, we should have an organisation which will take us forward. Since Satyagraha originated in South Africa, I think we should make them the Chairperson of this organisation. The current thought "Gandhian Philosophy in the 21st Century" came from India therefore India should become the Vice-Chairperson of this organisation. And together they should take us forward. But we have to bring in Pakistan also as we want to resolve issues. The organisation should have representation of all the continents, the entire world but bearing in mind that it should be fairly representative in terms of power. Keeping this in mind, I think the other members could be Germany and Sweden from Europe, Nigeria from Africa and Brazil from Latin America. Together as an organisation, these nations will not only be fairly representative in terms of power but will also bring the required balance. The organisation can then not only bring all of us together but lead us forward also.

Kefenste Mzwinila
Chairman, Youth Wing, Botswana Democratic Party, Botswana

We in Botswana for a long period of time had no military. We are fortunate that we never had any violent conflict or any form of internal strife. But unfortunately the environment we lived in during the 1960s and 1970s was such that all of our neighbours were actually in a state of political instability. This necessitated us to come to India and seek their advice as a peace-loving, peace-practising nation. The advice we received was that sometimes to defend yourself it is necessary to create a military force and have some sort of credible military deterrence. As a result our army received, and continues to receive, military assistance from India. What I would like to underscore is that on the point of militarisation or militarism it is very important for us to understand that we should not have catastrophic weapons such as nuclear weapons, but on the same logic we must also understand that in some situations, the environment you are in necessitates some level of credible military presence.

In conclusion, I would like to say that the best way to deal with militarisation or what is actually a credible military presence is through dialogue—dialogue with your security blocs, dialogue with the international community.

George Khutsishvili
Director, International Centre on Conflict and Negotiation, Georgia

It is observed that body and soul developed unequally in East and West. Western science and Western philosophy is all about body. Eastern philosophy, completely Indian, is all about soul. What is more important? Of course, both. But I would say that soul is more important. Weapons and disputed territories are material values. Truth, conciliation, and enlightenment are spiritual values. I want us to remember the words of the great humanist, Thomas Mann. In the novel "The Glass Bead Game" he said: "To those who are traveling East, today the impetus for peace, for conciliation, comes again from the East. And it comes from the mouth of Mahatma Gandhi." Gandhi's work has been the inspiration for me and my colleagues to fight nihilism and human disbelief in non-violence which is still prevailing in many regions, including my country. People don't understand how non-violence can resolve conflicts not because they like violent solutions but because they are convinced that the world works this way only. They believe in power based politics and power based solutions. They don't believe in non-violence.

People are tolerant and peaceful. People do not try to resolve conflicts by force. But they always speak about their doubts: Is it right to be non-violent? That is why they sometimes create the impression that they are preparing to retrieve lost territories by war, which will never happen. People should be bold and should be sincere to themselves. If they are tolerant, they should not be afraid or ashamed of it. This is what Gandhiji's philosophy teaches people and we should learn from it.

Charles Namoloh

Minister of Defence, Namibia

The world of today is a world of uncertainty and fear because we have lost peace in this world. We should ask ourselves as to what has gone wrong with our world. Are we slipping back to Stone Age? We seem to have become barbarians where we are today not only witnessing killing fields but we are also being divided in our approach to the problems of the world.

The issue of nuclear militarisation can be compared to human rights. There exits some double standards in approaching these issues. I think we need to be candid with ourselves in order to achieve our objectives with respect to this issue. There are evidences of those who possess these weapons of mass destruction and who have used them. But we have kept silent and suffered. We tend to condemn those who haven't even used them, to appease those who have used them. Today, technology is being used for deception. Gandhi said Satyagraha is about truth. We tend to be taken in by the lies. We are being deceived. People who have technology tell us all that they have information about a certain country which prompted them to take action against that country and we think that what we are being told is the truth. Later on revelations come that there was nothing of the sort. I think as people of this world we must fight in defence of peace and we must adopt the slogan: "Injury to one is an injury to all". We should all come together and start a peace movement that helps us reach a global understanding of the issues we face at the present time.

Declaration

Declaration

Declaration adopted at the International Conference on "Peace, Non-violence and Empowerment: Gandhian Philosophy in the 21st Century", 29-30 January, 2007, New Delhi.

The declaration was read at the Concluding Plenary by the veteran South African freedom fighter **Ahmed Kathrada** and was adopted by the conference by acclamation.

Declaration

WE, the representatives from 90 countries and 122 organisations, participating in the "International Conference on Peace, Non-violence and Empowerment: Gandhian Philosophy in the 21st Century", convened by the Indian National Congress in New Delhi on January 29-30, 2007, dedicated to the commemoration of the Centenary of the Satyagraha Movement launched by Mahatma Gandhi in South Africa, acknowledging the historical contribution made by him, and deeply cherishing the ideals of nonviolence and peace, which guided him in his struggle against injustice,

Having affirmed,

- That the values espoused by him are of enduring relevance, which continue to influence movements against oppression and discrimination across the world;

- That only just means can lead to just ends and bring an end to the escalating spiral of violence and bloodshed that the world is witnessing today;

- That 'Satyagraha' or the 'Force of Truth' can arrest the descent of humankind into fratricidal conflicts and lead to the path of peace and understanding;

- That the revival of eternal principles of love, compassion and fellow-feeling is indispensable for re-establishing trust and harmony in the world;

- That civil society has an important role in creating public awareness on issues concerning good governance;

- That violence and conflict are often engendered by widening socio-economic disparities;

- That despite tremendous economic advancement across the world, large sections of humankind continue to suffer in poverty, illiteracy, disease and hunger;

- That developmental activities must take adequate care to protect the environment and humanise the social order;

- That in spite of globalisation which has brought the world closer, regressive prejudices pertaining to race, religion and gender continue to prevail, leading to intolerance and fanaticism;

- That there is a strong reservoir of universal goodwill and common human values cutting across societies, religions and cultures through which humankind can address critical issues and instil confidence in the basic virtues that have brought human civilisation forward; and,

Therefore agree,

- That the basic concept of Satyagraha can carry forward the message of mutual understanding by reiterating its emphasis on:

    - tolerance and mutual respect for diverse cultures;

    - abhorrence of violence in thought, expression, belief and action;

    - the pursuit of Truth and promotion of ethical values and moral principles in public life;

    - the dignity of all human beings;

- That the way shown by Mahatma Gandhi a hundred years ago in his fight against injustice through his Satyagraha embodies the best principles drawn from all religions and beliefs; and,

- That his immortal precept that "violence cannot be dispelled by violence just like darkness cannot be dispelled by darkness" is as relevant today as ever before;

And urge people throughout the world,

- To re-dedicate themselves to the principles of Non-violence to resolve their differences through peaceful means;

- To ensure human freedom and equality;

- To mobilise public opinion against all forms of injustice;

- To promote the spirit of tolerance and mutual understanding;

- To act in concert in fighting the scourge of terrorism, which today afflicts all parts of the world;

- To empower the weak, the underprivileged and the oppressed to help them find their voice and become aware of their rights;

- To invoke the latent moral force of humanity by exposing the futility of adopting violent and coercive means to resolve conflicts;

- To help disseminate true knowledge for self-realisation and inter-cultural harmony;

- To dispel ignorance and misunderstanding through dialogue among cultures and civilisations;

- To ensure universal access to education and healthcare;

- To promote an equitable strategy to effectively deal with the phenomenon of global warming, which threatens the survival of humankind;

- To promote a democratic and multilateral world order, where consensus-building rather than unilateralism is the guiding principle;

- To strengthen the UN system as the principal mechanism for conflict resolution and the pacific settlement of disputes;

- To work for reforming the various organs of the United Nations in order to reflect the changes that have taken place since its inception;

- To appeal to the UN to declare Mahatma Gandhi's date of birth, October 2, as the **International Non-violence Day**;

And resolve

- To work towards:

  - A world free from hatred and violence;

  - A world united in mutual trust, harmony and friendship;

  - A world with more equitable access to global resources;

  - A world united in its struggle against poverty, illiteracy, disease, injustice and hunger;

  - A world free from nuclear and other weapons of mass destruction;

  - A world where territorial boundaries become irrelevant, where cultural frontiers are in an inclusive and ever-expanding mode, and where local values merge in the ocean of universal humanitarianism.

As representatives of the humankind, we take a solemn vow to nurture the values espoused by Mahatma Gandhi, to pursue Truth, to privilege peace and reject violence in all our activities, to respect diverse viewpoints, and to practise the philosophy of Non-violence to win over the forces of violence and injustice through tolerance, empathy and love.

The Conference | Photo Gallery

(L to R) Anand Sharma, Nasser al-Kidwa, Muhammad Yunus, A.K. Antony, Kenneth Kaunda, Sonia Gandhi, Lech Walesa, Ela Gandhi, Pranab Mukherjee and Mani Shankar Aiyar at the Inaugural Plenary of the Conference.

Prime Minister Dr. Manmohan Singh inaugurating the exhibition.
(L to R) Tara Gandhi Bhattacharjee, Ela Gandhi, Anand Sharma, Sonia Gandhi, Motilal Vora, Manmohan Singh and Savita Singh.

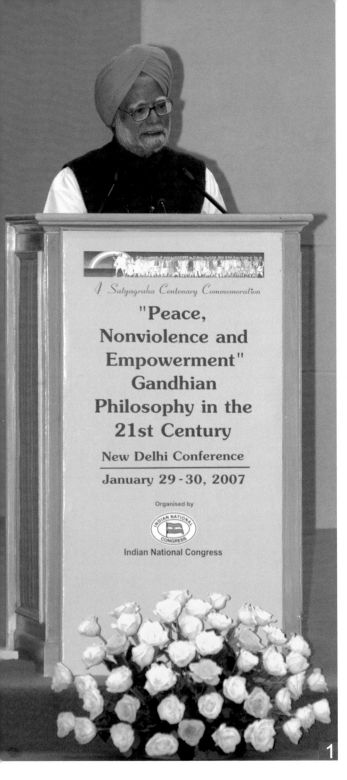

Photo 1: Manmohan Singh.

Photo 2: Kenneth Kaunda striking the World Peace Gong at Gandhi Smriti, New Delhi. Also in the picture: Tara Gandhi Bhattacharjee (R) and Savita Singh.

Photo 3: (L to R) Sonia Gandhi, Desmond Tutu and Lech Walesa.

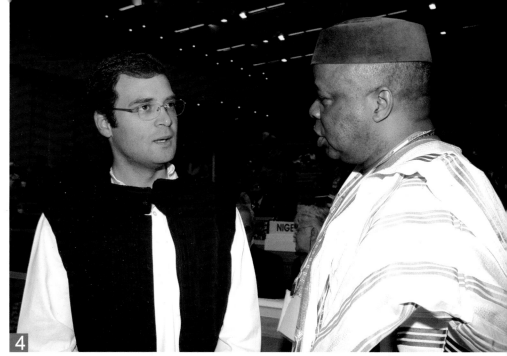

Photo 1: Muhammad Yunus.

Photo 2: (L to R) C.K. Prahalad, Chaiwat Satha-Anand and Bhikhu Parekh.

Photo 3: Lyonpo Khandu Wangchuk (C) with other Bhutanese delegates.

Photo 4: Ken Nnamani (R) with Rahul Gandhi.

Photo 5: Kirunda Kivejinja (L) with Tara Gandhi Bhattacharjee.

Photo 1: Kenneth Kaunda (L) with Sunderlal Bahuguna.

Photo 2: Delegates paying homage at Gandhi Smriti, New Delhi.

Photo 3: Farooq Sattar (R) with Rahul Gandhi.

Photo 4: (R to L) Sonia Gandhi, Manmohan Singh, Kenneth Kaunda and A.K. Antony.

Photo 5: Lech Walesa.

Photo 1: (R to L) Sonia Gandhi, Janez Drnovšek, Radha Kumar and Jusuf Kalla.

Photo 2: Johan Galtung (L) with Mani Shankar Aiyar.

Photo 3: Kenneth Kaunda (R) with A.K. Antony.

Photo 4: (L to R) Gene Sharp, Pawan Kumar Bansal, Lia Diskin and Rajani Patil.

Photo 5: (L to R) Bhikhu Parekh, Navinchandra Ramgoolam, Chaiwat Satha-anand and Jairam Ramesh.

Photo 1: Charles Namoloh (R) and other delegates.

Photo 2: Gene Sharp.

Photo 3: Margaret Alva (L) with Rahul Gandhi.

Photo 4: Desmond Tutu.

Photo 1: Tzannis Tzannetakis.
Photo 2: Manmohan Malhoutra (L) and Anand Sharma.
Photo 3: Sonia Gandhi.
Photo 4: Rahul Gandhi with Nasser al-Kidwa (R).

Photo 1: Hilde Rapp.

Photo 2: Kirti Menon.

Photo 3: A.B. Bardhan (L) with Prakash Karat.

Photo 4: Motilal Vora (R) with Kumari Selja.

Photo 5: Lalu Prasad Yadav, Sharad Pawar, Saif-u-Din Soz, Vasant Sathe and other senior Indian leaders amongst the audience.

Photo 1: (L to R) Shivraj Patil, D. Raja and Karan Singh.

Photo 2: (L to R) Jaipal Reddy, Priyaranjan Dasmunsi and Saif-u-Din Soz.

Photo 3: (L to R) Salman Khurshid, Essop Pahad and Manish Tiwari.

Photo 4: Ahmed Kathrada.

Photo 1: Anand Sharma.

Photo 2: Lord Navnit Dholakia (L) and Ahmed Kathrada.

Photo 3: (L to R) Tom Vadekam, Kumari Selja, Devendra Nath Dwivedi and Jayanti Natarajan.

Photo 4: Nirmala Deshpande.

Photo 1: (L to R) Mewa Ramgobin, João Cravinho, Rajiv Vora and Asfandyar Wali Khan.
Photo 2: Sumitra Kulkarni (L) with Ela Gandhi.
Photo 3: Ambika Soni (L) with Ashok Gehlot.

Photo 1: (L to R) Sheila Dikshit, J.P. Aggarwal and Suresh Pachauri.

Photo 2: Oscar Fernandes.

Photo 3: Sonia Gandhi amidst the audience.

Photo 4: (Front) Devendra Nath Dwivedi (L) with Ramesh Chennithala; (Rear) V. Naranyan Swami (L) and Vayalar Ravi.

Photo 5: Ahmed Patel (L) with Saif-u-Din Soz.

Photo 1: Kenneth Kaunda.

Photo 2: (L to R) B.K. Hariprasad, Johan Galtung, Bhubaneswar Kalita and Mani Shankar Aiyar.

Photo 3: AICC functionaries.

Photo 4: (L to R) Sonia Gandhi, Anand Sharma, Manmohan Singh and Savita Singh.

Photo 5: (R to L) Ahmed Patel, Kapil Sibal, Sheila Dikshit and Karan Singh.

Photo 1: A.K. Antony.

Photo 2: (L to R) H.R. Bhardwaj, Mohsina Kidwai, Satyavrat Chaturvedi, Mahavir Prasad and Jairam Ramesh.

Photo 3: Indian and foreign leaders at the Gandhi Smriti, New Delhi.

Photo 4: (L to R) Amrita Bahri, Ragini Nayak, Imran Kidwai, Amrita Dhavan, Sanjay Chandok, P. Anand Kumar, Yogesh Sachdeva and Hari Shanker Gupta.

(L to R) Anand Sharma, Nasser al-Kidwa, Ahmed Kathrada, Ela Gandhi, A.K. Antony, Kenneth Kaunda, Sonia Gandhi, Desmond Tutu, Lech Walesa, Muhammad Yunus, Pranab Mukherjee, Mani Shankar Aiyar and Mukul Wasnik at the Concluding Plenary of the Conference.

(R to L) Francesco Rutelli, Maumoon Abdul Gayoom, Navinchandra Ramgoolam and Janez Drnovšek along with other delegates.

Delegates at the Plenary Session.

Photo 1-4: Delegates at the conference.

Delegates at the Conference...

Idriss Jazairy
Algeria

David Holly
Australia

Gudrun Kramer
Austria

Wilfred Graf
Austria

Anwar Mohd. Abdul Rahman
Bahrain

Muhammad Yunus
Bangladesh

Enam Ahmed Choudhury
Bangladesh

Dipu Moni
Bangladesh

Reaz Rahman
Bangladesh

O. Laptenok
Belarus

Jos Chabert
Belgium

Paul Wille
Belgium

Lyonpo Khandu Wangchuk
Bhutan

Karen Balcázar Cronenbold
Bolivia

Binkie Kerileng
Botswana

Otsweleste Moupo
Botswana

Kefentse Mzwinila
Botswana

Lia Diskin
Brazil

Marta Suplicy
Brazil

Son Soubert
Cambodia

Ken Macartney
Canada

Gerardo Rocha
Chile

Liu Hongcai
China

Simón Gaviria
Colombia

Marija Lugaric
Croatia

Miguel Angel Ramirez
Cuba

Rául Valdés Vivó
Cuba

Theocharous Kariolou Eleni
Cyprus

Hawa Ahmed Youssouf
Djibouti

Mohamed Ali Hassan
Djibouti

Mohamed Abdellah
Egypt

Francisco Lainez Rivas
El Salvador

Marianne Mikko
Estonia

Abune Paulos
Ethiopia

Berhanu Adello
Ethiopia

Gerima W. Kirkos
Ethiopia

Shaista Shameem
Fiji

Jan-Erik Enestam
Finland

Philippe Humbert
France

George Khutsishvili
Georgia

Sebastian Edathy
Germany

Christian Bartolf
Germany

Willy Wimmer
Germany

Shirley A. Botchwey
Ghana

Barbara Serwaa Asamoah
Ghana

Joseph Godson Amamoo
Ghana

Atukwei Okai
Ghana

Johnson Asiedu-Nketiah
Ghana

Adams Iddie Kofi
Ghana

George Papandreou
Greece

Tzannis Tzannetakis
Greece

Paulina Lampsa
Greece

Katerina Georgopoulou
Greece

Lia Papafilipou
Greece

Theodoros Tsikas
Greece

Ilias Antoniou
Greece

Mamady Conde
Guinea

Carlos Eduardo Reina
Honduras

Margaret Alva
India

Rahul Gandhi
India

Ajay Maken
India

K.A. Sangatam
India

Kumari Selja
India

Jitin Prasad
India

Meenakshi Natrajan
India

Ramesh Cheninthala
India

Begum Noor Bano
India

Tushar Gandhi
India

Bharat Solanki
India

Jusuf Kalla
Indonesia

Arif Budimanta
Indonesia

Emir Moeis
Indonesia

Syamsul Mu'arif
Indonesia

Gembong Prijono
Indonesia

Chairul Tanjung
Indonesia

Pramono Anung Wibowo
Indonesia

Sumarsono
Indonesia

Mahdi Agha Alikhani
Iran

Mohammad Ali Tabarraei
Iran

Kieran Dowling
Ireland

Francesco Rutelli
Italy

Gianni Vernetti
Italy

Sandro Gozi
Italy

François Lafond
Italy

Raffaele Trombetta
Italy

Wykehem McNeill
Jamaica

Katsuyuki Kawai
Japan

Yasutoshi Nishimura
Japan

Yoko Kamikawa
Japan

Romin Madinov
Kazakhstan

Francis S.K. Bayah
Kenya

Thongsy Inthapnonh
Lao

Somphone Sychaleun
Lao

Samy Gemayel
Lebanon

Robert Y. Lormia
Liberia

Eugene H. Shannon
Liberia

George Wallace
Liberia

Mahfud R. Rahiam
Libya

Olga Murdjeva Skaric
Macedonia

Svetomir Skaric
Macedonia

Mohamed Ali Rustam
Malaysia

Anwar Fazal
Malaysia

Noh bin Haji Omar
Malaysia

Maumoon Abdul Gayoom
Maldives

Hussein Amir
Maldives

Ahmed Shaheed
Maldives

Mohamed Hussain
Maldives

Aishath Azima Shakoor
Maldives

Lubna Mohd. Zahir Hussain
Maldives

Aneesa Ahmed
Maldives

Jantsan Gulgou
Mangolia

Navinchandra Ramgoolam
Mauritius

Paul Raymond Bérenger
Mauritius

Pradeep Jeeha
Mauritius

Jávier Moctezuma Barragan
Mexico

Mariano Palacios Alcocer
Mexico

Aleksi Asatashvilli
Mexico

Saul Escobar
Mexico

Yeidckol P. Gurwitz
Mexico

Nouzha Chekrouni
Morocco

Jaafar Alj Hakim
Morocco

José Tsambe
Mozambique

Conceita Sortane
Mozambique

Charles Namoloh
Namibia

U.D. Nujoma
Namibia

Rajendra Mahoto
Nepal

Ram Chandra Paudel
Nepal

Sujata Koirala
Nepal

Pradip Giri
Nepal

Prakash Sharan Mahat
Nepal

Jhala Nath Khanal
Nepal

K.P. Sharma Oli
Nepal

Madhav Kumar Nepal
Nepal

Anil Kumar Jha
Nepal

Bharat Mohan Adhikari
Nepal

Bimalendra Nidhi
Nepal

Paul van Tongeren
The Netherlands

Camiel Eurling
The Netherlands

Jan-Jaap van Halem
The Netherlands

Graeme Waters
New Zealand

Ken Nnamani
Nigeria

Johan Galtung
Norway

Asfandyar Wali Khan
Pakistan

Farooq Sattar
Pakistan

Begum Ishrat Ashraf
Pakistan

Asma Jahangir
Pakistan

Zahid Khan
Pakistan

Nasser al-Kidwa
Palestine

Lech Walesa
Poland

Pawel Zalewski
Poland

Cezary Gajdamowicz
Poland

Danuta Walesa
Poland

Maria Iwinska
Poland

Piotr Gulczynski
Poland

Brygida Walesa
Poland

João Cravinho
Portugal

Hasan Ali al Neima
Qatar

Anton Niculescu
Romania

Teodor Melescanu
Romania

Cristian Diaconescu
Romania

Victor Bostinaru
Romania

Elena Musat
Romania

Dmitry Rogozin
Russia

Mikhail Margelov
Russia

Sergey Y. Glazyev
Russia

Dušan Prorokoviċ
Serbia

Sanda Rašković-Iviċ
Serbia

Momodu Koroma
Sierra Leone

Heng Chee How
Singapore

Hri Kumar Nair
Singapore

Diana Štrofová
Slovak Republic

Peter Bator
Slovak Republic

Janez Drnovšek
Slovenia

Valentina Flander
Slovenia

Ivo Vajgl
Slovenia

Ahmed Kathrada
South Africa

Desmond Tutu
South Africa

Essop Pahad
South Africa

Ela Gandhi
South Africa

Mosiuoa Gerard Patrick Lekota
South Africa

Mewa Ramgobin
South Africa

Kirti Menon
South Africa

Barbara Hogan
South Africa

Kidar Ramgobin
South Africa

Yvette L. Myakayaka-Manzini
South Africa

Fernando Reinares
Spain

Gustavo Aristegui
Spain

Ion de la Riva
Spain

Juan Moscoso
Spain

Ratnasiri Wickramanayaka
Sri Lanka

Ranil Wickremesinghe
Sri Lanka

Kumar Rupesinghe
Sri Lanka

Mangala Samaraweera
Sri Lanka

Sajith Premadasa
Sri Lanka

Harsha Kumar Navaratne
Sri Lanka

G.L. Peiris
Sri Lanka

Maithripala Sirisena
Sri Lanka

Lakshman Bandara Kiriella
Sri Lanka

Ravi Karunanayake
Sri Lanka

Farid Achmed Ketwaru
Suriname

Maud Olofsson
Sweden

Jürgen Störk
Switzerland

Abdul Aziz Al-Khatib
Syria

Bassam Janbieh
Syria

Haitham Satayhi
Syria

Hind Aboud Kabawat
Syria

Ayman Abdel Nour
Syria

Hazara Pindi Chana
Tanzania

Mahmoud Thabit Kombo
Tanzania

Benedict Elias Lyamuya
Tanzania

Casmir J. Ndambalilo
Tanzania

Muhammed Seif Khatib
Tanzania

Chaturon Chaisaeng
Thailand

Chaiwat Satha-Anand
Thailand

Phiraphan Phalusuk
Thailand

Montri Jiravaraphan
Thailand

Pimuk Simaroj
Thailand

Suwanna Satha-Anand
Thailand

Kantathi Suphamongkhon
Thailand

Sadok Fayala
Tunisia

Nepesow A. Begnejovich
Turkmenistan

Rejepow Mukhammetmyrat
Turkmenistan

Kirunda Kivejinja
Uganda

Amama Mbabazi
Uganda

Kintu Musoke
Uganda

Beatrice Wabudeya
Uganda

Mikhailo Kirsenko
Ukraine

Edward Samuel Miliband
United Kingdom

Hilde Rapp
United Kingdom

Indra Adnan
United Kingdom

Bhiku Parekh
United Kingdom

Mark Hendrick
United Kingdom

Navnit Dholakia
United Kingdom

Sandip Verma
United Kingdom

Gene Sharp
USA

C.K. Prahalad
USA

Jamila Raqib
USA

Patricia M. Mische
USA

Francisco Sesto Novas
Venezuela

Augusto Montiel
Venezuela

Wolfgang González Sequera
Venezuela

Desire Santos Amaral
Venezuela

Man Huyen Sam
Vietnam

Nguyen Hoanh Son
Vietnam

Pham Xuan Son
Vietnam

Kenneth Kaunda
Zambia

Michael C. Sata
Zambia

G.M. Chipare
Zimbabwe

John L. Nkomo
Zimbabwe

Saviour Kasukuwere
Zimbabwe

Chronology of Mahatma Gandhi's Life

(October 2, 1869 – January 30, 1948)

1869	Born at Porbandar, Kathiawad, son of Karamchand (Kaba) and Putlibai Gandhi.
1876	Attended primary school in Rajkot, where his family moved. Betrothed to Kasturba
1881	Entered high school in Rajkot.
1883	Married to Kasturba.
1885	Father died at the age of 63.
1887	Passed matriculation examination at Ahmedabad and entered Samaldas College, Bhavnagar, Kathiawad, but found studies difficult and studied only one term.
1888	First of the four sons born. Sailed from Bombay for England to study law.
1891	Summer. Returned to India after being called to bar. Began practice of law in Bombay and Rajkot.
1893	Sailed for South Africa to become a lawyer for an Indian firm. Found himself subjected to all kinds of colour discrimination.
1894	Prepared to return to India, but was persuaded by Indian colony to remain in South Africa and do public work and earn a living as a lawyer. Founded Natal Indian Congress.
1896	Returned to India for six months to bring back his wife and two children to Natal.
1899	Organised Indian Ambulance Corps for British in the Boer War.
1901	Embarked with family for India, promising to return to South Africa if the Indian community there needed his services again.
1901–02	Travelled extensively in India, attended Indian National Congress meeting in Calcutta, and opened law office in Bombay.

1931   Released unconditionally with 30 other Congress leaders.

            Gandhi-Irwin (Viceroy) Pact signed, ending civil disobedience.

            Sailed from Bombay accompanied by Desai, Naidu, Mira, etc., for the second Round Table
            Conference, arriving in London via Marseilles, met by C.F. Andrews.

            Autumn. Resided at Kingsley Hall in London slums, broadcast to America, visited
            universities, met celebrities, and attended Round Table Conference sessions.

            Left England for Switzerland, where he met Romain Rolland, and Italy, where he met
            Mussolini.

            Arrived in India. Authorised by Congress to renew Satyagraha campaign (fourth
            nationwide effort).

1932   Concluded "epic fast" with historic cell scene in presence of Tagore after British accepted
            "Yeravda Pact".

1933   Began weekly publication of *Harijan*.

            Disbanded Sabarmati ashram, which became centre for removal of untouchability

            Arrested and imprisoned at Yeravda for four days with 34 members of his ashram. When he refused
            to leave Yeravda village for Poona, he was sentenced to one year's imprisonment at Yeravda.

            Began tour of every province in India to help end untouchability.

1934   Launched All-India Village Industries Association.

            Resigned from Congress 'only to serve better in thought, word and deed'.

1935   Health declined; moved to Bombay to recover.

1936   Visited Seagon, a village near Wardha which eventually became an ashram for his disciples.

1937   Visited South India for removal of untouchability.

1938   Toured Northwest Frontier Province with Khan Abdul Ghaffar Khan.

1939   Began fast unto death as part of Satyagraha campaign in Rajkot.

1940   Launched limited, individual civil-disobedience campaign.

1942   *Harijan* resumed publication after being suspended for 15 months.

            Met Sir Stafford Cripps in New Delhi but called his proposals "a post-dated cheque"; they
            were ultimately rejected by Congress.

            Congress passed "Quit India" resolution—the final nationwide Satyagraha campaign—with
            Gandhi as leader.

            Mahadev Desai, Gandhi's secretary and intimate, who was under arrest, died at Aga Khan
            Palace.

1943   Began 21-day fast at Aga Khan Palace to end deadlock of negotiations between Viceroy
            and Indian leaders.

1944   Kasturba died in detention at Aga Khan Palace at age of seventy-four.

1946 Conferred with British Cabinet Mission in New Delhi.

Began four-month tour of 49 villages in East Bengal to quell communal rioting over Muslim representation in provisional government.

1947 Began tour of Bihar to lessen Hindu-Muslim tensions.

Began conferences in New Delhi with Viceroy (Lord Mountbatten) and Jinnah.

Opposed decision to accept division.

Fasted and prayed to combat riots in Calcutta as India was partitioned and granted independence.

Visited Delhi and environs to stop rioting and to visit camps of refugees (Hindus and Sikhs from the Punjab).

1948 Fasted for five days in Delhi for communal unity.

Bomb exploded in midst of his prayer meeting at Birla House, Delhi.

Assassinated in 78th year at Birla House by Nathuram Vinayak Godse.

Lead Contributors

Nelson Mandela : Veteran freedom fighter who spent over 27 years in prison during the struggle against apartheid. He led South Africa in its historic transition to multi-racial democracy in 1994 and became the first President of post-apartheid South Africa. Recipient of the 1993 Nobel Peace Prize, Mandela's contribution in upholding human freedom and dignity is universally acknowledged.

Sonia Gandhi : President of the Indian National Congress and the Chairperson of the ruling United Progressive Alliance. She was the Chairperson of the global conference convened by the Indian National Congress to commemorate the centenary of Satyagraha.

Manmohan Singh : Prime Minister of India and a distinguished economist. Dr. Singh is widely acknowledged as the principal architect of India's economic reforms, a process initiated in 1991 when he was the Union Finance Minister.

Muhammad Yunus : Nobel Laureate, Bangladeshi banker and renowned economist. Professor Yunus, the founder of Grameen Bank is known for his successful application of the concept of micro credit.

Desmond Tutu : Veteran anti-apartheid activist and recipient of the Nobel Peace Prize. Today, he is revered as a "moral voice" to end poverty and human rights abuse. Archbishop Tutu places great value on religious inclusiveness and interfaith dialogue.

Ela Gandhi : Prominent peace activist, she is Chairperson of the Gandhi Development Trust, Durban, South Africa. Granddaughter of Mahatma Gandhi, she was a member of parliament in South Africa.

Kenneth Kaunda : Led Zambia to independence in 1964 and served as the nation's president until 1991. He founded the Kenneth Kaunda Peace Foundation, dedicated to the establishment of peace and conflict resolution in the continent. Dr. Kaunda is now devoted to fighting HIV/AIDS and poverty in Africa.

Lech Walesa : Formerly President of Poland, Nobel Peace Prize recipient and a human rights activist. He co-founded Solidarity (Solidarnosc), the Soviet bloc's first independent trade union.

Pranab Mukherjee : Minister of External Affairs, Government of India. A senior leader of the Indian National Congress, he has also held several important portfolios in the Union cabinet.

Nasser al-Kidwa : Former Foreign Minister, Palestinian National Authority. He was Ambassador and Permanent Observer of Palestine to the United Nations.

Abdelaziz Bouteflika : President of Algeria and veteran of Algeria's war for independence. He is widely credited with having restored peace to the country and transforming its image internationally.

Gene Sharp : World renowned political scientist and author. Dr. Sharp founded the Albert Einstein Institution in Boston to promote research, policy studies, and education on the strategic use of non-violent struggle in the face of dictatorship, war, genocide, and oppression.

Francesco Rutelli : Deputy Prime Minister of Italy and Minister of Welfare and Cultural Activities. He has been the Mayor of Rome, and is president of the centre wing liberal party Le Margherita.

Ahmed Kathrada : Brave freedom fighter and a former prisoner of conscience. He was incarcerated along with Nelson Mandela in the struggle against apartheid. Kathrada is a practising Gandhian committed to the Mahatma's humane philosophy.

Radha Kumar : Director of the Mandela Centre for Peace and Conflict Resolution at Jamia Millia Islamia, New Delhi and trustee of the Delhi Policy Group where she runs a programme on Durable Peace Processes and Partners.

George Andreas Papandreou : Greek statesman and President of the Socialist International. He has served as the Foreign Minister of Greece and has been leader of the Panhellenic Socialist Movement party.

Maumoon Abdul Gayoom : President of the Republic of Maldives. His governance has ushered in a hitherto unknown period of social and economic success for the nation. President Gayoom is credited with introducing multi-party political system in the country.

Janez Drnovšek : President of Slovenia and the former President of Yugoslavia. He is a popular Slovene leader and statesman and is known for his crucial contribution towards democratic, economic and political developments in the country.

Jusuf Kalla : Vice President of Indonesia and Chairman of the Golkar Party. He has been instrumental in resolving several inter-religious conflicts in the country.

Abune Paulos : Patriarch of the Ethiopian Orthodox Tewahedo Church. He has been instrumental in encouraging interfaith dialogue in his country. He is also President (Oriental Orthodox) of the World Council of Churches.

Bhikhu Parekh : Member, House of Lords, United Kingdom and Fellow of the Royal Society of Arts and of the Academy of the Learned Societies for Social Sciences. He is also a Professor of Political Philosophy at the University of Westminster.

C.K. Prahalad : Globally recognised business guru and thinker. He is Professor of Corporate Strategy at the Ross School of Business, University of Michigan.

Navinchandra Ramgoolam : Prime Minister of the Republic of Mauritius. He is the son of Sir Seewoosagur Ramgoolam, the Father of the Nation. Before starting his political career he trained as a doctor in Dublin, Ireland and later studied law at the London School of Economics.

Edward Samuel Miliband : Minister for the Cabinet Office and Chancellor of the Duchy of Lancaster. Previously, he was the chairman of the Treasury's Council of Economic Advisers, which directs UK's long-term economic planning.

Gianni Vernetti : Deputy Minister of Foreign Affairs, Italy. In charge of international relations for Le Margherita, he has been working on building a network of democratic political parties around the world.

Hawa Ahmed Youssouf : Minister for Advancement of Women, Family Welfare and Social Affairs, Republic of Djibouti. Under her guidance, health and education services for women and children have received a special thrust in the country.

Asma Jahangir : Leading human rights activist and an advocate of the Supreme Court of Pakistan. She has twice been elected as Chairperson of Human Rights Commission of Pakistan and is also co-chair of the South Asians for Human Rights.

Marianne Mikko : Member of the European Parliament for the Social Democratic Party. She is also the head of the European Parliament's Commission on Cooperation with the Republic of Moldova.

Essop Goolam Pahad : Minister in the Presidency of the Republic of South Africa. His political career began in 1958 when he became a member of the Transvaal Indian Youth Congress. He was part of the South African liberation struggle and served on the leadership structures of African National Congress and South African Communist Party.

Mushirul Hasan : Vice-Chancellor, Jamia Millia Islamia, New Delhi. He is one of India's most erudite historians. He is also Director, Academy of Third World Studies, Jamia Millia Islamia University.

Asfandyar Wali Khan : Leader of the Awami National Party in Pakistan. Grandson of Khan Abdul Ghaffar Khan, he has served as Member of Provincial Assembly and Member of National Assembly.

Rajiv Vora : Well known Gandhian and eminent interpreter of Gandhi's works. Professor Vora has a long standing association with the Gandhi Peace Foundation and he is also the founder of Swarajpeeth, a Gandhian centre for non-violence and peace.

Mewa Ramgobin : Renowned social activist, he is Chairperson of Phoenix Settlement Trust, South Africa. He has been President of the Natal Indian Congress which was founded by Mahatma Gandhi.

Mahdi Agha Alikhani : Secretary General of the Youth Party of Iran. He has also been a member of the Central Council of Islamic Republic of Iran's House of Parties and the director of its International Committee.

João Cravinho : Secretary of State for Foreign Affairs and Cooperation, Government of Portugal. Formerly, he was Minister of Equipment, Planning and Administration.

Johan Galtung : Norwegian professor, founder and co-director of TRANSCEND. He founded the International Peace Research Institute in Oslo and is recognised as the pioneer of peace and conflict research and peace journalism.

Mani Shankar Aiyar : Union cabinet minister for Panchayati Raj and Youth Affairs and Sports, Government of India. A former diplomat, he is a senior member of the Indian National Congress and is also a well-known author and political columnist.

Chaiwat Satha-Anand : Professor of political science at Thammasat University, Bangkok, and Director of the Thai Peace Information Centre at the Foundation for Democracy and Development Studies. He is known for his contribution to theory and activism of non-violence.

Tzannis Tzannetakis : Former Prime Minister of Greece. He continues to be a member of the parliament and is also active in New Democracy (Greece) organisation.

Paul van Tongeren : Founder and executive director of the European Centre for Conflict Prevention, Netherlands. He has been involved in the activities of numerous Dutch NGOs in the field of development cooperation, peace and environment protection. He is also the executive director of Global Partnership for the Prevention of Armed Conflict.

Jos Chabert : Vice-President and Minister of Finance and Foreign Relations for Brussels-Capital Region. He is also President of the European Popular Party in the European Regions Committee.

Anand Sharma : Minister of State for External Affairs, Government of India. A former spokesman of the Congress party, he is recognised for his proactive participation and contribution to the struggle against apartheid.